A GLIMPSE OF JOY
(Journey with the Divine)

A GLIMPSE OF JOY

(Journey with the Divine)

(In Three Volumes)

(Volume 2)

Khurshid Dabdi

A Glimpse of Joy (Journey with the Divine)

ISBN : 978-81-7835-969-4 (Set)
ISBN : 978-81-7835-971-7 (Vol. 2)

Published in 2013 in India by
Kalpaz Publications
C-30, Satyawati Nagar,
Delhi - 110052
E-mail: kalpaz@hotmail.com
Phone : 9212142040

Laser Type Setting : Shah Computer Graphics, Delhi
Printed at : G. Print Process,Delhi

Contents

Foreword

God had blessed me with His presence in my life and expected me to go by the voice of my conscience. With the help of acquired knowledge from His messages, He wished that I should learn to discern good from bad. Yet, as you must have read in the earlier part of Volume I, I consistently erred, suffered due to my own faulty thinking. Baba did not impart spiritual knowledge to me during that time but waited for that moment when I awakened to His call. He waited till I was able to surrender to His will by cultivating and adopting the humility required to be able to do so.

In the first half of Volume I of the series of 'A Glimpse of Joy', I have shared with you details of that part of my life that I had never been able to bring myself to talk about to anybody. As a survivor of emotional and physical abuse I had often experienced a sense of isolation. I had trouble expressing my feelings to anybody. Writing the books had been a release from my pain. It had been a way to get my thoughts and feelings out, in a way I was not able to with anybody.

As the books progressed over the years it was wonderful to look back and see how far I had come. The series of 'A Glimpse of Joy' was a place where I could express myself freely, without having to worry about blame or disapproval. Writing had actually helped me heal from the effects of emotional trauma. Earlier I had just put it all behind me and tried to deceive myself that nothing negative had ever happened in my life. But by compelling me to put it all down on paper, my guru had given me an opportunity to address the damage that the abuse had done to me. It had not been an easy process. There had been ups and downs, days when I had found it difficult to put it down on paper.

As you read through the Volume I and reach the last chapters of the same, you will note that it was just the beginning of my journey to God. **Hence, sharing the latter part of Volume I has meant sharing with you (the readers) some learnings in life. It is an account of the continuous cycle of my rise and fall in His sight, and yet His constant reassurance that I was worthy of His love.** Baba played the role of a mother in my life. Over the years, I realized that it was love, not time that could heal all my wounds. Love that went beyond my parents' love or even that of my dear guru. Their love no doubt was supportive and helped me on my way to healing. But the most important love I needed to discover as I healed was a love for myself. Love for the child that I once was. The one who had erred. This kind of healing had taken a great deal of effort.

The first half of Volume II would speak of the Divine insights that I received from Baba during my one year stay in His presence at Parthi and Whitefield. And His encouragement that helped me make a commitment to free myself from the effects of the different kinds of exploitation I had gone through – via expressing my feelings through the books that I penned during that period. It took time and courage. To learn of ways to cope through the healing process and beyond. To invest time and thought in self-study, as I watched myself grow – grow into not only a self-confident, self-sufficient individual, but one who with His grace could even experience her own inherent divinity and that of every human being.

Back in Mumbai and with my family, **the latter part of Volume II relates how I put His teachings into practice and made it a way of life.**

During my life-time He did not make me undergo any rigorous learning. **His teachings, I understood, were meant to be practiced. (That part of my life is penned in the Volume III.)** My Lord advocated living in the world as a necessary environment for helping me along on my path to self-realization through karma yoga, through service to Him in the form of the underprivileged children living on the construction sites, slums and the pavements of the city of Mumbai. Sunbeam, a Public Charitable Trust, born of my tireless efforts, was a wonderful opportunity via which He made me do so.

I asked myself questions like: How can I use my past difficult experiences in life to my advantage? As if in response to this question, God provided me with multiple opportunities in life to be of use to my family. Thereafter, He blessed me with opportunities to serve humanity at large. **Volume III will speak of my life devoted to the underprivileged children living in the slums and pavements of Mumbai.** You will notice from this Volume, i.e. Volume II onwards, how my level of self-doubt dropped and was replaced by a greater sense of trust in humanity and in my own inherent goodness. Over the next two decades Baba helped me transcend my petty self and look beyond – to spend my life in serving others. I actually began to get acquainted with my higher self – the spark of the divine within me.

Today, in the year 2011, with my autobiography penned in III Volumes, I wear no mask. Neither am I an extraordinary human being just because I have chosen to take responsibility of the well-being / future of over a thousand underprivileged children, nor am I just the person who had erred during her youth. I am a child of God who has consistently throughout my life endeavoured to live up to His expectations. I am still in the process of walking towards my goal – self-realization – by realizing God in one and all. Dear readers, I hope to be remembered as someone who made every effort to outgrow her human limitations in order to grow into His image.

Acknowledgements

The reason that led to this book has many roots. One of the most important was my eagerness to share with you, the innumerable spiritual lessons taught to me by my guru, Sri Sathya Sai Baba during my 10 month stay in His ashram.

- Within that span of less than a year, He appeared in my dreams and visions innumerable times to help me visualize Him in one and all (including myself) and to also guide my steps on the path to becoming His image. It is no wonder then, that with so much loving, spiritual energy, the writing of this book flowed harmoniously and filled me with joy.
- My dearest dad, with his complete trust in the fact that the series of 'A Glimpse of Joy' were meant to see the light of day, understood and supported my need for the long break – away from the family. His short trips to Whitefield and Parthi added warmth to the moments of bliss in this memorable period of my life.
- Particular gratitude goes to Nargish Aunty for her overwhelming demonstration of selfless love – leaving Mumbai to give me company during my period of trial. Being a mother, cooking nourishing meals for me, she took utmost care of me while writing consumed my time.
- Special thanks goes to Aban for her ongoing support to the series of 'A Glimpse of Joy', for providing invaluable assistance in giving the final touch, drawing my attention to important details that I had missed out earlier.
- Deep appreciation to Vivek who, with his wealth of insights, helped me to bring the book to its present level. I owe a debt to him who enriched this book.

Synopsis

In this Volume, I have recollected my most vivid memories of my 10 months' stay in His spiritual abode. It's with pleasure that I share with you the magical effect His love in the form of daily teachings via dreams and visions had on me. He laboriously taught me to expand my definition of divinity. My attempt is to give you a glimpse into the spiritual consciousness wherein my soul so often experienced the love of my guru.

He consistently made it a point to remind me that all throughout He expected me to be focussed on the Divine. This meant not only during the short span of daily meditation or bhajans but also while writing His books, having meals or interacting with another human being.

Each day I learned something new about myself, and in doing so I was never again the same person. Each experience of this blissful period brought me greater fulfilment, closeness to divinity in its different forms – both divine and human. Ultimately, oneness with all humanity.

My guru inculcated in me pure, unalloyed loving devotion to the Divine in His multiple forms. Then He made me recognize Him as a spark of the Divine dwelling in every human being. Through His daily teachings He made me understand what a life of seva and spirituality meant. He briefed me on the path of karma yoga – of loving service to our fellowmen. At the same time, He stressed on the importance of the path of Bhakti – devotion to the Lord in the form of prayers and meditation. The series of 'A Glimpse of Joy' are meant for ordinary people like me. I hope that the experiences shared herein succeed in unfolding the spiritual truths with simplicity for them to be understood easily.

Each time He appears in dreams and visions and I correctly interpret them, they invariably provide helpful information to me.

(Visions are different from dreams. These are the Lord's visitations to me in a wakeful state, mostly during meditation and bhajan time.) This book is also an attempt at bringing forth the Lord's endeavour to teach me that life is an opportunity to overcome defects, weaknesses, limitations, and transform human nature into divine nature – therefore, utilize life well every second. He has been my best friend who has always believed in me even before I have had a chance to prove that I deserve His trust; a friend who continues to encourage me to dream the impossible dream – to become His image.

Friends, I want you to know that I am not to be a teacher for anybody and that I can only share my experiences, relate what I have done in life and what I have gained from it. Please note that in this life of mine (with Baba holding my hand) I am attempting to find my way. I am still at a formative stage, where the space and scope for improvement is considerable. Working on me patiently, Baba wants me to progressively change the situation in my life to better and faster spiritual progress and cultivation of feelings of love for one and all. Very often He places me in situations where it is painful to see myself reflected in my adversaries. Sometimes it is as though these individuals are mirroring aspects of my own self that I would otherwise be unwilling to confront, and that is the reason these people exist in my life. In short, He not only brings to my notice my limitations but also helps me overcome them.

My dream of becoming a good human being is perhaps coming a little closer to fulfilment. But His dream of making me reach perfection will materialise only after a prolonged struggle on my part along the lines in which He wishes me to move; rather more of a struggle on His part is what He seemed to express on 3rd September '95. Let me quote a part of His message as He appeared to me in His Shirdi Sai form. While actually adjusting the pupil of my eye with His own divine hand, He declared, "Khurshid, I am referring to that inner eye of yours. Whenever your inner eye shifts from its place blocking your vision, I set it right so that it may focus only on what it should. Khurshid, the change won't come about overnight. For the next few years I'll be quite busy setting your vision right. So till such time you may carry on with your work and let me do mine."

Though I can't predict what your reactions to my writings will be, at least to my own self it is clear that I have written these Volumes in submission to His Will. There is a possibility that the sharing of a few of the lessons taught to me in my life could help you discover your strengths as well.

1

My Faith in Baba's Protection Put to Test

Baba Provides Shelter at Affordable Rates

The Lord had predetermined the path He wished me to tread. Enthusiasm had led me to enlist myself in His service. But soon I found myself admitting that if the service would begin with a rigorous training of detachment, then I longed to back out. To cut myself off from a world I was rooted in (my family) required a lot of courage. Later, begging His forgiveness, I decided to surrender myself to His will and obey Him at all costs. He in turn helped me to evolve His message in the form of the series of 'A Glimpse of Joy'. He took over my charge and I spent a blissful period of 10 months in His presence.

On 18th May 1993 I had set off for Whitefield, Bangalore. My companion, Santosh Aunty (an acquaintance from Mumbai who attended the same bhajan group that I did) chattered on and I listened, relieved that she did not inquire of me as to what had led me to leave my family to be on my own in Whitefield/Parthi. In my emotional fragile state, I did not want to try to explain. I was going there with no confirmed accommodation, without enough funds for bare necessities in life and with very personal notes in hand. A small knot of fear gripped my stomach. I was entering an unknown world. But I would soon be in the company of my guru and that was worth any amount of inconvenience I'd have to put up with on a material level.

Although I had not known it at that time, the move to Parthi/Whitefield did mark an important step in the preparation for my own future. It removed me from 'home', from the protection that my family could have offered me. I understood it was a time for letting go of the past and move on.

Landing in Whitefield, Bangalore, I felt vulnerable, alone. Yet, I felt compelled to decline the offer made by Santosh Aunty to stay with her, despite free boarding and lodging at the residence of Leela Amma, an acquaintance of hers because Baba had not given me the permission to do so. At the same time, I did need alternate decent accommodation. I could see the hotel rooms easily available but couldn't afford the rent. Wandering into Kadugodi village, with quick steps, my heart throbbing with joy, my feet hastened to Nagu's residence. Nagmani was a young village girl, about 16 years old, addressed as Nagu by all. It was at her residence, in the spacious flat on the first floor that I had spent a few days on one of my earlier trips to Whitefield. This time however, it was already occupied. They had given it away on lease for a year. But they were gracious enough to offer me a room on the ground floor, provided I didn't mind using the common bathroom. Nagmani had three brothers, one studied in college and the others were still school-going. Her elder sister was married and stayed in a close by village but currently was staying here with her little one year old daughter. Krishnabai, Nagu's mom, was a very accommodating lady. It overwhelmed me to hear them say they could keep me at very nominal rates, (the same that the ashram had to offer). Their next offer surprised me even more and brought tears to my eyes. They told me that there was no need for me to stand in long queues at the ashram canteen and I could have my meals at their house at less than ashram rates, or whatever that I could afford.

My soul was seeking permanent anchorage with Him, with whom it had begun to realise its oneness. I had a sense of being on a definite mission. Besides doing the writing work, I devoted myself to rediscovering my true nature and the relationship of my soul with the all pervading spirit of God.

Time sped by quickly at the feet of my guru. Although I was deeply happy, those 10 months of training were not without struggle. Our Lord was lovingly but firmly engaged in transforming a weak human being into an exemplary disciple. What remains vivid in my mind are the daily teachings He imparted to me via dreams and visions and the experiences that followed to confirm the same. I no longer craved for my family as intensely as before, as I daily sat in His presence experiencing bliss. So began the second phase of my life, being given the opportunity to be at His feet. During the first phase, His glory had been partially concealed from me. During the second phase, He was helping me turn inwards, visualising Him within me. And this, dear readers, merged into the third towards the end of the year 1997, during which His radiance – in the form of 'Sunbeam' shone like the midday sun on all who benefited from it. (Sunbeam is a Public Charitable Trust catering to the educational and psychological/emotional needs of 1000+ underprivileged children in Mumbai. In 1997, as the Founder Trustee of the organisation, I had started off with a handful of children and, the numbers multiplied over the years.) At that point in time, it was known as the CRY Neighbourhood Project which later was christened as Sunbeam in the year 1999 and got registered as a Public Charitable Trust.

My dear guru had no plans (at least none in the immediate future that I could foresee) to make me perform any penance and austerity. To put it quite simply, one of the important lessons He taught me was that I needed to dutifully remain in this world. That fulfilling my earthly responsibilities need not separate me from God because I had to attempt at detaching myself from worldly desires and play my part as a willing instrument of the Divine. Here, He was referring to my immediate family as well as the larger family – His children. Renunciation did not mean abandonment of home. True renunciation on my part would be renunciation of my desires, passions and attachment. By guiding me to lead a balanced life, after my return to Mumbai 10 months hence, He was teaching me the simple yet profound truth that oneness with the Divine, self-realisation is dependent on inner, rather than outer, renunciation.

Via His daily teachings, my guru guided me into the path of devotion, action and wisdom. He had no plans to keep me in Parthi forever but release me for an outward mission – which was to take the form of Sunbeam of which I was not aware then. The hole in my heart I had thought would never be healed. Yet, today a time had come when I had finally been enveloped into the fold of the warmth and affection of my Divine parent.

I came deserving my own destiny. And when it wasn't a good one, I had been given this chance by Him to change myself. He wanted me to change because of His love. He helped me in altering my destiny. Before taking my life any further, I resolved to work on myself.

Feeling Vulnerable and Rootless without Family, Home and a Steady Job

Dear readers, let me take you through my journey as I experienced it right from day one. Away from my family, my secure job at CRY and the familiar city of Mumbai, I admit for many days I felt rootless, wondering where I belonged. But in the days to follow, doubts were replaced by faith and conviction that I was at home in the company of my Divine parent.

With my Lord having taken care of my boarding and lodging at Whitefield, what reason had I to complain? He wished that I focus on my writing work. But my mind was in chaos. Wasn't I staying in Nagu's house without taking prior permission from Him? Did He will that I stay at Nagu's house, or had He other plans for me? After spending three nights at her house, I could not take His silence any longer and appealed to Him to respond to me, whatever it be to convey – His pleasure or displeasure at my decision. On 22nd May '93, at 1.30 a.m., I sat writing down the dream before I could forget His message.

Thousands of devotees had gathered for a glimpse of our Lord. But avoiding the crowd, He walked up to me. "One minute, my darling daughter." I was overwhelmed hearing Him whisper these words into my ears. Yes, I was startled at Him having addressed me so lovingly. And what He did next took me to a near ecstatic state. My dear parent came closer and rubbed His cheek against mine. This was perhaps His way of preparing me for the trial He was about to put me through, one that was to test my faith and surrender to His will. "Baba, when I follow you to Parthi, may I stay with Mrs. Jasawala inside the ashram?" He clearly expressed His displeasure at that query and pursing His lips, nodded His head in the negative. To ensure that I had got the message right, I repeated my query and His response was once again the same as before. Fear gripped me. Full of anxiety, I asked, "Baba, yes or no?" His response was in one word, "No", after which He was absorbed in deep thoughts. His face had taken an angry look and He was staring into what appeared to me as empty space but where in some near future He could apparently see how wrong my action of living with Mrs. Jasawala could prove to be. This was news that put me in a dilemma. Where would I stay if not with her? "Baba, in that case, shall I stay outside the ashram?" This I asked being fully aware that the ashram authorities would certainly not allot me a room for a long period. "Why outside, my dear? You shall stay inside the ashram."

Baba's message brought fear in its wake. His sweet, divine voice and the endearing terms 'dear' and 'darling' that He had uttered were the only consolation. Not to stay with Mrs. Jasawala was an unexpected response. He certainly didn't want me to stay with the only lady inside the ashram who was willing to accommodate me for 10 months at a stretch. (Mrs. Jasawala was a long-time permanent resident at His Parthi ashram who had been kind enough to give me shelter in her own home during my short trips to Parthi in previous years.) At the same time He wished that I live within the ashram premises. Who then did He want me to approach for accommodation? In mute agony I watched the form of my Lord as He walked away. Further and further He receded till I began to lose sight of Him and as a person in some dreadful fear of the future, I ran after Him. "Baba, Baba, wait for me." He immediately stopped in His tracks and turned to look at me. It was a look of compassion. "Baba, it's you who has been writing my book all along. You have been guiding me on innumerable occasions in writing these volumes. Isn't it so?" What a sweet smile of approval He gave me, a smile that dispersed all the dark clouds gathered in my mind. With that the dream came to an end.

Though Nagu's family had provided me with lodging and boarding facilities, the responsibility of keeping my spirits high fell on my dear guru. His little expressions of love had a healing effect on me. My relationship with Baba – my parent, was very sweet, intimate and one filled with devotion. He was helping me know that I was someone whom He loved dearly.

Even though ours was a divine relationship, by His expressions of love, He taught me that love did not survive under constant verbal neglect. Hence, I resolved to never fail to express my love in all my relationships. My dear guru understood my need for reassurance from Him without which I'd perish. Therefore, He consistently nurtured and strengthened our bond of love.

In His own way He was doing His best to lessen the pain and loneliness in my life due to separation from my family. My dear guru was sewing a small thread of continuity into my currently insecure life with no guaranteed roof over my head. He knew I felt uprooted from the soil of my family and missed them a lot. After His instructions that I couldn't live at Jasawala's residence, I was a complete bundle of nerves. He had given no concrete, helpful alternative suggestions either. And I cried myself to sleep, upset that He should test my faith so.

My Guru Sheds Tears at My Vulnerability of being on My Own

There was something aloof about Him. Sitting in a corner among the thousands who thronged His ashram, He appeared inaccessible to me – personal interviews is something I could not dream of being blessed with, at least on a physical plane. Well, He compensated for it by granting me multiple interviews in the dreams.

Since He had not given me any alternative but to wait in suspense about my accommodation problem once I followed Him to Parthi, I had begun to feel forlorn and neglected. Overcome by delusion, I had not realised how much pain He underwent each time I wept.

Getting worried about basic needs in life such as accommodation at Parthi or the meals was something that my Lord certainly did not approve of. Yet, He understood my need for His love and guidance, and my expectations from Him to provide for my worldly comforts. Hence, within 3 hours of the earlier dream, He once again appeared to me in a dream.

"Baba," I called out softly, expecting Him to be pleased to see me. But to my dismay, He turned His face away. "Baba, are you fed up of me?" I enquired expecting to receive a negative answer. My guru, visibly irritated by my excessive need for approval and reassurance, spoke with evident exasperation, "Of course." There was something so terribly earnest in His tone that I sobbed wildly, "Baba, please don't ever turn away from me like this." Now His eyes were full of compassion and tenderness; His face expressed love – that of a mother who had forgiven an erring child. He was actually smiling and it was a mischievous smile. Immediately mustering courage, I asked the question uppermost in my mind. "Baba, since you don't want me to stay with Mrs. Jasawala, who do I go and stay with?" Absorbed in His own thoughts, His only response was, "Hmmm." So I repeated my question and this time His response was even more confusing than before. "Go to Radhika's house." To confirm if I had the name right, I asked, "To stay with Radhika?" Pointing out to me and looking at me ever so gently as though I were a wounded child, He whispered more to Himself than to me, talking about the two of us in the third person, "When she cries, Baba also cries with her." A tear actually slid down His eye as He said so. Someone, whom I assumed to be a devotee, rushed to ask Him the cause of His grief but Baba never disclosed it. I was moved by His touching gesture. My dear guru who had only a moment ago seemed so angry with me, was now shedding tears because I had done so. This kind of behaviour on His part immediately put my mind to rest. He cared for me and that was all that mattered. And I woke up happy and content that He was there to lead me out of uncertainty.

Baba allowed me the freedom of speech. With Him I could talk, express my feelings and forever expect Him to love me unconditionally. Full of remorse as I was, for bothering Him over such a trifle issue as accommodation at Parthi, I silently prayed to be forgiven.

Lost and Utterly Lonely Among Thousands of Devotees

My routine was set. I woke up at 6.15 a.m. to be in time for the morning darshan. My guru was seated in my heart. That was one of the reasons why I didn't feel the need to sit in the token number queues. His regular visits in dreams to answer my daily queries left me with no unsolved problems to be checked with Him on a physical plane. After morning darshan, I sat and wrote right up to 4 p.m. except for the half an hour break that I took for lunch. On my return to Nagu's house once again after evening darshan, I carried on with my writing work for a few more hours. At 7.30 p.m. I had my dinner and was in bed by 9 p.m.

23rd being a Sunday, the crowds swelled even further. As per my habit, reaching the hall quite late, I was about to take my place in the vacant space at the far end of the hall. A lady volunteer walked up to me and insisted that I leave and take a seat outside the hall. It was with a heavy heart that I followed her instructions and moved out of the hall. I had no idea why the volunteer had been so rude to me when there was still ample space in the last enclosure.

How I longed for a seat inside the hall. Unlike others, I did not have the luxury of time to sit in long token queues, given my writing work and the fact that I kept indifferent health. Actually I had multiple tumours all over my body, very visible lumps with the one on the neck being the most painful. Only if this inexhaustible stream of devotees would vanish for a day, I'd get an opportunity to get closer to Him. Soon I was chiding myself for my wishful thinking. My anguish could not be justified by any logic. Like me, every devotee sought the source of Divine love – Baba. My chain of thoughts was suddenly interrupted by the sight of my dear guru walking in my direction. He walked right up to where I sat outside the hall. Soon He was standing right before me. My cousin brother, Kaikobad, had given me a letter to be handed over to Him which I placed in His outstretched hands.

The Gloom Lifts as Sainath Acknowledges and Appreciates My Presence

One day I made a resolution. My goal in life would be to become His image and I decided to completely surrender to His will. Baba's response brought tears to my eyes. This one little resolution of mine, according to Him had made me worthy of reverence. At least, His response the next morning in a dream gave me that impression. Standing before me with joined hands, He bowed to me in reverence. Even before I knew what was happening, He bent low and touched my feet! It was indeed the most humbling experience I had had till date. I couldn't allow my guru to be at my feet and immediately took a step backwards. "Baba, are you happy to see me?" I questioned. "Yes, I am happy. Very happy. Happy indeed that you have come," He replied softly. His beautiful eyes were fixed on mine as He said these words. What divine joy flashed into them, making them sparkle all the more.

All I had to do was to keep my commitment of total surrender and never let my faith waver. That was my only weapon at a time when I had no other source of support. His response in the above dream brought peace and filled the void created in my heart at the separation from my family.

Baba was happy that I had heeded His call. What more could I ask for. Gradually I understood that till I lived enveloped in sorrow or fear of loneliness for want of human love or in the bondage of the senses, I would never realise the true nature of my soul. My guru had called me to impart spiritual training, to help me get rid of all my attachments. My devotion, my unending flow of love for the Lord, mingled with a deep knowledge and conviction of His unconditional love for me was what helped me on my path to self-realisation for the rest of my life.

My Lord had already planned my future. This one year was to be the preparatory period. He had resolved to take my hand and lead me to my true self and beyond. In the months to follow, blessed by divine insights, my understanding of myself and my connection with the Divine increased manifold. He consistently helped liberate my mind of its worldly bonds and attain the level of absolute oneness with the Divine.

By my total faith in Him, surrender to His will and remorse for past actions, I sought His forgiveness, and tried to work out my karma that had until then made me unready to be in His company for divine wisdom.

My prayers did not go unheard. To my amazement, on 1st June '93 I woke up to find myself completely cured. The multiple tumours that I had all over my body for quite some time and had caused me considerable discomfort had vanished miraculously. The spiritual method of healing by God's power was the greatest and was instantaneous. Perhaps earlier my faith was lacking and I had not been receptive to His healing power.

Our guru wanted me to have one-pointed attention on Him so that I'd not be inwardly affected by changing circumstances in my outer life. Disappointments did not have to move me. I had to learn to accept whatever He had to offer without being too elated or too discouraged.

Though the tumours had subsided, the whooping cough persisted and so did the bleeding from my mouth. So one day I consulted a doctor at the hospital in Whitefield only to be told that I was suffering from Tuberculosis. The medical reports confirmed the diagnosis. Because I foolishly believed that I suffered due to my own karma, I decided not to take medication.

Baba appeared to Nagu in a dream. Until then, she had not been aware of my ailment nor the fact that I had resolved not to take any medicines. Our Lord informed Nagu that I was not paying heed to the doctor's advice and not taking the tablets as prescribed by him. Baba also gave her the details of the exact doses of the tablets that I was supposed to take.

His above message to me via Nagu was an eye-opener. Yes, it is true that to a large extent the cure of a disease depended on my karmic condition – the sum total of the effects of my past actions. But it also depended on the antidote taken for that illness. Thinking that my karma predetermined me to suffer, I decided to give up on medication and accept the inevitable. That, of course, was being fatalistic. God helps those who help themselves. Of course, I had to have faith in the power of the mind to heal myself, but He also wished me to give credit to medical science and not to disregard it completely.

"Can You take over My Job of Cleaning the Path to the Temple?" Baba Asked Me

One morning, in the beginning of June 1993, He came up with a strange request in the dream. The scene was of Prashanti Nilayam. As I walked up to the main steps leading to the Prashanti temple, I spotted our Lord with a broom in His hand and a bucket of water in the other. Upon approaching Him and enquiring with Him about the unusual job He seemed to have undertaken, in soft but sad tones, His response was, "This is my hospital, my child. Most of my patients here are in the habit of quarrelling with each other." "But Doctor, why do You do such odd jobs instead of sticking to Your role of curing people?" I asked out of curiosity. "See how dirty they have made the steps that lead to the main gate of the hospital. Besides treating the patients for their ailments, as a Doctor I also ensure the cleanliness of the hospital premises." And His eyes softened as He brought the broom and the bucket up to me, "Would you like to take up the job of cleaning the steps that lead to the place where my patients finally get healed? Do you mind taking over my job?" "Not at all," I answered quickly, taking up a broom and joining Him in His current role. It was a back-breaking task as I had to bend all the time while cleaning the path that led to His temple, His temple that He referred to as His hospital. At long last I managed to clean all the steps leading to the temple and looked up at the main gate, satisfied at the results. To my dismay, a few individuals whom I presumed were His patients, climbed down the steps with soiled footwear and they quarrelled with each other like little children. I was horrified to see that the cleanliness that I had so laboriously achieved had gone to nought. The entire path leading to the temple was soiled as before. With tears streaming down my cheeks, I turned to Baba. "Doctor, what's the sense in cleaning the path if they are going to spoil it again and again?" He responded by asking me a counter question, "Do you expect everyone who comes here for treatment to get healed or overcome their weaknesses? No, it does not happen that fast. You should never lose hope but start afresh. Perseverance will help you accomplish your task one day." Neither very hopeful nor focussing on the end result, I once again set about with the cleaning job, praying that this time the patients leave His hospital with clean shoes and not muddy ones as before. But I was hoping for too much. The dream went on with me bending all the time, cleaning the path over and over again while the patients, as before, soiled it. The only thing that kept me going about with what seemed like a thankless task was the fact that He had requested me to give Him a helping hand. The dream ended.

Baba did not want me to be content living in Divine consciousness. He wanted me to stretch myself to the service of the Divine; by serving our fellowmen. No doubt, I had begun with devotion to the Divine but He didn't want me to stop there. He desired that I strive to translate that adoration into action.

Baba wanted me to take over His job. Even if I would be able to achieve a fraction of what He did for mankind, I'd consider myself blessed. Yet, I wasn't clear what role it was that He wished me to take on besides writing these volumes and taking care of my immediate family upon my return to Mumbai. Gradually as the months rolled by in His divine company, months full of insights that led me closer to Him, experiencing the divinity that pervaded all around me, I learned the following lesson. It was not enough for me to eliminate the desire for the fruits of my action and surrender them to the divine. I also needed to give up my personal choice of the kind of work to be done. It was Him who had to determine the work I had to do.

The above dream also set me thinking about Baba and me – the unique relationship that I had always shared with the Divine. I recalled the umpteen number of times He had forgiven me, held me in His compassionate embrace despite the fact that I had failed Him time and again. I thought of the numerous times I had let Him down and yet He had never given up on me. I could also easily recall the relief I felt as I could sense Him forgiving me each time and saying that it was OK as long as I resolved not to repeat the same mistakes. His soothing, comforting words flooded me with relief. At my disobedience, in utter exasperation, He had also punished me by closing His door on me for a day or two. Angry with Him, even though I knew I had been at fault, I had spent such days thinking about the defence I could make. But most unexpectedly, He'd reappear, pained at our separation. He would then go on to explain that I had to grow up and learn to be as forgiving in my life with others as He was with me. I was accepted unconditionally. No matter what errors I made in life, He never stopped trusting me. He firmly believed that I'd strive to become His image and succeed at it. All my life He had conveyed the message that He loved me, no matter what.

Today, He wanted me to try playing His role! Our dear guru was holding out His hand to me in the form of a request that I take over His job, even if it meant the smallest fraction of it, at my own level. If as He had appealed to me in the dream, He wanted me to take over His role, would it ever be possible to measure up to His expectation – of having the large-heartedness to continue to shower His children with unconditional love no matter what? I could sense He was giving me an opportunity to prove to myself that no task on earth was impossible if I put in the required effort. And I was determined not to let Him down. At least, I could make an effort in that direction.

One more form in which I viewed Baba was as a leader who inspired me with confidence, courage and a sense of mission. He had actually asked me if I were willing to take up His job of cleaning the path that led to His temple, the path that was time and again soiled by His students who simply couldn't learn to love each other. Of course, I would offer myself at His feet and accept whatever role He assigned to me as His gift and as an opportunity to prove my love for Him. I'd take up the role with a true sense of mission, a sense of sacrifice and strong values.

The pride that came along with being recognised by my guru led me to strive diligently for a life of greater heights. Unlike at home and at the places where I had served, here in His presence, I lived with His consistent affirmations of my worth as a human being whom He could entrust with His job. His trust in me stimulated me to try harder and do better at the job He had assigned to me. How could I ever betray the confidence He had so willingly placed in me, the recognition He had given me?

Just like our guru calls each of us in our own way to success, He was calling me. This success of course would have little to do with the world's assessment. While the writing of these Volumes could have been the grand vocation He had in mind, I believed He had another higher vocation planned for me, that of serving Him in mankind.

An Unfortunate Event at Parthi

On 4th June '93, our dear guru left for Parthi. I should have followed Him but some instinct held me back. The uneasy feeling within me persisted that I better not leave Whitefield till I received a clear sign from Him to do so. Santosh Aunty had been a donor at Baba's organisation and, as per ashram rules, would be allotted a room for the fortnight that she wished to stay at Parthi. The dear lady had generously offered me to share her room, upon my return to Parthi. But the dream I had had in the recent past had left me with an uneasy feeling of an impending danger and I prayed to Baba that till such time that He wished me to stay back at Whitefield, He should appear in my dreams on a daily basis. The day He didn't give me darshan in the dream, the very same morning I'd leave for Parthi, taking it as a sign from Him that it was time I could do so. There was a feeling that I shouldn't be leaving before the 7th morning. This strange intuition remained an unsolved mystery till a few days later when I was actually on my way to Parthi on that very day. On the 7th of June, He didn't grant me darshan in a dream or even a vision. Hence, I immediately packed my bag and was soon at Brindavan gate from where I was supposed to board a bus to the Bangalore station and from there another bus to Parthi. "Baba's driver has been murdered. Therefore, bus services to Parthi have come to a stand-still at least for today." This news did not deter me from my resolution to leave for Parthi. Nagu's younger brother pointed out to a vehicle saying, "This man is about to leave for Parthi. Why don't you join him and his group?" They were a group of Kashmiri men who owned shops in the Parthi village but who always followed Baba to Whitefield whenever He came here. I was fearful of joining a group of strangers but cast aside my doubts and approached them with the request to allow me to be a part of their group on their journey to Parthi. Initially, they responded to my request for a lift with incredulous looks, but later let me enter their car. They tried to make me change my mind by giving me a detailed account of the news that they had heard from others. "There have been murders at the Prashanti Nilayam temple last night. Swami's driver, cook and others lay injured and the murderers, who also happen to be His students if I have heard it right, have been shot down by the police." After this little speech, the Kashmiri stranger gave me a keen look. And the silence that followed spoke as if to say that I better abandon the idea of going to Parthi for a while. Once again I requested them to let me join them and this time they did so without another word.

The Tragedy at Parthi Compounded my Accommodation Problem

Upon reaching Parthi, I was at a loss to locate Santosh Aunty and had no option but to move to the common shed inside the ashram where I was instructed by the accommodation authorities to go to. The scene that met my eyes as I passed by the mandir grounds was that of a few devotees cleaning up the space right from the steps of the mandir.

There was tight security all over the ashram. Even when Baba did come to give darshan, the police followed Him in order to grant Him protection. At least that is what they believed they were doing. Each devotee had to pass through a security check before entering the grounds for darshan. Things that a week ago would have been perceived as a significant inconvenience to Baba and the devotees were now being perceived as essential security measures. Devotees claimed that the whole question of this attack and its aftermath must be understood within the paradigm of good and evil.

Though He has a large number of followers all over the world, there are even larger numbers who are either not aware of His presence or lack faith in Him. This tragedy had given further impetus to this lack of faith in His divinity. Twin fears of my family/friends' opinions of Him (as they coaxed me over the phone to return to Mumbai) and the accommodation problem at Parthi gripped me and I was in a shaky frame of mind as to where to seek shelter in Parthi.

Ashram Regulations Overruled due to Baba's Grace

The next morning after spending a restless night in the overcrowded shed, He appeared in my dream. "Baba, when will you meet me?" (Here, I meant a personal meeting on a physical plane.) In response He changed His form to that of a toddler and crawled on all fours. Soon the Divine babe was at my feet, waiting to be taken into my arms.

The above dream was no consolation. A single girl wanting to stay for so long in an ashram seemed especially prone to suspicion. My life it seemed was ruled by no roof over my head, fear and unpredictability. But my memoir of the months to follow is a story worth narrating, a story of my Divine Parent's love for me that was expressed by Him in a million ways.

One morning, after meeting her in the darshan grounds, I stayed with Santosh Aunty for a week by moving from the common shed to her room inside the ashram. On the last evening I didn't know where to go once she would leave. Baba's command given to me in a dream on 22nd May '93 had been that I had to live inside the ashram till such time that I met Radhika. In the highest sense, if I believed in Baba and had complete faith in Him, there was no reason to ask Him to arrange for my accommodation. My dear guru knew my needs better than I, with my limited human understanding. To pray for myself, therefore, was a contradiction of my own faith in my guru.

The same evening His divine drama started unfolding itself before my eyes as Santosh Aunty introduced Dolly, a young girl who sought our permission to be allowed to spend the nights with us. We explained to her that she could stay for a night with us but next morning we were supposed to vacate the room. "Khurshid, you don't have to look for accommodation outside the ashram. I have been allotted a room in the South Wing, S2 A6. You are most welcome to stay with me for a month." Her answer brought relief that words cannot express. But since I was curious to find out why she wanted to spend the night with us she let us know that currently the room allotted to her did not have a fan and since she had made friends with Santosh Aunty during the darshan time, she had made this strange request. Listening to her, I was sure it was Baba's leela to send her to our place for one night and then to make her offer me accommodation for a month.

He Approved of My Efforts at Writing my Autobiography

One day I carefully smoothed out some paper on my desk, then picked up a pen to write. Initially, I struggled to find the words to express my thoughts and feelings. But eventually, the writings began to take shape.

In Parthi I read the introduction to the book and the few pages that I had written and found them satisfying. But many blank pages lay before me. What if I never got it right? I wondered grimly. Baba gave me the required courage. I scribbled a few lines. Parthi's environment was such that its seeming magic invariably helped me think things through and now I decided to seek His blessings.

The next time our guru appeared to me in a dream, I held out my books to Him, requesting Him to bless them by saying, "Baba, please bless my books." My Lord immediately placed His divine hands on my books, in a gesture of blessing.

That morning I woke to the realisation that I was not alone. And that He approved of my efforts at writing. Feeling confident again, I resolved to focus on my writing. It was a happy, productive time, before and after daily darshans. I spent days, months in utter bliss, completing the handwritten manuscripts by the end of my stay on 28th February 1994, thus covering a decade of experiences in life and my gradual spiritual progress.

My Guru Intimated Me that I'd Soon be Staying with Foreigners

It was too early to know all the consequences of Dolly's offer to provide accommodation in Parthi within the ashram premises. But a gesture of this magnitude evoked in me more than the desire to give a simple thank you note. I needed to repay her generosity. And what better way could I do so than by acceding to her request that I become 5 year old Poonam's guardian during my one year stay in Parthi. This was to be her dear child's first year in Baba's boarding school at Parthi and my presence in her life every Sunday would lessen her pain at the separation from her own parents. I couldn't imagine letting Poonam sit alone and desolate in the schoolyard while the other children ran into their parents' arms and got enveloped in warm embraces.

Knowing that within a month Dolly would be gone and that would leave me without a roof over my head, I decided to check it out with Baba well in advance. On 11th June, in a dream, after much hesitation He finally granted me permission to touch His feet. Later, as I went closer and rested my head on His chest, I found Him smiling as though that was certainly permissible, more than being at His feet. He seemed to be in an extremely happy mood and said, "If you want to ask for something, go ahead and speak out." With that sort of an invitation from my Lord, I could not resist myself. "Baba, where shall I go and stay after a month?" (Here what I meant was after Dolly left and after my 10 days stay in the shed – the maximum period that the authorities would allow me to stay inside the ashram.) "You shall stay with foreigners." With that reassurance, the dream came to an end.

On the 13th of June, Dolly was requested by the ashram authorities to shift to S2 C2. To Dolly's relief and to my dismay, it was a room with a fan. I was running temperature almost every evening and hence shivered under the fan that was kept at full speed throughout the night. With pride she announced, "Khurshid, influence works. You have none so you'll be in the common shed for a few days after I leave and then without a roof over your head. For devotees like me who have influence with the right people in Baba's organisation, it is no problem to demand and receive rooms in the wing closest to His temple and for any length of time."

Surrendering to His Will and giving Priority to His Books

The dream on 15th June '93 was a strange one. I found myself in hiding, far away from my family. At my home in Mumbai, my family members were in tears. Baba went to console them. Our relatives, neighbours and family friends all seemed upset with me, claiming that I was not bothered about the well-being of my family and had no right to shirk my duties. They also maintained that I was a coward who had run away from my duties. To my shock, I found myself behind bars. Baba was in tears and His eyes were red and swollen. "Baba, my imprisonment was inevitable but you need not cry for me. It is a great consolation to me that you are aware that I am here with the books out of self-defence and not with the intention of hurting anyone." Baba continued to cry and the others carried on with their taunts.

The above dream of my imprisonment did not have to be taken in the literal sense. In reality, I was indeed in a sort of a jail, imprisoned by the consequences of my wrong actions. But I could break out of this prison and be one with God again. I was behind the bars of my own fate, bars of my karma, emotions and attachments. It was neither God nor anyone else who had created the jail but me. By surrendering to His will and with the saw of wisdom provided by Him, I could severe the bars of this jail in which my soul was imprisoned.

No matter how many incarnations of bad karma I had, His grace combined with my sincere devotion would be enough to bring into my consciousness the light of God, burning away the darkness of the errors of the past.

He Willed that I Stay in His Company Till End February ' 94

Almost every alternate day, He appeared in my dreams or visions. But there were those unlucky periods when almost for a week He would vanish, leaving me wondering at it, leading to an introspection and consequently corrective steps on my part. On 18th June '93 He blessed me in a dream but there was no special message. (Of course, I did have daily darshans, and that too four times a day but that was during darshan and bhajan time – morning and evening. These were mere glimpses of Him as I sat at the far end of the hall or outside the hall at the steps of the South wing from where I could see Him as He walked from His new residence somewhere above Poorna Chandra Hall on to the darshan grounds.)

On 20th June '93, in a dream as I bent low to touch His feet, He stopped me by asking, "Khurshid, how often have I told you that you should not be touching my feet?" Before He could move away from me, I once again checked out with Him if He wanted me not to leave for Mumbai before March '94. He confirmed that it is what He willed.

How remote my family, the office, the world seemed, as I spent my days at the feet of my guru here in Parthi – the abode of peace. It was sheer joy to know I could stay here till as long as March '94.

If I wished to make my life happy I had to learn to live in the present. I was living too far into the future, or oftentimes weighed myself down with regrets of the past. My present was full of happiness and that's all that should have mattered to me.

The Veil of Maya Lifts to Receive His Grace

During His next visit to me in a dream on 21st June '93, I could not see His face clearly. Everything seemed hazy, my vision had grown dim. But to my joy, my vision soon cleared and He blessed me with a few toffees.

As shown in the dream, maya came in my way and distracted my attention from Him. He would certainly test me, carrying on playing with His divine sport. But I had to keep my sight fixed on Him, seeking no other.

I resolved to bring under control the mind, the reasoning faculty and the senses which roamed behind objective pleasures. All I had to do was to train myself to follow the course of one pointed disciplined attention on Him.

Granting Me Continuity of His Protection Among all the Uprooting

After the 25th June, Dolly was supposed to vacate the room inside the ashram. Since I had still not been fortunate enough to find my Radhika, the person whom Baba had instructed me to live with, in utter desperation, I got carried away by the promises of Anuradha, an old lady who informed me of good decent accommodation outside the ashram. She assured me that the rent would be only Rs. 500 per month just as I would have spent on a room within the ashram premises. Conveniently forgetting Baba's instructions of not seeking accommodation outside the ashram till He so permitted, I sought His permission in a dream on 26th June '93 beginning with, "Baba, Baba, I am unable to find accommodation." He took me by surprise by asking, "Why, hasn't someone promised you a room today?" Thrilled that He was aware of my efforts, I proudly questioned Him, "Are you referring to Anuradha?" "Yes, yes. Go, go." Happy beyond words, after prior permission, I had padnamaskar. He then moved on to the other devotees. Coming back to me, He gave me a pleasant surprise by placing in my hands a bouquet of flowers! Once again He took a round meeting devotees gathered in the hall only to return to me. Materialising another bouquet of pink and white flowers, He gently placed it into my hands. I also noticed with delight a beautiful white rose on the top of all those flowers.

My joy knew no bounds. I took the above dream message as a green signal from the Lord to go along with Anuradha, believing that my problem for accommodation was solved once and for all. That lady simply told me that if I was still interested in that room, I'd have to pay rent not @ Rs. 500 per month that she had offered earlier, but @ Rs. 6,000 per month! I was devastated because I felt cheated not just by her but by my guru who had said, "Yes, yes. Go, go." Why had He put me through such humiliation?

The moment Baba perceived that I desired anything in preference to God (who alone I had to seek), He put every possible obstacle in my path to awaken me from my delusion. He took it upon Himself to help me recognise and overcome delusion; His mission was to make me into His image.

My immediate task, therefore, was not to find who was to be blamed for a given set of unfavourable circumstances, but to see what part I myself had had in bringing about that particular situation. A close and sincere self-examination showed the defect in myself – that of lack of faith in Him as the provider. Once again I was full of remorse.

How much of my time I had wasted in planning and working for my own material comforts. I was hopelessly preoccupied with the bodily needs. Baba knew that my folly and lack of surrender to His will could be overcome only by hard blows. So, He had changed His earlier instructions of not allowing me to stay outside the ashram (at least till I met Radhika) and resorted to agreeing with me, in going to the place Anuradha had recommended.

My ambitious hopes for decent accommodation within my means were shattered. I was devastated. But with determination I set to repair the damage I had done to myself and sought accommodation in the shed. There were fresh disappointments too, but I knew one thing now: I would never return to Mumbai till He permitted me to do so. The person behind the window of the accommodation office told me in no uncertain tones that he would allow me to stay in the common shed for 10 days and no more. He added that I need not even approach him for extending my stay in the shed. I gratefully accepted his offer and walked up to the common shed carrying my meagre luggage with me.

Baba had kept a reserve of flowers for me, various gifts – spiritual ones – that He had planned to offer to me one at a time in the months to follow. But He also had in mind flowers in the form of very sincere friends who were to make my well-being their priority. Flowers in this form, He knew, would give me some continuity amidst all the uprooting. Throughout my stay in Parthi/Whitefield He saw to it that I never experienced loneliness.

Our dear guru was extremely patient with me; He loved me unconditionally. His divine love was not so insubstantial that if I did something wrong or was not always able to live up to His expectations, He'd forsake me. He taught me to view the world as a nurturing place in which something good would always turn up and therefore I need not fret much about my needs being taken care of. I resolved to offer Him my heart with the flowers of devotion and purity.

Days Spent in the Appalling Conditions at the Common Shed

The conditions in the shed were appalling. I stood staring all around in horror at the common hall packed to its extreme by devotees who had spread mattresses all over. Upon checking with the volunteer in charge, I was told to spread out my mattress in the narrow space of 2½ feet in between two mattresses. On seeing me sweep the floor and realising that I'd be sleeping next to him, the man to my left started singing a Hindi film song, which was in bad taste.

I looked around the hall with its cold vastness and people, both men and women sprawled on their mattresses. As it was noon-time, they were resting. It was a hall with no sign of beauty or comfort in it. I was still cleaning the floor space I was to use when another man joined the earlier one in the singing.

None of the women in the hall appeared to be living by themselves as I was. They were with their families, hence, secure. Once again my eyes moved round all those people, some chit-chatting with family and friends, others snoring away and a few having their meals on their beds. Entirely forgetting my previous determination to go through all that might happen to me with patience and unflinching nerve, I now sat down on my narrow camp-bed very, very angry with myself and with Baba for making me live in a place as difficult as this one.

The circumstances there tempted me to catch the next train to Mumbai. Yet, with God's grace, I was able to stick to the parameters I had laid out for myself and succeeded in my endeavour of surrendering to His will and put up with this ridiculous situation till such time that He chose to send flowers my way – flowers in the form of genuine, caring human beings who would not mind giving me a decent roof over my head.

In the next few days, the crowd in the shed had reduced a bit, but that was the only consolation. In the general shed where I lay and had spent a few nights, each time I woke up I heard the rushing and pouring all around; the rains had come. Over my head and at many other places in the roof there were cracks and the water seeped through, so that from half a dozen patches of roof in the shed water dripped in and I had to often creep out of my bedding in order to shift it enough to make place for the jug that I set to catch the drops. No, it wasn't funny at all. It was an extremely frustrating experience, more so, because I was down with burning temperature and diarrhoea. In the middle of the night, with an umbrella and a torch in hand, I had to go to the common toilets outside the shed.

Amidst the appalling conditions that I lived in, He wanted me to see the Divine, to adapt to all kinds of hardships in life, to practice patience and to come out of my self-pity mode. My eyes welled with tears. "This is just way too much for me," I thought. My worst fears began to race through my mind, and soon I was sobbing. At the moment, I wondered if I would ever find the strength to see it through.

I was always striving to be rewarded and noticed. One day, convinced that my worth was not being duly evaluated by Him, I gave voice to my discontent. But He wanted me to be cheerful under all circumstances, at all times. Wherever He willed that I live, it was up to me to make heaven of it. All it required on my part was one-pointed attention on God and on my writing work and the surroundings wouldn't matter any more.

At His response, I hung my head in shame. In the dream, a child walked up to me with His message, "Why do you sit with your back bent in this manner? Learn to sit straight with your head held high. Baba has sent me with the message that if you stop complaining of any pain in life, He has promised to give you the first row today and to give you flowers." This dream was enough to teach me to be content with whatever life had to offer me.

In the Prashanti grounds that morning, the crowds were still the same. Yet, it was different during this darshan. For once I had got up early and gone and sat in the token queues. To my great joy I got token number one. As I sat in the front row and Baba stood before me, I was in a state of bliss. He continued to look at me penetratingly for almost half a minute. The divine spark of illumination from my guru touched me deeply. The message of peace and inner tranquillity was clear and took over me.

No matter what happened, my guru accepted no excuse for my becoming mentally ruffled. He did not want me to make a fuss of anything. Whenever I got disturbed, I was deepening the delusion in me.

Thus, after regarding me with silent compassion for almost half a minute, He slowly moved away, leaving me to my tears and reflections.

At the Mercy of a Stranger who Gave Me Free Shelter

On my way back after His close darshan, I recalled my experiences of the past one month in the company of Dolly and Poonam.

Dolly had always taken delight in harassment tactics. She had woken me up at midnight, at 3 in the morning – at any time I slept – and ordered me to press her feet. She had expected me to wash the tiffins whenever she, her sister and daughter had their meals at home. She claimed that she would be able to leave Parthi in peace knowing that I was to be her child's guardian. For that she would have to introduce me to the Principal of the school. But she added that she'd be ashamed to even walk by my side, let alone introducing me to anybody as her child's guardian – ashamed of my faded clothes, ashamed of my poverty, ashamed of my low status in life as compared to her own. (Of course, she had no choice but to introduce me to the Principal for the sake of her own child.)

Consequently, I had found myself sulking at the assault on my self-esteem. But soon I'd recover, each time telling myself that such childish behaviour did not become of me. As long as I devalued myself, so would others. I had to know where to draw the line and not let anyone take me for granted. Dolly would not cross her limits with me if I didn't allow her to do so.

Dolly understood pride as different from how I understood it. To her, arrogance and an exaggerated sense of self-importance meant pride. To me it was self-respect and values relating to myself. Seldom did a day pass when I had not been submitted to such demeaning, condescending experiences. Yet in all fairness to Dolly, I have to admit that she had at least trusted me, a complete stranger, to allow me to share her room in the ashram for almost a month.

I felt obliged to say yes when I should have been saying no. But I wondered now why I didn't refuse gracefully. Very often I had ended up doing her bidding. Lack of enough money for securing accommodation outside the ashram had snatched from me the right to say 'no' to her demands. Besides, people like Dolly had influence through which she had secured the room within the ashram. I had none. Baba had wished that I stay within the ashram premises till I met Radhika. This again was one more reason that made me put up with the indignities, the insults, the inhumane treatment in silence.

The Divine is manifest in everyone. By awakening the Divine within me, He was opening my eye to recognise the Divine in others as well. Once I understood this principle, a new kind of consideration entered into my relationship with others.

I had always been more fortunate than perhaps the majority of His devotees. Had He not taken the trouble to guide me at every step in my life, I'd have perhaps (if not always, then at least occasionally) been just as insensitive to others' feelings as Dolly was with me. Thinking on those lines made it easier for me to develop a more compassionate attitude towards others.

An incident that took place one day remained imprinted in my mind. Poonam was to leave for Baba's boarding school that same day and Dolly was to leave Parthi in a few days time. We had to vacate the room the same day though but I could not follow Dolly outside the ashram premises. "I'm worried about Khurshid Aunty, not you, mum. As for me, at the boarding school Baba is there to be my mother and father. But where will Khurshid Aunty go to live?" A knot had formed in my throat as Poonam, her daughter, repeated her concern about the lack of roof over my head. There had been a glistening in her eyes, as if tears were pooling at their edges. After so long I had heard someone say she was concerned about my well-being. My heart had felt fuller than it had ever been.

Poonam was a simple kid like any 5 year old. What set her apart and kept her memory warm and alive in my mind, though, was her complete faith in Baba and the equanimity with which she had accepted separation from her parents. She had taken Baba to be her parent and said she was actually looking forward to spending her childhood in His school at Parthi.

The child's attitude in life had been an eye-opener for me. She taught me: Self-pity weakens, but concern for others strengthens human nature. In times of distress I often contemplated on this lesson.

Sai Teaches Me the Virtue of Forgiveness

Now as I continued to tread the ashram grounds, I recalled my experiences with Jasawala Aunty who, as I have mentioned earlier, was a long-time permanent resident of His ashram. They were memories full of pain. She was in charge of one of the shops in the shopping complex within the ashram premises. Assuming that it was Him giving me an opportunity to work in His ashram, I had taken up her invitation to help her in her seva of serving the devotees visiting Parthi.

Her attitude towards the devotees in general and towards me in particular, was strange. She suffered from an inflated ego and claimed that being a permanent resident of His ashram gave ashramites like her superiority over other devotees. Whatever it be, since she was short of staff at the shop and needed assistance in sales during peak hours i.e. after darshans / bhajans, I had grabbed the opportunity to repay her earlier kindness of having given me shelter during my trips to Parthi in previous years.

I was myself surprised at the fact that I had actually managed to continue to work at the shop for a few hours for almost a month instead of quitting the very first day. Every single day this lady made it a point to insult me in public. She would give me clear instructions that I should request people for change. When I did so, that too in very polite tones and only when we were really hard-pressed for change, she'd stun me by apologising on my behalf to the customer. Then she'd turn around and tell me to stop harassing the public. Within minutes, she'd think of a new way to insult me in full view of the ashramites and other devotees.

On another occasion as requested by her, during free time, whenever for a few minutes there were no customers at the shop, I'd spend my time fruitfully in the role of packing that she had assigned to me. The moment she'd see a foreigner or a well-to-do Indian walk up to our shop, she'd address me in the most exasperated tones, "No matter how much I try to change you for the better, I see no hope. What will you gain in robbing me? Don't think I am not aware of your sly ways. This time I've caught you red-handed at robbing things from our shop." Turning to the purchaser, she'd say, "Don't imagine that all who enter this ashram are saints. There are robbers like her as well. We who are true devotees have to learn to forgive people like her. But one day she will pay for her sins." The customer sympathised with her, made the purchase and moved on, giving me disgusted looks.

On yet another occasion, due to shortage of change, I could not return a small amount of 25 paise to a customer. The devotee told me not to bother much but carry on with the next client. After that person had left, our dear lady made a big issue out of it. She never once mentioned the amount and the fact that even though I couldn't find the coin, it certainly was lying in the ashram account only. In a very harsh tone, she called out in a voice loud enough for all to hear, "Your lust for money is going to make you fall in the Lord's sight. We ashramites don't swallow what belongs to others. You will certainly not be able to digest such ill-earned money." A crowd of devotees soon gathered and she continued shrilly, "What else can one expect from girls who have led their entire lives in a city like Mumbai and not in the holy atmosphere of Parthi?" Baba wanted me to learn to forgive others, to love others and I forgave her then and there, telling myself that I'd give in one last try and talk to her in private the next day. But that next day never came. Before that an incident took place which made me resolve never to offer my seva at that shop again.

This time I felt myself really choking with anger when I heard her say, "I am aware why you wish to stay in the shed instead of taking up my offer to stay in my house where all comforts are available. I have my doubts you have been sleeping with men in the common shed." I was too aghast to respond. Ultimately, I left the scene when she asked me, "Can you tell me how many men have you slept with since you have come to Parthi?"

As I walked back to the shed, in tears and in anger, of one thing I was sure. I'd never again do any seva at that particular shop in the ashram. Besides, I demanded of Baba to appear to me the same night and give me an answer right away as to why I was being put through so much of humiliation.

In a dream the same night, I called out to Baba who had worn the Doctor's coat over His usual robes. "Doctor, doctor. Please cure me." In a trice He was by my side. I wept for quite some time, complaining to Him about the innumerable wounds I had received. "Please do something about the wounds I am receiving." "Let me inform you that I am the Doctor to inflict wounds on you." For a moment or two I was nonplussed at this strange, cold, unexpected response. Finally, I dared to ask Him, "As a Doctor I expect you to cure me and not cause me more pain." This time He responded in very soft tones as though to a small child, "Look deep within those wounds and you shall find some dirt lying therein. In order to give you an opportunity to remove that mud from your system I give you these deep wounds. And I expect you to heal yourself which is possible provided you are willing to clean the dirt from within."

The little dirt still to be removed from my system was the dirt of body consciousness, of my ego being hurt, of being ruffled at another's words. Whether I liked to accept it or not, whatever was happening to me at that moment was a result of the choice I had made. When someone insulted me wasn't I making the choice of being offended? Wasn't that a choice I could have made differently by remaining unperturbed and immersed in Him? Therefore, after the above dream, I resolved that I would not let my reactions be automatically triggered by people and circumstances in the choices I would make henceforth. Each time I'd make a choice, I'd first check with myself whether that choice would bring happiness to me and to others. If not, then I'd not make that choice.

Going by the dream and His instructions to me, Baba turned out to be my most beneficial physician. He was teaching me to be kind and forgiving by getting away from smallness. If others were unkind to me, He expected me to try to win them with love. If that didn't work, then to give the problem to Him and forget about it instead of brooding over another's words and action and causing myself pain.

I resolved never again to let any thoughts of resentment or anger to enter my heart, because I'd realised that if I had to become His image, I had to cultivate in me a high degree of forgiveness. No matter what Jasawala Aunty did to hurt me, I should be forgiving and compassionate. Yes, I had the power to change her feelings towards me if I practised that.

After the above dream, I resolved to send her loving thoughts of forgiveness and once again extend my hand of friendship to her. I learned and grew from this experience because I was beginning to love her unconditionally the way my guru loved me. And I resolved not to give up doing the few hours of voluntary work at Baba's ashram shop of which she was in charge.

Radhika Comes to My Rescue

The same morning after the dream (wherein I had been promised flowers from Baba), as I walked out of the Prashanti grounds after our guru's darshan, I felt at peace at my above resolution.

All of a sudden, through a sea of heads, I saw Nargish Aunty and Yasmin Aunty walking towards me. I couldn't believe my eyes till they were standing opposite me. I heard Nargish Aunty's voice as if from far away, from heaven. There were no words sufficient for that moment. I stammered something: we hugged and she said, "Khurshid, how ill and tired you look. Where are you staying presently? Please move in with either of us."

They could certainly provide me with the much needed shelter. But Baba's command had to be obeyed. He wanted me to live with Radhika and none other. I would therefore have to refuse their offer at the cost of having nowhere to go. The moment I'd complete 10 days at the shed, I'd have to move out from there as well – as per the existing ashram rules.

Just then Yasmin Aunty met up with an old acquaintance of hers and left us for a while. This is when I shared my predicament with Nargish Aunty. To my great surprise, she began to laugh and said, "Khurshid, if I say so, you may not believe me. So ask Yasmin Aunty yourself. She just shared with me on our flight here that of late she has been getting strange calls at home when everyone has been calling her Radhika. And she also firmly believes that Baba too addresses her by that name. So please join us without any hesitation." Upon her return, Yasmin Aunty confirmed the same. I walked trembling into their house, completely humbled and grateful to my guru.

These two wonderful ladies took it upon themselves to look after me. It was touching to experience both of them as mothers, who had made my well-being their prime concern. Because of the experience of total deprivation of the bare necessities in life in the past 10 days, now I felt that the vegetables they cooked for lunch were the best I had ever tasted, the hot water bath the most cleansing, the privacy to be on my own the biggest reward from God.

While Nargish Aunty sponsored the rent of my room, Yasmin Aunty who was all love and kindness, took over the charge of my meals. She took the trouble of buying a stove and providing me with home-made Parsi dishes! This saved me the trouble of standing in the long queues at the canteen. Being as good a cook as Nargish Aunty, she gave me nourishing and tasty meals. This lady from Singapore, before and after darshans was busy cooking for me. A miracle took place. Though she didn't know a single influential soul in Parthi, she was actually offered a seat among the VVIPs every single day, and at times, was offered the chair right at the entrance from where our Lord entered the grounds. She and I believed it was Baba's grace and blessing to her. As our guru would pass by her while coming from the auditorium (where He now lived) to the darshan grounds, He would at times smile at her or glance over at her. That is all she needed to keep her in high spirits. I was indeed glad for her.

Both my aunts (i.e. Sai family aunts – not related to me) could look through the tough exterior of an individual who had left her all to live in Parthi for a year. They looked upon me as a child; they could easily unearth the little girl within. Life had changed for me ever since these two dear ladies had resolved to fulfil my material needs. All I knew was that after the hard work I had been through for the past 6 years, I deserved my share of rest and unconditional love from friends like them.

I was not suggesting to myself that I become completely self-indulgent. But I did need a little self-indulgence from time to time. And it was a nice feeling knowing someone was there to take care of my needs while I sat working upon these Volumes. For once, instead of feeling selfish or guilty, I actually enjoyed being pampered.

Seeking Lord Zoroaster's Blessings

Early morning, on 4th July '93, upon waking up, I was blessed with a beautiful vision of our dear guru who then changed to the form of Lord Zoaraster.

As I gazed at the benevolent face of prophet Zoaraster, my prayer to Him was simple. "O Lord, I seek to attain purity of thought, word and deed by controlling my inner being through discipline. Be with me in my efforts to tread the path shown by you."

Within 3 days of the above vision, Baba again blessed me, this time in a dream on 7th July '93 – 3.30 a.m. On this occasion He had let me be at His feet and allowed me to press those Lotus feet into my eyes.

No Better Company than My Divine Parent

As I had mentioned earlier, if not daily, my Lord had made it a point to bless me with darshan at least every few days. On 9th July '93 at 4 a.m. as He stood before me in a dream, I asked, "Baba, within a month Nargish Aunty and Yasmin Aunty will be leaving for Mumbai/ Singapore respectively and once again I'll be left all alone. Whom do you want me to stay with then?" "Call your mother or brother to stay with you," He replied. He gently lifted me by the hand and led me to the devotees waiting for His darshan. Addressing the public, He said, "I have called her to Parthi. I want her to stay here." My hand was held by Him in a tight grip. His eyes were full of compassion as He looked at me. "Yes, Baba, you are my mother, father, brother, friend, child and guru. Please stay with me. Don't leave me." Reading my thoughts, He smiled for a moment before enfolding me in His loving embrace. Taking Him to be my parent and best friend, I clung on to Him.

Before I knew what was happening, the Lord and I were dancing, yes, dancing! How secure I felt in the arms of my Divine parent. Soft music of the flute could be heard all around. We swooped over the temple grounds. Then, we were suddenly spinning. These were rare moments with my guru. And I could do almost anything to prolong them. There were no more worries of who'd give me company after Nargish Aunty and Yasmin Aunty left. For a long time, we were spinning, lost in time. After a while I was breathless. He was making me spin at such a speed that it made my head reel. So I pleaded with Him to go a bit slower. In His mercy, He did lessen the speed and I could breathe more freely!

I had always had a vague idea of what it meant to be one with the Divine. But these were moments no one had prepared me for. He was playing the role of my father, mother, brother, sister and child – all combined into one. He meant to me more than my family in Mumbai. With Him by my side, I no longer needed human support. This was clear to me. And with this very strong flash of insight I kept on dancing so the spell wouldn't be broken. I felt thrilled and proud that He took time off just to let me experience the bliss of love divine. Those were magic moments spent in the arms of the Divine parent, moments I'll cherish forever.

This particular dream of mine left me shaken. On waking up I could still feel His arms around me for a few seconds, though I could not see Him. Had it been a mere dream or an experience at another level of consciousness?

With my Divine parent I could be expressive of my affection for Him and blissfully remain in His protective arms for eternity. It is from my guru Himself as I had experienced Him in the past and did so even now, that I learned an important lesson. That where words fail us in our efforts to understand and be understood, reaching out with kind gestures of support was the most direct form of communication we have. It conveys the message to the other person that you are there and that you care.

My Guru Desists from Acknowledging My Presence in Public

"Baba, is it only in dreams that I shall continue to meet you? What about actually calling me close to you once at least?" This prayer of mine was answered via a dream on 10th July '93 at 4 a.m. which I shall describe now.

He was giving darshan where the men were seated. He moved about freely among them, getting close to someone or the other, giving a pat on the shoulder to one and / or holding another's hand for a while. But the minute He came to the ladies side He maintained His distance. Unable to resist myself, I ran to Him. Just as I was about to put my arms around His neck, He stopped me from doing so by saying, "Not now. Not here." And in order to be more explicit, He turned His face towards the public, moving His eyes among them and by gestures told me that I should not expect such closeness with Him in front of them as they were not aware of our divine relationship - a relationship that was built on the pure love of a mother and child. Yet, in order not to disappoint me completely, He did place His hands into mine and held them tight. And, He also let me kiss His hands and press them into my eyes.

This dream was His way of telling me that if He chose to embrace me in public, there was a possibility of our relationship being misunderstood in case someone attributed it to the physical plane and that would indeed hurt both of us. To understand our relationship, one needed to have a spiritual knowledge far surpassing all material wisdom. Having chosen me as His mother and knowing of my maternal feelings towards Him, and also my devotion to Him, it wasn't surprising then that He regarded me as His own and hugged me – a gesture of the affection that was mutual. My Lord knew that it might appear strange to the superficial observers but quite natural to one who had the knowledge of the bond between us, the bond of a mother and child.

Also getting caught in the web of maya, it took me a long, long time to reconcile myself to the idea that during this lifetime of mine it would not be my privilege to meet Him on a physical plane. But then I found myself lacking in faith if that condition of His brought sorrow or grief. Was there any need to meet Him on the physical plane, when almost on a daily basis at a spiritual level, He came to visit me? I was blessed with the Divine company of the Lord on a spiritual level – our Lord who held my hand in a firm grasp and walked by my side every step of the journey to self-realisation – the goal He had set for me.

Negligence on the Doctors' Part at the Parthi General Hospital

The first clue that something was wrong with Nargish Aunty slipped by unnoticed. It came one evening after darshan. "My stomach aches," she said. Vomiting and loose motions began. As days went by she was only on fluids and went into a steady decline. Then she had no strength left to move about and lay in bed soiling her clothes. Medicines proved ineffective. Dark circles ringed her eyes, and she seemed to be losing consciousness fast.

Once at midnight I woke up at the sound of a tiny voice calling out to me. "Khurshid, help me." It was Nargish Aunty who hadn't spoken a coherent sentence in over four to five days. I rushed to the bathroom from where the sound came. By the time I reached her she had slipped into a state of coma. I gave her body a proper wash. Because I didn't know a soul in Parthi and Yasmin Aunty had shared with me that she herself was a heart patient, I had no one to assist me in helping her to the bed. I had to almost drag her there. She regained consciousness on and often for a few minutes. Unspoken, but understood, was that neither Yasmin Aunty nor I knew if she would make it even if we did manage to shift her to Baba's general hospital next to the primary school.

Early next morning, I shifted her to the Sathya Sai General Hospital. Over there, the scene was not as we had anticipated. Initially, I had felt relieved, believing that now she was in safe and caring hands of doctors and other staff at the hospital who were long-time devotees of Baba. Nargish Aunty was in a delirious condition. She couldn't recall what had landed her in that hospital.

The attitude of the staff at the hospital (at least as I personally experienced it), right from the doctors down the line up to the nurses and even maids was not at all humane towards Nargish Aunty who was in a semi-conscious state, struggling for life. The hygiene of the ward seemed to be nowhere on the priority list of the hospital authorities, to say the least. When chances of her survival seemed negligible, without a day's notice, she was discharged from the hospital. It was an extremely bitter experience for me. And even more so for poor Nargish Aunty who suffered at their hands.

Let me share my experience in brief: While completing the formalities for admission at the hospital, I was in agreement with the doctor who claimed that it was wrong on my part to have brought her so late. She was moved into a room that had two beds. One of the doctors immediately put her on the drip to avoid further dehydration. The doctor on night duty read her papers, and using some medical terms, claimed that aunty was perfectly all right and in no need of any medication whatsoever! Then she pulled at the pipe, detaching it. She screamed at me that the medication being given to her by the daytime medical staff was not the way it should have been. "Why don't you speak up girl? You should not have let the day doctor give her those tablets and why is she still on saline?" I was totally flabbergasted at such ridiculous statements from a responsible person like her. Once again the doctor who came in the morning spoke roughly to me as though I was the one responsible for the removal of the drip! The very next minute she was put back on to the drip.

It was 24 hours since I had been at the hospital at aunty's bedside. Therefore, when one of her acquaintances offered to stay with her for an hour, I decided to go to the lodge to have a wash and a meal. So often had I heard the Sai devotees take special pride in talking about the cleanliness maintained in the Super Speciality Hospital. But at least in this hospital, located at just a few minutes walking distance from the Prashanti Nilayam, the condition in our ward was pathetic. Within an hour I was back in the hospital and found that I could not stand the offensive smell even for a few seconds without feeling nausea. The patient on the next bed, an old lady who lay in a semiconscious state, had no family members at her bedside or anybody from the hospital to attend to her. Her bed was soiled and nobody had changed the bedspreads. For the next two hours or so that I was present, no one came to help her change. The drip was on and the saline in the bottle had finished. No one bothered to come and have a look despite my repeated reminders. The old lady was unaware of the numberless flies all around. Not a single nurse was to be seen and the maid responded by rudely telling me to mind my own aunty and not bother about the patient on the next bed. The only time the same maid spoke to me in polite tones was to ask for a tip though she had not attended to Nargish Aunty even once. But that was not surprising.

I had barely overcome the shock of the dirty state in which the lady on the next bed lay, when Nargish Aunty, who suddenly seemed fully conscious for a while, said something which made me lose my speech altogether for a minute or so. My conscience was put to test and I knew not how to react when with great effort in hardly audible tones, and with tears in her eyes, aunty said, "Khurshid, take me home." The only thought that occurred to me was that she was fed up of the hospital, but never in my wildest dreams had I considered what actually made her say so, not until she clarified. "I have been discharged from the hospital." Aunty had not even regained full consciousness for long periods, let alone enough strength to be able to sit on her own. The motions had not yet abated and the dehydration had worsened. But the doctors were relentless. They ordered me to make her vacate the bed immediately. They spoke amongst themselves in voices loud enough for me to hear that chances of her recovery were dim.

In all humility I approached the doctor in charge to request her to permit Nargish Aunty to remain in the hospital at least till such time that she could take fluids without throwing up – but to no avail. Despair overwhelmed me as I paced the hospital corridors for a while. Ultimately, my optimism of a recovery faded as the doctor in charge unceremoniously ushered us out of the hospital. The strain of dragging her feet even a few steps – up to the gate – was immense. It was painful to see her being treated so shabbily. We dragged her back to our guesthouse. She sobbed silently and I was furious at the callousness and heartless behaviour of the so-called doctors who claimed to be doing seva at our guru's hospital.

As I moved her from the hospital back to the guesthouse, I believed, I had left her in the protective custody of my Lord, moving her from an unsafe hospital to a safe home. She had been compelled to leave the hospital even before she could reach the low risk category. Now that she was out of the hospital and with no medical assistance, she was totally at the mercy of God. What could I do? I had no knowledge of any way to bring her back to health. The gastro-enteritis persisted and she stopped consuming even fluids such as electral or glucose water. Yet, in one way, I continued to believe, defiantly, hopelessly, that somehow all would be well. That flicker of trust and hope was as obstinate as Nargish Aunty's own fighting spirit and her will to live.

The mysterious footstep of death appeared to be catching up with her. At the guesthouse for days Yasmin Aunty and I took turns in sitting at her bedside and watched her condition deteriorate, both of us powerless to help her in any way. Finally, Yasmin Aunty called up Mumbai and told Nargish Aunty's brother to catch the next flight to Parthi / Bangalore and take her to Mumbai for treatment.

One morning, Yasmin Aunty assured me that she would not leave her bedside till I returned, so I went for darshan. I returned to the guesthouse with a heavy heart only to find Nargish Aunty sitting and munching a buttered toast with a steaming cup of tea held in her other hand! Yasmin Aunty stood next to her, coaxing her to have one more toast. How strange that she had recovered so miraculously! I was overtaken by emotion at the scene. Doctors had written her off but God had given her a rebirth. Yes, even today, looking back I can only say that aunty's revival was like being born again. We immediately made a call to Mumbai and informed her brother about her miraculous recovery so that he need not rush to take her back to Mumbai.

"A dazzling light fell on my eyes. On opening them, I found the same light filling the entire room. And who did I see but our Lord Sai standing at the door with gold dust descending on Him. Khurshid, our room was illumined with the light that surrounded our guru. Though I have had a few visions in my life with open eyes, none was clearer," Nargish Aunty said. Her body seemed to have resumed normal strength. Her time to leave this earth had apparently not arrived.

17th July '93 was a day I spent in joy. All the ridicule and humiliation I had endured at the hands of permanent ashramites, devotees having influence in the ashram, the staff at His hospital – was wiped off my memory with His reward – of coming in my dreams and visions almost every other day to express His love for me. This time He gave darshan for a few seconds before changing His form to that of a little child who then gently placed His head on my shoulder and let me stroke His face and pass my hand over His soft curls! That morning I sat for an hour or so thinking of nothing, except that beautiful vision of our closeness.

On the 22nd we followed Baba to Whitefield. Nargish Aunty came and stayed with me at Nagu's place whereas Yasmin Aunty booked a room closer to the ahsram.

Our Guru Addressed Aban, My Best Friend as 'Masi' (Mother's Sister)

Aban, my dear friend from Mumbai, came for Baba's darshan and stayed with us at Nagu's place. I was thrilled at the opportunity to spend a day or two with her after a period of so many months. In the past few months her letters had given me great joy, especially when she mentioned about Baba's visits in her dreams. From one particular letter let me quote a line that gave me immense joy, this assurance was given to her by Baba in one of her dreams: "Aban Masi, if I shall not hear your prayers then whose prayer shall I listen to? Because you are very special to me." She, my dear friend, whom I loved as much as I loved my sister Jasmine, had still not read any of these Volumes. Nor had I revealed to her that Baba always addressed me as His mother. Hence, it was but natural that she could not guess why Baba addressed her as 'Masi'. The term 'Masi' in Gujarati language (which is our mother tongue), is used for 'Mother's sister' and indeed, she was to me a sister. Then what else could the Lord address her as? And of course, she was thus very special to Him as He had Himself said so!

Before I move to the next message of His, let me share with you a little about my relationship with Aban, my best friend. In 1991 when I had rejoined CRY, she was one of the employees who had joined recently. My daily journey home from office was in her company and I made my way into a new friendship. In the 18 years since then (i.e. till date in 2009 when I am editing this Volume), we have been really close. At first, we seemed unlikely candidates for such an enduring friendship. Yet, our friendship has grown because of how much we have shared and because of our common love for Baba. But the times I've leaned on her, come to mind. She is someone who has shared my joys and sorrows. Later when Baba approved of my desire that she edit the series of 'A Glimpse of Joy', she agreed to do so. She is someone who has encouraged my dreams of becoming His image and also my dreams of Sunbeam. (Sunbeam is a Public Charitable Trust that was founded by me in 1997, one that catered to the educational and psychological / emotional needs of over a thousand underprivileged children in Mumbai.) In 2001, she ultimately gave up her job to join me full-time at Sunbeam at less than half the pay she received at CRY. Once again this was in surrender to His will.

Very often in the company of my dear friend, I felt in the presence of my guru. I felt it was Him speaking to me through those intimate chats. Just like Baba, she too loved me unconditionally and was committed to my happiness. And I treasured the gift of her friendship.

In a few days she left for Mumbai.

Baba's Presence Eliminates my Longing for Human Company

"Khurshid, whatever belongs to me belongs to the Sai in you," Nargish Aunty said modestly. Her compassion and sacrifice were unstinting. She spent all her money up to the last rupee on my comforts.

I learned a lot from that dear aunt. I learned how to be there for people when they need you. From her I learned how, without using words, we can reach out to another human being. All it requires is a shoulder to cry on, a gentle touch, a sympathetic heart, a listening ear.

My guru's love for me was all encompassing and I would have ended up imposing limits on it by seeking to define it. Yet, my idea of love needed redefining and He helped me do that. He taught me that as guaranteed as it was, my love for others still needed expression. Didn't the unique expression of His love for me always make me feel complete? Then why was I being stingy in giving expression to my own love to each and every member of His family?

On 4th July '93, Yasmin Aunty and Nargish Aunty left for Mumbai. This opened a wound that nothing could heal for the next few hours. With Baba choosing to be indifferent to me – at least on a physical plane, I felt neglected, especially when on a daily basis I witnessed Him granting personal interviews to a chosen few devotees (even though to a different group each time). Feelings of alienation and discoura-gement often threatened to break my resolve of staying in Parthi/Whitefield till March '94. To be left all alone was, I see now, a blessing. But at that time I looked for solace from Him. I longed to have company, company of my father whom I now missed terribly. My first day without the two of them – despite close darshan of the Lord – was full of sadness. That night I had severe chest pain.

Early in the morning He appeared to me. But today, darshan in a dream did not satisfy me. So, upon waking up, I stood before His calendar praying that during the morning darshan (I now am talking about the public darshan) He should come and talk to me in these very words, "How are you feeling now, mother?" And so that nobody should guess about our relationship, He could put that question to a lady sitting on my either side. Would He do me that favour?

Darshan time on 5th July '93: As usual I went at the last moment, just when He was about to come for public darshan. The hall was full, and, with the other late-comers, I sat outside, in the very first row, at a prominent place, from where the Lord would pass by to enter the hall. Baba walked straight in our direction and I suddenly woke up, as if from a trance, upon hearing His voice as He addressed the lady to my left. He asked her (in Hindi), "How are you feeling now, mother?" His next question followed by a piercing look that He gave me, was, "And how is your son?" After the emptiness of being left all alone and pain of the previous night, the warmth of His loving voice brought tears to my eyes.

He was standing right in front of me. Overcome by emotion, I disregarded His earlier warning of not touching His feet. As I bent low to do padnamaskar, the lotus feet were not to be felt though visible! He stood there and let me search for His feet that could be seen but not felt! At last when I overcame the bewilderment of not being able to feel His feet, I gazed up at Him only to find Him laughing away merrily. I made yet another attempt but His feet were not to be felt! As I wondered what to do, I made eye contact with my guru only to find Him laugh gleefully like a child happy beyond words. His eyes were twinkling with mirth. Almost half a minute had passed by, with my search for His feet still on. As I once again stared up at Him mutely, He burst out laughing and with slow steps entered the hall, leaving me in tears at His leela. I was moved by His love.

I tried to concentrate on my writing work but I missed dad terribly. It seemed like eternity since I had last seen my family. I missed them, especially dad. So during this close darshan, as my guru stood before me, enjoying His leela, I spoke to Him endlessly (silently – in my mind) about slices of life from an almost imaginary homeland. I appealed to Him to make arrangements for dad to visit me at Whitefield within 24 hours. My Lord actually nodded in affirmation as though He had decided to gratify my wish and made prior arrangements for dad's forthcoming visit of which I was in the dark.

Immediately after darshan I asked the lady sitting next to me whom He had asked, if she had been unwell since Baba had asked her how she was feeling now. "Of course not, I keep excellent health. It so happens that I am a long time devotee of His and it's only natural that He should come and talk to me," she boasted. This only confirmed that my guru's question was meant for me and not her.

2

The Beginning of My Journey to Him

Upon My Request, Sai Summons Dad to Whitefield within 24 Hours

The feelings evoked by the sight of my dad actually standing before my very eyes, in less than two days after my prayer, stunned me into silence. It took me some time to accept the fact that I was always being too bossy with my Lord and Him tolerating me and complying with my demands!

"Khurshid, how are you?" Dad's soft voice brought me out of the stupor and I stepped aside to let him in. "Papa, how come you've made this sudden trip and that too all by yourself?" I queried, still unable to believe that it was not a dream but an actual happening, that there stood before me the one person in this world whose secure company I craved for whenever I felt lonely.

I have always been resistant to change and it had been very difficult for me to accept the idea of staying for ten full months without daddy. "Khurshid, Yasmin Aunty had an urgent parcel of photographs to be sent to Verena Huber (our German friend who is a permanent resident at the Parthi / Whitefield ashrams). Since Yasmin Aunty is unwell, she requested me to make this trip and has sponsored the airfare both ways."

Dad had come only for a day. As his car moved out of my sight taking him to the airport, though it made me feel sad that he had to leave so soon, I was grateful that the Lord had heard my prayer.

Made to Undergo Utter Depravation to Test My Faith in Him

Was I taking my welcome for granted? Would He provide me with an opportunity to repay Nagu's family's generosity? I wasn't aware of the unpleasant surprise that was in store for me the very next morning and Baba must have been chuckling at the thought of the test of my genuineness of feelings to repay another's kindness.

Right from the very next day, I was systematically starved. Daily rations for lunch became a few spoonfuls of pulses or a few spoonfuls of vegetables. For dinner even that stopped and I was told to make do with burning hot chutney or pickle with wheat bread. I felt like a famine survivour.

Life was harsh, food was scarce, the result of Krishnabai's wrath. (Krishnabai was Nagu's mum.) There were days when I felt blessed when for dinner they offered a few morsels of vegetables in place of the hot chutney to which I had still not grown accustomed. Somehow I had got used to not having proper dinner. Then they stopped breakfast, telling me that the milk, porridge and noodles that I purchased were given away to their own children.

My hunger for love and kindness which I occasionally did suffer from was always fulfilled by Nagu. By cooking a hurried meal for me and coaxing me to eat it before her mom could return from the market, she provided me not just with food but love which was the required nutrition for me whenever I was feeling lonely and abandoned. In her it was He who fed me.

A crisis developed when Krishnabai felt enough was enough and I had to move out of my room with immediate effect. The ever-growing shadow of destitution deepened as I tried to think of ways to please Krishnabai. She looked at me with disdain and announced one morning, "We'd love to help but we can't let you carry on at Rs. 1,000 per month towards your boarding and lodging at our place. You'll have to shift into the passage. Now we will rent out your room to foreigners who can easily give us Rs. 100 to Rs. 200 per day." I had no choice but to do as she bid. Again, that sense of embarrassment is what I experienced. I felt I was an irritation. I was no longer the person who had left all to be at His feet. I was a beggar, a person living on others' mercy.

I shifted into the passage which had no proper light or ventilation. Each side of the passage opened the doors to a room now occupied by someone or the other. One side of the passage also led to the common bathroom, thus leaving me with no privacy whatsoever. I consoled myself that I should be grateful for that 3 by 6 feet sleeping space.

In silence, in that passage, I unpacked the few contents of my backpack: a spare set of clothes, a bed-sheet to cover myself with, a sweater and my books. As I lay in that stuffy place with a motorcycle taking away the much required space, huge doubts assailed me. I moved this way and that on the mattress in a futile attempt to find lasting comfort. Halfway into the night I wore the sweater for extra warmth. I resolved that in the morning I'd abandon the whole absurd venture; I had made a mistake, I should be going back home. But after His darshan in the dream that I had that night I woke in better spirits. I couldn't give up, that was certain.

My faith in Him was still lacking because I did not possess the perfect confidence in His will in all things. If I loved Him deeply, unconditionally, with implicit trust in His love for me, I would not care what condition He kept me in. No matter what came my way, my consciousness had to remain unperturbed, unruffled.

Baba wanted me to discipline the body and not give it too much attention. The purpose was not to torture my body, but to save me, His child, from all the troubles that would beset me if I believed that comfort came from material things. Only if I'd change my own attitude I'd not feel any discomfort. He was helping me make my life simpler instead of getting myself accustomed to the comforts in life. He wanted me to be disassociated with whatever happened to me and spare myself unnecessary mental anguish.

Utter poverty, like I experienced, brought a dreadful sense of alienation. It threw my life into a totally new perspective. I changed a lot. Deprivation made me understand for the first time how lucky I had been in life, in Mumbai, how I was sheltered from many of the miseries that underprivileged people had to undergo. At home, I'd never had to worry where I'd sleep each night; and never in my life had to go hungry. This long stay in Whitefield / Parthi, living at the mercy of others, taught me many important lessons in life.

Yet, the poverty of material things I could easily put up with today because, surrounded by His love and affection and His Divine wisdom that He consistently blessed me with, I was certainly no longer experiencing the poverty of the spirit, of loneliness, of being unwanted.

On the 11th August '93, as I sat writing, a shadow that fell on me made me look up, only to find two Australians – Andrew, a young gentleman and Gladys Peacock (who was addressed as Glad by her friends), a lady in her fifties standing before me. Andrew enquired of me if any rooms were available. My heart beat quickly. A longing to tell them to look elsewhere was strong in me. But my conscience didn't permit me to say any such thing. It took me only a few seconds to regain my composure. Krishnabai was not at home so I called Nagu instead and informed her that these people had come to seek accommodation. Nagu, who could not converse in English, requested me to negotiate the terms of stay with them! O my God – that was a real test for me. A choking sense of tears was in my throat as I translated for Nagu these words: "This is the room that is lying vacant and you may rent it at Rs. 200 per day." As the two foreigners looked at each other and then at me before saying anything, a vague terror began to possess me. How money-minded I must have sounded to those two who were not aware of what I was going through just then. Glad sounded incredulous as she addressed me in polite but firm tones, "The rate you quote is exorbitant for a room without any bed and one that has no attached bathroom." They were looking steadfastly at me and I dare not meet their gaze. With an effort, I raised my head, turned to Nagu and translated to her what Gladys had just said. The haggling went on with me playing the role of the interpreter, until finally they settled at Rs. 100 per day. They left, saying that they had booked a room at a hotel in Bangalore city but travelling up to Whitefield twice daily for darshan was tiring and would like to shift from the next day itself to this room. After they left, it took me a few minutes to gain control over my nerves and continue with my writing work as though nothing was amiss.

Andrew came back the next morning to say that he would be renting the room but would be coming alone. Nagu's eyes had an indignant expression in them as she told me to tell him that her father would not allow a single man to stay in their house! Now it was his turn to be astonished for he had been utterly unprepared for such a statement. For a moment he looked taken aback and at a loss for words. However, recovering his composure, that dear fellow, who didn't want anyone to look at him with disfavour or suspicion, tried to explain by gestures. He took out his lock and showed that he would fasten the front door and pointing to the back door, showed that he would lock it from within! And then he said in slow, simple words that we need have no fear on his account, "You all won't see my face from 6.30 a.m. onwards. I shall be returning only in the nights." From his appearance and general bearing it was easy to make out that he was a very good man at heart and it embarrassed me to deny him accommodation though, in my heart of hearts, I never wanted to part with my room. And as for the agent who had brought Andrew here, he was so vexed with our stupid condition that he screamed at me, little knowing that I did not want to insult Andrew or anybody else. Once again I apologised to Andrew who did not seem to have taken offence and left without another word, but only to come back with two ladies this time, Glad and Helen! Ultimately, it was the two ladies who occupied this room.

Surprise overtook dejection when after spending a night or two at this place and upon realising that I wasn't an inmate of that house, they put forth a proposal that suited all of us. They requested Nagu's mother to allow the two of them and their entire group of Australians to conduct bhajans in their room for an hour every evening and that for the rest of the day and night I could stay in that room. The rent of Rs. 100 per day would be borne by the Australian group.

From among all those in the group who sang with devotion, Hans and his wife were the best bhajan singers. I was astonished and bewildered at the devotion of all these foreigners. How could they survive the innumerable adjustments they must have had to make to stay in an Indian village after their reasonably luxurious life back home in their land, if not for their immense love for Baba? The thought of their sacrifice made me feel small for having grumbled so often for want of comforts.

Sai Ensures My Family's Welfare in My Absence

"What about the salaries of Rs. 4,000 per month that you'd have earned and given to your family had you not left your job in mid May?" Santosh Aunty had asked me seriously. But for once I did not feel guilty though I had been able to give dad only a small sum of Rs.10,000 on the day I left Mumbai. For 2 reasons: Firstly, because it was at His command that I was here without a steady income to send home to family. Secondly, He had taken care of the monetary problem at home in 2 ways. My maternal uncle who had sold off granny's room had given mum a cash gift of Rs. 20,000. Later, another amount of Rs. 20,000 was deposited in my account towards the Provident Fund that I received from CRY and my parents were free to use that.

I had Failed to Realize Our Guru's Divine Powers

"Stop where you are! Don't touch me because you won't be able to absorb the power emanating from me at this moment!" These were His very words of warning when I tried to touch His feet in a dream on 14.8.93. This dream also set me thinking. More often than not, I took Him to be my father, child and friend, not as my guru with Divine powers. This kind of a message from Him also brought me back to reality and my good fortune of being so close to Divinity.

"I Meet Khurshid Quite Often," Baba Told Nagmani

In two days time He again appeared in my dream. This time I found myself hesitating to get closer to Him in order to avoid bringing the wrath of the volunteers upon me. He, my dear Lord, bent towards me and stretching out His hand, gently pulled me by the waist. None of the volunteers objected to my closeness to Him even though I had not been among the front row because our Lord Himself had called me, taken me close to Him.

The dream came true within hours during the morning darshan itself. During darshan, as I sat outside the hall, in the far end, with Nagu's letter in my hand, our Lord stood looking in my direction. With my failing vision, I could not make out that the person He was calling out to was none other than myself, till such time that devotees sitting next to me encouraged me to get up and go to Him. The volunteers were aware that I wasn't breaking any discipline but from the far end walking up to Him because He had called me. As I made my way through the thick crowd, He steadfastly looked at me with a smile and waited patiently with His outstretched hand to receive my letter. Nagu had given me this letter almost a week ago, which I had been carrying daily but dared not to hand over to Him because I would always get the second or the third row instead of being right in the front. But today it was as if His hand had been on my waist, pulling me to Him. Addressing me in Hindi, He said, "You are eating too much sweets, reduce eating sweet things, reduce the intake of sweet things at least a bit." Saying so, He accepted Nagu's letter from my hand and blessed me by offering me a few toffees before moving on to the hall where the public awaited His darshan.

I felt I was in heaven long after Baba had moved away from me. My guru had spoken to me, this time not in a dream but in reality. I experienced sheer bliss at thus being blessed.

I had no clue why it was so important to Nagu that He accept her letter through me. Her eyes sparkled and then moistened on hearing how the Lord had eagerly asked for her letter. Only after hearing me out did she narrate her dream to me, a dream in which our guru had appeared to her just a day or two prior to my coming to Whitefield! "Khurshid, you are aware that my family members are not believers in Baba so they do not allow me to come for His darshan except on rare occasions. A day before you reached my home in the month of May, Baba had appeared in my dream and told me that a few sparrows were to come and stay at my house. That all except one would fly away in a few days. And that the name of that sparrow, He said, was Khurshid! He also told me that He met up with Khurshid often and that I could send my letters through her since my family did not approve of my longing and desire to go for darshan. All these days when you came back without handing over my letter to Him I started doubting my own dream, started doubting whether He does come to you as often as He claimed."

My heart was overjoyed at these words of confirmation. Yes, wasn't He appearing to me almost daily in dreams and visions? I, His sparrow, had won the grace of my guru.

Resist the devil in the form of Earthly Temptations – the Lord Tells Me

Via a dream that I am now going to recount, Baba let me know how easily I could fall prey to maya, to the temptations of the world! The dream began with Baba and the devil facing each other, ready for combat! They stood at extreme ends of the stage. The spectators were people from all over the world, all of whom, including myself, sat on the side of the devil, leaving our Lord all alone at the other end, though there was enough open space at His side as well where we could have seated ourselves. In order to have a better view of the battle that was to ensue, step by step I went nearer to the stage, with the result that I was hardly a few feet away from the devil!

My Lord's voice as He called out to me had urgency and a note of caution in it. "Khurshid, don't come any closer because chances are that the devil might attack you." But His warning was already too late and I was caught off guard as the devil struck me from behind. The drama had begun and the world watched the three of us in action!

The devil had struck me with great force, making me fall. As I lay on the ground the pain was unbearable. It was not physical pain though. It took the form of mental anguish that I experienced at my failure despite several attempts to raise my head enough to look at the Lord in the eye. Getting back on my feet seemed an equally impossible task. No matter how hard I tried, I could not have His darshan even though He stood at such close quarters. Our dear guru could feel my anguish and in His mercy, came to my aid. Most unexpectedly, this time He pierced my back and now it was extreme physical pain I had to endure. Only when it became unbearable, did I cry out to Him. Initially His response sounded quite strange as He replied in very calm tones, "The snake has bitten you. Shouldn't I remove the poison before it spreads all over? I understand that it is a painful process to undergo but you have to let me remove the poison completely from your system and silently bear with the pain, if you desire to have my darshan." Saying so, He pierced my back exactly where the devil had bitten me, and much deeper. After what seemed like an eternity, I found myself cured and standing on my feet, facing Divinity! He, my Lord, looked at me with compassion and also with satisfaction at having succeeded in curing me. As I thus stood basking in His love, once again the devil took me unawares by attacking me from the back. The entire drama repeated itself. As before, the Lord came to my rescue. This time when I finally stood upright, I pleaded with Baba to have mercy upon me because I was too tired, too exhausted of playing that role over and over again. And He responded with, "Since you are very tired, you may take a break from this. Consider it as an interval."

The above dream set me thinking. My dear guru did not want me to stay satisfied with being a mediocre disciple. Hence, I dare not set standards by the rest of the world. I had committed enough mistakes in the past. Baba had always been forgiving. But I could no longer ask for concessions. Any lapse on my part could cause Him so much pain.

I had to move away from any thought, word or action that took my mind away from God, drew my consciousness down into restlessness and anger. I had to strive to live in such a way that I thought, spoke and did only those things that were uplifting to my consciousness.

At the same time, I was still finding it difficult to let go of the hand of Satan – of all wrong thoughts and feelings that caught up with me from time to time. These took the forms of the demons of self-pity, attachments to family and friends, anger and the inability to easily forgive the wrongdoers. Thus, until such poison was not removed from the system, I'd be unable to grasp the hand of the Divine.

Sometimes He appeared very harsh. But He was tearing away the veil of maya so that I could see the truth even though I may not have liked to see the truth about myself. He wished me to cast all my desires into the flame of one desire: to behold the face of Divinity.

Gathered together on the battlefield of my consciousness were my good qualities and my unwanted qualities. Each day I began to ask myself how I fared. Did I make the mistake of going close enough to the Satan to be stung by him, leaving me with his poison in my system and, as a consequence, ashamed to meet my guru's eye? Or did I conquer my unwanted qualities by being open to His treatment, painful though it was, and let Him suck the poison out of my system, leaving me proud to meet His eye?

A battle between the good and bad was going on within me all the time. It felt as though I was standing at the centre being pierced by Satan as the negative forces that pulled me to itself and from the other side by God as the positive forces – God ever ready to suck out the poison from my system. The only way of not letting negative forces claim my consciousness was to remain alert all the time. God had bestowed me with the discrimination between good and evil and also with free will to accept or reject that which was unwanted. I chose to completely surrender to His will and co-operate with Him. Yet, on some days the dragon won. Fortunately, the dragon didn't always win. And I was doing whatever I could to see to it that he and the evil he represented won less and less.

Glimpses of the Lord Dwelling in One and All

17th August '93 – 5 a.m., i.e. within two hours of the above dream in which my Lord had promised to grant me an interval, interval of pleasure between two periods of pain, He reappeared to me in a dream! There I sat catching the lotus feet of my Lord, my eyes glued on them. Strangely enough, His orange robe changed to a printed saree with a green background. It had a beautiful print of white flowers and leaves on it! As I turned my eyes on to His face, I found Him laughing away. He seemed to be quite amused at my astonishment, to find Him dressed up in a saree and, moreover, decked up in all finery. O dear, I thought I was going crazy and looked around to find out if others, too, had noticed the difference in our Lord. As though that was not enough, He surprised me even further by saying, "Here, let me come closer to you so that you may have a proper look at me. This is in order that you may find out that not only do I dress up in a saree and apply lipstick, but also apply powder and perfume as well!" I blinked my eyes to have a proper look at Him, still wondering whether I had heard and seen right.

My Lord's instructions varied according to the nature of the individual being taught. And knowing that I had still not grasped the significance of His strange behaviour, He now spoke in gentler tones, "Khurshid, don't pay any attention to the dress. Always keep your mind fixed on ME within. Underneath all that beauty and finery, can't you see me? Do one's looks or dress really matter when you become aware of the fact that the one before you is none other than ME?" With that the dream came to an end.

Coming back to Nagu's place after darshan that morning, my mind was still full of misgivings about accepting what I had dreamt that morning. Just then I heard Glad's voice say, "Hello. We have come with sarees. Would you mind help us drape them over ourselves?" For a moment or two I stood speechless. Eventually, it was Nagu who taught them the art of wearing sarees in an elegant way. Looking at that scene before me, I learned that material benefits did not necessarily deter one from being spiritually close to the Lord. In fact, it had to be these two friends of mine my Lord must have referred to when He spoke of applying lipstick, etc. I wondered if by making me experience this dream materialise within hours of having seen it, the Lord had any other purpose apart from demonstrating the profound truth in action. Nagu excused herself and left the room for a while and I sat narrating my dream to Helen and Glad. I shared with them that the only thing about the dream that didn't come about in exact details was the colour of the saree that Baba had worn. Neither Glad nor Helen's saree matched that colour and print of His saree. Hardly had I completed my sentence when Nagu entered the room and the sight I beheld struck me dumb. She was wearing the saree of my dream, the one my Lord had draped around Himself. Exact colour and print! What simpler way could He have taught me to believe that it was Him in whose company I lived, whether it was Glad, Helen or Nagu.

This particular incident within hours of His message in the dream illustrated His eagerness for me to make the transition from the love and devotion of duality to the blissful serenity of oneness. After the wonderful experience mentioned above, my consciousness began to expand. There awakened a longing to behold Him in all human beings. Momentarily at least I found the secret veils of maya lifting, and glimpse the reality of bliss. In the months to follow, as I gained more and more access to Him through the dreams and visions, I knew it was a rare blessing. It was as if He was offering Himself to me to be unmasked as the indweller of all.

The World Shall have Proof from Me of My Visits to You

The dream of 18th August '93 – 1.20 a.m.: Of all the people present, my Lord came and stood facing me. I touched His hand lightly whereupon He immediately placed both His hands into mine! "Khurshid, if you so desire, I shall follow you from Whitefield, Bangalore to Parthi tomorrow itself." His words stunned me! Was He implying that He knew I was, of late, not too well looked after at Nagu's place and was referring to my feeling of discontentment at the spicy food and other things that I could not adjust myself to? And did He mean to say that in case I wanted to go to Parthi, He would accompany me there?

I stared at Him bewilderedly, for a long, long time and He kept His gaze fixed on me, love pouring out of His eyes, the love of a divine mother. "Baba, no one believes me when I say that you come and talk to me," I complained. "Nobody believed me the last time when, as per your wish, I had been to the Secretary for accommodation. What they require is proof that you do visit me so often. Everyone feels that my imagination is playing tricks on me. And I have nothing to provide them with by way of proof of our meetings – our meetings that have never been anything but private ones, hidden from the public eye." "Ah! So they want proof! Is that so?" For a second or two He simply smiled. Then in a determined tone, He added, "Well then, they shall have proof from me. Here you are. I shall myself write it all down." Saying so, He took a paper and a pen and began writing something, His sweet face lit with mirth. When once or twice He looked up at me, He must have found me staring at Him incredulously but that didn't seem to bother Him one bit. So engrossed in His writing was He that it seemed as though He was oblivious of the time He spent on it. Thinking it most improper to sit idle while He worked, I told Him to hand over the job to me. "Baba, let me do this work for you. And if you want me to type it all out, I shall do that as well." "No, no," He replied hastily, "There is no need for you to start typing any of it, not yet. You may for the time being just carry on with the writing part of the work. You may copy it down, the exact words that I give you." My Lord did not wish to conceal from others our daily meetings but He wanted them to know of it in His own way and at the appropriate time. And it is simply astonishing to think how, in a tone of authority He then said, "Khurshid, this is the proof I shall provide for one and all who doubt your word about my visits to you. I am putting it down on paper so that none will ever disbelieve you when you say that I come and talk to you so often." And the dream came to an end with this beautiful message!

Consistently being in touch with my guru on an inner plane was worth more than the few personal interviews that He could have granted me the way He did to others. That was my personal belief. But as far as other people's opinions about my relationship went, it was almost uniform. My family, relatives, acquaintances, friends, colleagues pitied me for the seeming indifference of our Lord towards me on a physical plane. No one knew of the kind of deep relationship I shared with our dear guru. None believed that all my life I had acted as per His will alone. Baba had said that's precisely why He was putting it all down on paper.

Hopefully, these Volumes of mine, my autobiography will bring to light the truth that despite never once meeting Him on a physical plane for a private interview, on a spiritual level I met Him almost daily; that we shared a deep divine bonding.

Our Relationship is that of a Mother and Child, You are My Mother

One of the ways by which I could really know if I was progressing spiritually was to analyse myself honestly. Each time I checked where my consciousness was, the results brought a rude awakening. More often than not my consciousness was not engrossed in silent communion with God, but with worries about my own needs of accommodation at Parthi now that the time to leave for Parthi was approaching.

By surrender to His will I meant complete entrustment of myself to the Divine. Without any reservations I decided to lay myself at His feet. I told Him I'd stop taking any protective measures on my own, that I left the responsibility of my well-being on Him. Now it was left to Him to provide me with a decent roof over my head and make preparations for my stay in Parthi prior to Himself leaving for Parthi. Of course, I would take normal care of myself and trust Him to do the rest.

On 19th August '93, i.e. the very next day He appeared to me in a dream. This time He came and placed His head on my lap as I sat cross-legged on the floor. Very gently I lifted His dear face, keeping one hand under His head for support. A lady came and placed some cash at His feet. Pointing out to the cash, He told me, "The relationship between you and me is not based on money. Certainly not." Unable to grasp the import of His words, I said, "Baba that is not my money. Someone must have given it to you for Narayan Seva. As for me, I have been only demanding from you monetary assistance and not vice versa." He was not one to be satisfied with my answer and drew my attention to the flaw in my vision. There was a pause. Then His voice, calm, clear and very gentle, vibrated on the silence. "To put it that way too is incorrect. Money does not play any part whatsoever in our relationship." Then He encouraged me once again to think deeper,

"Khurshid, what is our relationship?" His tender voice brought tears to my eyes. After some hesitation I dared to speak out my mind, "Baba, our relationship is that of a mother and child." This answer seemed to have pleased Him and for long moments the two of us just continued to gaze at each other. Finally mustering up enough courage, I put forth the question half wistfully, "Baba, you are my child, isn't it so?" His reply was in a language I couldn't understand and seeing the look of disappointment on my face, He immediately translated it for me in gentle tones, "Well, that means you are my mother." What joy it brought to my soul to hear Him say so. Our guru calling me His mother was indeed a bestowal of a grace unparallel to what I had known Him bless others with.

But the next minute my mind switched over to my uncertain future stay in Parthi and I asked Him to give me the earliest date when I could go back to Mumbai. In very soft tones, He said, "In the month of March." "May I leave before March, say by the end of '93?" I asked hoping for a positive reply. "No, you can't return to Mumbai before the month of March '94," He said resolutely. "When I follow you to Parthi, where should I stay? Last time also I went exactly according to your instructions but none at the ashram office believe me. They are not willing to hear what I have to say about your message." My Lord's dear face that was still held in my arms, took on a concerned expression and turning to a man standing close by, He said, "See to it that she gets some place to stay in Parthi." The man nodded his head, bowing to His will.

For a few minutes He quietly lay on my lap smiling contentedly, then got up and moved away, leaving me in the company of that man in order to take down details about the house he could offer me. On asking his name he told me to write it down on a piece of paper.

The dream had ended but each time that I recalled His words, 'You are my mother' a blissful peace came over me.

We associate 'giving' with money. Of course, money may to some little extent be important in human relationships with duties, responsibilities and obligations towards each other. But in my relationship with Baba, money certainly did not play any role. Yes, material comforts it could have offered me had He blessed me with money. But no amount of material wealth could have bought me the value of Him accepting me unconditionally, always concerned for my spiritual growth. My dear guru wanted me to seek the deeper meaning of our relationship. His role in my life went way beyond the provider of material comforts. He was a very loving nurturer who was there to fulfil my spiritual needs.

When we measure people, situations and relationships in terms of money, values become secondary. The more we measure life in terms of money, the less room there is for love. Moreover, in our divine relationship, how could I grudge Him for not showering on me the material comforts when He was willing to open the doors to the treasure of self-realisation for me? Money played no part in our relationship. Material possessions or prestige could not have any role whatsoever. None of those things would enable me to make my life a gift worth placing at the feet of the Lord.

Mother Sita Blessing My Sister

His message in the above dream had also left me puzzled as to who that man in my dream could have been. Would I be meeting him soon? His face was not a familiar one. Being a stranger, would he help me find accommodation at reasonable rates? Looking at the watch and knowing it was only 4.35 a.m., I went back to sleep, only to find myself face to face with God once again. This time He appeared in the form of Lord Rama with His consort Sita, in all her splendour.

Mother Sita came and stood before me. Pointing out to my sister I told Her, "Mother, please give your blessings that Jasmine, my dear sister gets happily married." She turned Her gaze, full of compassion, on to Jasmine. Then gently lifting one of my hands, She passed Her fingers from over my wrist almost up to the elbow saying softly, "Her hand won't remain thus without bangles for long. She shall be happily married." What a relief it was to hear those assuring words.

Thus, almost every day my Lord appeared to me in dreams and visions, and I felt His love as never before, His loving warmth directed towards me day and night.

A New Friendship Materialises – with Rama and Sairama

On the 21st August I had our guru's darshan in a dream.

That evening I witnessed with astonishment the sport of my Divine Mother Sai. Just after the public darshan, as I looked for Rama, a newly made friend, at our usual meeting place i.e. near the Saraswati statue, she was not to be seen there. Instead I found her a few feet away, talking to a middle-aged man. Again and again I rubbed my eyes for I could hardly believe what I saw. It was the man I had seen in the dream, the man whom Baba had instructed in the dream to ensure that I got accommodation in Parthi! Rama introduced him to me as Bala Krishna, her maternal uncle who was a permanent resident at Parthi and stayed in Sai Ram Colony outside the ashram. She further informed me that presently he and Lata, (his niece who was to be in Parthi as a nurse in Baba's Super Speciality hospital), were in need of accommodation at Whitefield. They intended to stay for a week or so and could afford to pay up to Rs. 70 per day.

Here was my chance to prove my devotion to the Lord and repay this man in advance for I was sure he would be instrumental in arranging accommodation for my stay in Parthi from October '93 till I left in March '94. Of course, I never let him know that I would be shifting out in order to make room for him and his child. Lata came with me while he went to collect his luggage and follow later. When Bala Krishna uncle returned in 15 minutes, (by which time I had shifted my luggage and bedding into the inner room), his hands were free of any baggage and his face was beaming with joy. He related to me how unexpectedly he had come across a friend of his at the Kadugodi Post Office who had invited him and his child to stay at his house for as long as they wished. I shifted back to my room and 'Uncle' – that is how I addressed him – insisted that his niece Rama, Sai Rama (her sister-in-law), Lata and myself accompany him to a hotel to celebrate the good tidings. There I was dining at the expense of Mr. Bala Krishna, the man whom I had never seen before and who assured me of trying his level best to find accommodation at reasonable rates (obviously I didn't tell him about the dream). And he was true to his word. On going back to Parthi, he had taken over the responsibility to find clean, decent, economical accommodation for me and kept me informed of the developments by sending me telegrams at Nagu's residential address! The second telegram was with the happy news that he had booked a decent room at Sai Ram colony, 3–461, with self-attached bathroom. Moreover, it was a terrace flat. The rent was just Rs. 1,000 per month.

He Responds to My Prayers Each Time

On 22nd August '93 – 5 a.m., in a dream, as I handed over my book of experiences to Baba along with a pen and while He scanned through the pages, my mind was busy trying to find a solution to my immediate problem – accommodation at Parthi. I asked Him anxiously, "Baba, when you go back to Parthi, may I go and stay at Mr. Bala Krishna's place?" "Yes, you shall be staying there itself and nowhere else," was the gentle response of my Lord.

His words stated a reality. Every time I had called out to Him, He had responded. Not once had He failed me. He loved me unconditionally and had provided ample proof of it. By making me an instrument, He would be (via these volumes) conveying the Divine love and relationship between a guru and a disciple, between one who was the very embodiment of divinity and a human being who struggled to become His image. Above all, ours was a relationship between two souls covered in human frames, those who never ever met on a physical plane (except for having padnamaskar or exchanging a few words during darshan time), during their lives, yet consistently experienced their oneness at a spiritual level. The self within became the focus of my attention as I lived in the awareness of this truth. Absorption in the inner self brought peace and tranquillity. Ultimately, I was able to transcend the desire to be publicly acknowledged by Him during my lifetime.

Experience Sai beyond His form

The next morning (i.e. on 23rd August '93) when He appeared in my dream, He allowed my sister to touch His feet. When I believed it was my turn to do so, He pulled His feet away and asked, "Whose feet do you want to touch?" I found Him smiling all the time. "O Baba, yours!" I exclaimed in some surprise before placing my head on His lotus feet.

His question in the above dream set me thinking. I realised that once again I had got caught into the web of maya. He and I were one. He was the indweller of every human being. Hence, after analysing His question thoroughly, I came to the conclusion that it was necessary to give up the need to seek God outside of me. It wasn't easy to do so though. It seemed that to put that profound truth into practice it would take me some time.

"You're a Little Less in Your Head," Baba Told Me Good Humouredly

The dream on the 23rd had more to it than just padnamaskar. I had enquired of Him, "Baba, may I call Nargish Aunty from Mumbai to come and stay with me?" In very soft, loving tones, Baba said, "Yes, call her." Not sure if He had heard me right and, finding it hard to believe that I could be lucky to have the company of that dear lady, I repeated my question, "Baba, you want me to call her. Isn't it so?" "Yes," He replied very gently and then added, "Send for her. Call her." "O Baba, I am so happy," I exclaimed in ecstasy and the next moment a sudden doubt crept into my mind, making me quite nervous. "But Baba, will everything be OK when she comes?" (I was hinting at her health because she was 71 and the last time she was at Parthi, she had gone through a lot of pain.) "Of course, everything shall be OK when she comes." My Lord put my mind to rest by His reassuring words. And then I saw His eyes twinkle and in a mischievous mood, He said, "It is for your sake that she has to be with you." After a pause He finally decided to clarify by adding, "Because in any case you are a little less in your head, as good as 25 p. less in a rupee. That is why it shall be very beneficial for you to have her with you." He saw my shocked expression and had a hearty laugh. When He was about to leave, I made a special request, "Baba, please let me hug you once, just once before you leave." To my surprise, He relented. "OK, just give me some time." Pointing out to some place, He continued, "I shall be going there for a while. Upon my return, you may have your wish fulfilled." With that the dream came to an end.

In time, I discovered that beneath her tough exterior Nargish Aunty was one of the warmest human beings I had known. Even more remarkable than her motherly affection towards me, was her stamina at the age of 71. Yes, Baba had recommended the perfect person. From her I learnt that love expresses itself in different ways. Nargish Aunty gave of herself selflessly for my well-being. I was stirred by her unconditional love for me.

Months later, on my way back to Mumbai, I could say with conviction that Baba could not have recommended a better human being. I have no words to express my gratitude to aunty who lived with me through my tantrums and broken heart each time Baba hid Himself from my view for a while. She was someone without whose daily contribution of emotional support, (besides the material one that she provided), I would have found it extremely difficult to revive my faith in the goodness of human beings.

At My Guru's Feet on the Parsi New Year

When it was our Parsi New Year, with timely news from Verena, my German friend (and a long time permanent resident of the ashram at Parthi / Whitefield), I took my seat in the front row among the Parsis. Verena claimed Baba was expected to come to wish us a Happy New Year! Within minutes, during darshan time, I was actually at my guru's feet! Long after the darshan, I remained in that blissful state.

His Unique Sense of Humour

Baba watched over me with the tender care of a mother nursing her child. That's the role that my dear guru played in my life. And I prayed for His special attention on a daily basis! So I decided to bring up the topic the next time He would appear to me.

Within days, He responded by appearing to me in a dream. I found myself sitting face to face with my Lord who sat cross-legged on bare ground. As I dashed forward and fell at His feet, He hurriedly hid His feet beneath His robe and pushed my hands away roughly. Hurt to the very core of my heart, I asked, "Baba, are you angry?" My voice was barely above a whisper. "Of course, I am," He said, but because His eyes were smiling mischievously I also played at the game by repeating the question, "Are you very angry at me?" Again He feigned anger by answering in the affirmative and laughing at the same time. "Is it wrong on my part to wish to be with you at all times? I am your child, am I not? If so, then does that relationship with you not give me every right to demand your consistent presence in my life?" I cried somewhat unreasonably. After demanding for His undivided attention towards me, I was unsure if I should have uttered those words. I believed, I had carried the matter too far and could have annoyed my dear parent. But instead of expressing resentment, He seemed to have become serious. He surveyed me with mild criticism. Then suddenly His smile was warm as though He was in agreement with me and yet wished to convey His helplessness to me. So He went on to actually justify at length His inability to give me His undivided attention. In a very patient tone, He addressed me thus, "But I am not a bachelor. Just look around." This was the last thing I had expected to hear Him say and the strangeness of the statement pushed me into silence. I turned round to where He had been pointing. Thousands of women, young and old, Indians and foreigners, each one dressed like a gopi, sat waiting for the Lord, with their hands stretched out with a bright burning flame of light on their palms! They were obviously the brides of my divine parent, in the sense that they had dedicated their lives to Him. Now pointing out to the men dressed as gopas who sat in equally large numbers, in the same serious tone, He added, "I have got to attend to so many people whole day long. Daily after exerting myself beyond limit, I feel utterly exhausted by night. So you should understand and not keep on calling out to me every now and then." Instead of paying heed to His plea since He was almost imploring me to leave Him alone, I was unable to comprehend the gravity of His words. I took it all very lightly and had a hearty laugh, telling myself, "Imagine Him who is the Lord, ever getting tired!" Ah, here was my omnipresent and omnipotent Lord trying to tell me that there were times when He could also feel tired! Moreover, each time I recalled His words 'I am not a bachelor', I found it amusing and could barely control my laughter. Imagine how my poor guru must be coping with the infinite number of gopis craving for His attention!

To hear Him speak thus in the dream was to become acquainted with one whose love encompassed all humanity. His love was reaching out and embracing all. The scene of the gopis with flames burning on their palms was a sublime expression of the yearning of these souls and of their joyous fulfilment in God.

The Leela of the Lord, His divine sport was beyond my comprehension. The smallest act of my Lord was saturated with supreme sweetness. Today, it resembled the divine drama that He had chosen to reveal to me.

I looked about in the darshan grounds. One look at the thousands of gopis patiently awaiting their turn and I could see in their eyes an upsurge of affectionate adoration. Now I turned my gaze to the gopas whom He had claimed equally needed His attention. Their eyes as well were full of devotion and love for our Lord. Suddenly it was all so clear. The Lord was one with the gopis and gopas. In their hearts, He was permanently instilled. No doubt, I was His child. But that didn't give me any exclusive right to have His undivided attention. The affectionate, devotional yearning of the millions the world over had to be responded to by Him. And, today, as per the revelation in the dream, from among those whom He'd be granting personal interview, would be the Australian group as well, including Glad. Right enough, that's exactly what took place. It was sheer joy to see my dream materialise within hours and see Glad and her group from Australia walk in for an interview with Baba after the morning darshan.

The Lord Wished that I Rejoin CRY and not the Corporate World

The Lord had drawn a curtain between me, and my distant future. He was teaching me to live in the present, to live wisely and selflessly today, knowing that only good would come of it. Just as my present situation was the result of my past thoughts, words and deeds, what I thought, spoke and did in the present would be shaping my future. Instead of wasting my time being preoccupied with the future, I resolved to make realisation of the self – my priority in life.

When I observed my life minutely I realised that I had always tried to live in reference to my past and in the hope of the future, totally neglecting the present which was most important and valuable.

It was with a very heavy heart that I slept that night after the dream in which He had said, "I have got to attend to so many people whole day long. Daily after exerting myself beyond limit, I feel utterly exhausted by night. So you should understand and not keep on calling out to me every now and then." Though not wanting Him to forsake me, I did not dare to call Him either, since He had Himself said that I let Him stay in peace. Yet, in a dream the very next morning, we were standing and talking as before! Always known to have consulted Him prior to taking any decision in my life, I resolved to find out whether on my return to Mumbai, I could join the corporate world instead of an NGO. My Lord was not in favour of any such step concerning my future. Hence, on my insisting (in the dream) that I would love to serve in a corporate organisation like my brother or sister, He looked very grave and said, "Khurshid, you can't, because your future is so uncertain. Isn't it?" This answer left me wondering.

The lesson was twofold. I needed to have the discrimination to see what would be best for me in the long run, and the will to make wise decisions when a lucrative job presented a more attractive alternative as compared to rejoining CRY.

After His above message, I was happy living in the present, embracing the present. Joy was building within me. Day by day I learned to give up the burdens of resentment and defensiveness. The past was history. It no longer mattered. The future was still a mystery. But the present was glorious and I basked in His love, love that He kept demonstrating in a million ways. I experienced peace, fulfilment and freedom.

Lending a Helping Hand to Sairama

In the eyes of my guru, no spiritual exercise, no vigil on my part would have greater significance than removing the misery of others, stretching out a helping hand to the less privileged. Service to fellow human beings would be the highest form of worship. And I prayed to the Lord to bless me with such an opportunity.

On 31st August '93, I was running temperature and very early in the morning I had even vomited blood. This had me worried and I wasn't sure whether I was in a fit condition to go for darshan – yet I did go.

The same morning, after darshan, my friend Rama insisted that I accompany her to her house and finally I relented, even though I didn't feel like walking that long distance. I could sense that something was amiss. On reaching her house I saw Sairama, her sister-in-law (brother's wife) leaning against a wall – her face full of pain and eyes staring at nothing in particular. She seemed as one in a trance of misery. On my repeated questioning, she roused herself at last and said, "The lump under my armpit needs to be removed. Twice before I had been operated for the same but it has emerged once again and since last night the pain is unbearable." "In that case, you should be consulting a doctor immediately," I told her. In a sad tone it was Rama who clarified, "You being our close friend, I don't mind revealing our personal difficulties. In fact we would love to take her to a doctor, but have no means to do so. At the moment, all that is left of her meagre income from tuitions, is ten rupees. Since the past so many months my brother has been without a job and tuitions is the only thing we could fall back on. Recently I have taken up a job but it will be days before I receive the salary. Sairama insists that we allow her to go to her mother's place for treatment and rest, but knowing my brother's nature she is scared to do so. Hence, there is no solution." "But why should it upset your brother?" I argued. To that she came up with the selfish explanation that he did not wish to remain under his mother-in-law's obligation and that he would stop talking to Sairama if she were to go against his wish. I was amazed at the insensitivity of the husband.

But presently I put aside all other considerations, and only pondered on one thing - how best I could help them. The inner compulsion to relieve misery and assuage pain came very close to being my deepest urge and the thought of Rs. 1,000 that lay in my purse came to my mind. It was a very small amount but they could go to a close by government hospital. Why not give it away to them? Though I knew it would be spent on a noble cause, I saw the advantage of retaining it as well. Torn between the yearning for financial security and the desire to be of help to my friends, I sat worrying. But in a few minutes my mind was made up; the money had to be given away. I had won my own battle. But how do I persuade these friends to accept the same? How could I convince them of my own financial security and that this was a way of expressing my love towards them by giving them a little of what I could spare? "Sairama, don't cry," I said. "Treat me as your own. What I give you belongs not to me but Baba. He gives me more than my immediate requirements and I gladly give it back to His children. So don't hesitate. But I shall be highly obliged if Rama could come with me to my room to collect the same since I am not feeling too well." Actually I was feeling so weak that it took great determination and will-power to walk back to my room at Nagu's place. As I handed over the amount to Rama, all that I was left with was a sense of satisfaction that I had done only my duty towards my sister Sairama.

With the lump in her armpit removed, she felt much better in a day or two and it brought me immense joy to see her smiling once again.

I Learnt not to Get Lost in Rituals or Limit God to any Form

On 1st September '93, the group of Australians presented me with a huge laminated photograph of our guru. And I had no words to express my joy at possessing such a life-size photograph of my Lord. It was a personal token of friendship which I accepted easily in that spirit. However, the night after that, when I got to know that Nagu desired to have a photo like this, I should have gladly parted with it instead of holding on to it, justifying my action to myself.

By my attachment to a material object I had hurt my Lord. In a dream the same night, no matter how I tried, I could not reach out to my dear Lord since there emerged from nowhere a huge iron gate of bars.

I did not have to get lost in the externals of religion – in rituals or forms. How could I have got so attached to a mere photo of His to have disregarded the joy its parting could have brought to my dear friend, Nagu? That morning I firmly resolved that at each step of my life, I would ensure that no iron gate of desires remained locked to bar my entry into His garden. With warm wishes I handed over the photograph to Nagu.

My Dream of Years ago Coming True

One day I received a very warm letter from my brother, Peshotan. It was full of wonderful news. He had sent me a photo of Nandini, a lovely girl, to whom he was to get married. That he was to get married to a Hindu girl and not a Parsi did not come as a surprise to me because long time back I had already seen his marriage take place while performing the ceremony as per the Hindu custom.

Gladys Providing Me with the Much Needed Warmth and Affection

Gladys and Helen often came to visit Nagu and me, to have a friendly chat. On the day the group was to leave for Australia, I thanked Baba for their lovely company and told Him that I'd miss them, to which my dear Lord immediately answered in a dream, "Khurshid, I am aware that you begin to shiver if scantily clothed. Hence, I provide you with warm covering. You shall continue to feel the same warmth in the future as well." With Him to provide me with the warmth of love what more could I ask for? Divine love – experiencing Him in one and all is not only possible, it is the most complete love of which we are capable as human beings. I was warm in God's love so how could I shiver with the cold of loneliness? It was God's love in the form of all the wonderful people who in turns took care of my needs. The same morning Glad came up with a pleasant surprise. She had extended her visa and had decided to stay back.

That day just after morning darshan she overwhelmed me further by holding my hand and in a trembling voice, with tears brimming in her eyes she said, "One does not need to be a blood relation to make one fond of another. And words are inadequate to express how I felt today when I saw you enter the hall just before darshan." And I was equally happy to know that she was going to stay back for a while. As I was lost in my thoughts she gently said, "I shall stay in India, not just for a few more days but for two months."

Now coming back to 6th September, in the dream Baba did not allow me to touch His feet but offered to give me whatever else I desired. All I asked was for some vibhuti.

For the next two months that Glad and I shared a room, in Whitefield and then in Parthi till Nargish Aunty came from Mumbai, she always expressed her love in action.

"There is no Separation for us, my Beloved Child."

It was 12th September '93, exactly a week since my Lord had last appeared to me and I was feeling as though darkness had enveloped me. Why had He not come to me in the past week? Surely, I had done something wrong to have displeased Him. Overwhelmed with grief, I wrote a letter to dad telling him to pray that He never stop coming to me, that the gap between us never widen and that He remain by my side always.

Once again forgetting His divine message to me through the earlier dream of the gopis, I was deeply hurt. Baba was ignoring me. I believed He was moving away from me. My guru and best friend, Baba was not annoyed with me though for writing a letter that indicated my lack of faith. By my letter to dad, I had given a soul call to my Divine parent. He could no longer remain indifferent. He manifested in Nagu's dream the same night.

The letter had not even reached the letter-box by which time Baba went to Nagu in her dream with the following message. On 13th September '93, early morning Nagu came running to me and in an excited voice she narrated to me her beautiful dream. "Khurshid, Baba was sitting in the main room of our house with you at a short distance to His right. After taking His permission I sat to His left and while doing so my foot slightly touched His, upon which He moved closer to you. He inched towards you little by little till He was so close to you that His arm touched yours!"

How wrong I had been in believing that my Lord was being evasive, always hiding; and I was always being side-tracked. By His message to me in Nagu's dream, He had proved me wrong. The fact was that it was I who once in a while lost sight of Him, but He never lost sight of me, never once moved away from me. It was as if via Nagu's dream, He was saying, "There is no separation for us, my beloved child."

My dear guru was the very embodiment of kindness, love, forgiveness, and compassion. He had not forsaken me. His blessing was ever present; my receptivity had been lacking. Hearing Nagu, my heart was filled with joy eternal. The little cup of my heart could not contain the love that overflowed as I heard her out. I was overcome with joyful relief. I no longer felt the continuous torment that had kept me nearly sleepless for days; at His loving, reassuring message the agony vanished as though it had never been.

As a child of His, I needed to reflect upon my own attitude and the expectation I carried in my own heart about my guru whom very often I limited to His human frame, completely forgetting His omnipresence, even if momentarily. Baba had once again reaffirmed to me that one of the few things about His love for me, that was constant, was His promise that He'd never move away from me, His child who had left all to be at His feet. His messages to Nagu each time He appeared in her dreams to respond to my prayers (prayers that she was unaware of) were powerful ways of reinforcing that affirmation.

I had not expected the Divine experiences that were to happen in the months to follow. Never had I asked for or craved for spiritual experiences. I had simply asked that He forever continue to grant me special darshan in dreams and visions as a sign of confirmation that I was on the right track in my thoughts, words and deeds. My joy came from the fact that He loved me unconditionally and had promised never to leave me; I sought no other reward in life.

His Humility and Divine Friendship Moved Me to the Core

I find it so difficult to put into words my experiences with the Divine. And yet I've attempted to do so in order that I may share to the best of my ability the joy I experienced in His company.

The dream: Taking long strides I reached the main gate. When just about to enter the grounds from the ladies side, I had a quick look in the Ramesh Hall and was relieved to note that Baba had not yet arrived. But when I turned my gaze to the inner gate from which He always appeared, I was amazed to find Him peeping, His eyes scanning the crowd in search of someone in particular. All of a sudden, He caught sight of me and the look of joy and rapture that came over His face brought tears to my eyes. Then He came running to me in order to receive me at the gate! By gestures, He graciously welcomed me into the hall. And the dream came to an end.

That morning I once again recalled the dream with joy. Such was His humility and perfect expression of what divine friendship meant that my eyes blurred at the memory of that dream.

I did not have any material comforts – thus my life was not so easy. But I did have the treasure in the form of my guru waiting at the gate to receive me. The very thought of the months that lay ahead in the company of my guru filled my heart with immense joy and gratitude. Even today, (on 23rd February '02) when I'm editing this Volume, I still cannot forget the feeling that came over me every morning as I trudged from Nagu's place to the ashram.

My Guru Emphasised that He was My Parent

In the dream on 18th September '93 I saw that I missed my father and hence sobbed uncontrollably. And then a gentle voice calling out my name made me look up hopefully only to find my guru sitting cross-legged on the floor right in front of me. "Khurshid, sing a bhajan." The choked feeling in my throat was making it difficult to speak and yet amidst sobs, I said, "No, I can't! No more can I sing now that..." It was an involuntary cry of anguish. And my voice trailed away into silence. My Lord did not give up. Very gently, He continued to coax me to sing. "Sing, Khurshid, sing. Sing for me, my child." And after a pause, "Did you pray today?" "No Baba. I..." I broke off and put my hands over my eyes. "Then pray, my child. A little prayer of four lines at least. Come on, little one, start praying right away." "Baba, I can't," I wept and protested. "And why can't you?" I could never hide the truth from Him. For a while though I avoided His gaze, I knew there was no escape, so I said in a repentant tone, "That's because I have never in my life endeavoured to pray. Hence, without referring to a prayer book how can I possibly do so? Besides, I do not wish to sing or pray at all." In having to live without my dad by my side, I felt I had lost my greatest friend, blessing and comfort, for he had always been that to me. Others in the room looked aghast at my reply that I could not even pray a few lines, but my Lord, the all-forgiving one, was full of love, "O why do you cry out that life without dad has no meaning for you? Am I not your father? Am I not your mother? With this parent always with you, what makes you still say things like – life has no meaning for you and is not worth living any more?" He protested with a touch of petulance and I could make out that I had wounded Him deeply. But the softness still lingered in His eyes as He almost whispered into my ears, "All you have to do is just call out to me once and I shall be there with you. I shall respond to all your prayers. With me by your side you need never consider yourself alone, my child."

Was it the death of my attachment to dad that Baba had been referring to? He wanted me to look at the process of death with the eye of wisdom so that I could see it merely as the soul changing its robe – rebirth or gain freedom from this continuous cycle of birth and death – liberation.

Today, in June '09, when I'm re-editing the book, my dad is living a happy and fruitful life. Even though Baba understood my longing for my dad's presence, he wished that I should overcome the absence of my earthly parent by keeping my focus on Him alone. I had to learn to maintain equanimity in the face of loss of a dear parent.

Baba wanted me to pray. This was not the first time in my life that He had made that request. After performing his family and social duties, dad still had the time for meditation and prayers. His harmoniously balanced life should have become an inspiration for me. Well, I actually did pray once in a while, and my prayers had taken many forms. Sometimes I had prayed for explicit outcomes and at other times for nothing specific.

Love for my family and attachment to them (especially dad) were different things. Attachment clouded my understanding. Baba was teaching me to have divine love for them, love that would never bind. By telling me to sing for Him, He was implying that I cross over the river of delusion instead of longing for my dad's company. Till now I could not completely succeed in abandoning the desire for a family. He was aware of it and helped me overcome the same by simply expanding the normal idea of what a family was until it embraced all humanity.

Baba was certainly not telling me to give up close, loving relationships. The precious teaching He was imparting here was that when I gave up my attachments to loved ones, I could draw closer to them than ever before. It would be only by knowing and realising the indwelling spirit, within that, the habit of identifying myself and my loved ones with the body would cease.

Sai Proved that He would not Forsake Me

Hardly had a day or two passed after the above dream, that He once again put me in a situation that had my blood boiling against someone who had shown disrespect to me. It also was an incident that made me feel deserted by Him. Ramu, Sairama's husband was at my door at Nagu's place where I lived. Before I knew what was happening, he had walked up to me and tried to misbehave with me. (But I pushed him away.) As if that was not enough, he demanded money from me, and that too for alcohol. He justified his demand by saying that if I could offer monetary help to his wife for medical expenses, then I could very well afford to sponsor his alcohol expenses!

For a long time after he had gone, I could not control my tears. Had I learnt to live without any feeling of identification with my body, nothing would have hurt me, and my faith would have kept me far removed from all the shadows and turmoil in life. But wounded as I was, I dared to challenge Him! "Hadn't you promised that I have only to call out to you and you'll respond? And had you also not said that with you as my parent, I need not cry but sing bhajans for you? Today you have to prove your love for me, your dear child, by coming and staying in my room throughout the night so that I know I am not alone. If, as you claim, you are my parent who has heard my cry, give me proper evidence that you shall stay with me tonight!"

After the initial outpouring of rage and anger, voices of reason suggesting that I was behaving childishly were surfacing. Yet, within moments I was distraught, once again demanding proof from Him that I was not alone in life, that He was willing to spend at least one night in the company of someone whom He loved dearly and called His one and only mother. I cried silently from the depths of a tormented spirit. With that silent prayer from a bleeding heart, I went to sleep. As usual, there was an absolutely instantaneous response from my dear guru who appeared in Nagu's dream. (My dear girl Nagu was unaware of my unpleasant experience with Ramu.)

My prayer to my guru was that I no more be deluded by this world and its maya. Just then, Nagu entered the room all flushed and breathless with what she had recently dreamt about and in hushed tones began to disclose it to me. Let me quote her in her own words:

"Khurshid, you were sitting cross-legged on the floor, yes, it was in our house, and Swami (Baba) came and lay on the ground with His head on your lap! Very surprised at the gesture of so much love and affection towards you, I was gazing at the two of you when you suddenly took the form of my mother and then were back to your normal form. And, it was now easy to understand it all. He was sleeping on mother's lap." Too eager to hear more of the dream, and very relieved that she had not understood what the Lord was trying to disclose, I said, "Do carry on with your dream."

And she continued by saying, "Now you were once again back to your own form as He lay on your lap. After a while He moved on to my lap! As I placed my hands under His head, I could feel the soft curls. Just then, the pundit (later, Nagu clarified that she had meant the man who walked behind Baba during darshans, and to whom Baba handed over the letters of the devotees every time they became a handful) entered our room. He questioned Swami upon His unusual behaviour of sleeping in a stranger's house and on the laps of strangers like you and me. Swami merely smiled at that remark and remained with us in the same position for a long time. Just before dawn broke, He got up saying that He better be on the move to reach out in time to the thousands who awaited His darshan!"

Damaged egos require healing. Baba understood my need for reassurance. He never let me remain in a state of despair for long. He was always there to love me. I didn't have to keep testing His love and constantly demand for proof of it. Armed with this reality, I felt at peace.

Sai Foretelling His Arrival in the form of Sunbeam Children

24th September '93 – 3.45 a.m. – dream. A dream that left me confused and guessing, I finally decided to just note it down in my book and leave it at that. It was as follows: Room no.14 in my house at Mumbai, on the wall adjoined to which my bed was, there hung a huge wall calendar of my Lord Sathya Sai. As if from my room, suddenly I was transported to heaven, I stood facing Him among the clouds. He was actually standing on the clouds. His feet were not visible as they were hidden under those beautiful clouds that were always on the move. He kept rising higher and higher up into the sky. And I gazed, not understanding the significance of the event as He disappeared altogether into the clouds, but not before giving me a date – 25th May '97. Though I remember the date quite clearly, I just could not recollect the rest of our conversation on waking up. But that was not all that I dreamt. In the latter part of the dream, I saw my Lord descend on earth once more, slowly, gradually till His feet touched the ground. He was again in my room. Now at His feet lay not the clouds, but flowers. Yes, it appeared as though He was standing in a flower garden! Flowers of all sorts bloomed at His feet. This flower-bed had sprung up next to my bed! The feeling of sharing the news was strong in me, and I wanted to let my friends know that Baba was in my house, and a new garden had sprung up. He stopped me by saying, "No, don't call up your friends. Keep quiet about what I have said." And also by putting a finger on His lips, He once again let me know that I should keep quiet.

Today, after almost a decade and a half since the above mentioned dream, I surmise that His arrival in May '97 that He had prophesised in 1993 was actually His arrival in my life in the form of the first batch of 8 children with whom I formed a friendship via the CRY neighbourhood project in 1997. Later on, that informal beginning took shape of a full fledged project that was christened Sunbeam in December '99. Sunbeam – a public charitable trust that catered to the educational, psychological and emotional needs of the underprivileged children in Mumbai.

To Genuinely Love and Grow Spiritually, I Needed to Become a Forgiving Person

In a dream on the 25th September '93, I received a strange command from the Lord. By gestures He was telling me to go in a particular direction that He was pointing out to. He kept repeatedly doing so. What wasn't clear to me though was, where did He want me to go? Within hours of the dream, Glad, who was unaware of my decision to never again step into the house of my friends Rama and Sairama, enquired if I could accompany her to that place, since she had something to offer to them.

Angry at the very thought of entering the house of the very people who had insulted me, I was about to refuse her. Just then, I was blessed with a very clear, consistent vision of the Lord telling me to go, exactly as He had done in the dream the same morning! Now I had no choice but to accompany Glad to Rama's home.

Two days ago, Sairama had said many things that wounded me deeply. Firstly, she believed her husband was not capable of showing any disrespect to a woman. More outrageously still, she added that if as I claimed the incident had taken place, she could easily guess why her husband must have behaved so with me. Didn't he have to be sure of the kind of company his wife kept? That she believed gave him the right to come to my house at night to test my character. And she further went on to say that since I hailed from Mumbai and not a holy place like Whitefield, it was all the more necessary to be sure of my reputation! Her words wounded even more deeply than her husband's attempt at misbehaviour with me. I was bitter, hurt and shattered. On no account was I willing to maintain friendship with Sairama. I found endless reasons to be angry with her. But Baba wanted it to be otherwise.

I had to be able to step aside from my prejudices, step into Sairama's shoes, look at life through her eyes rather than my own. Only by doing so would I be able to clearly see how to serve those needs of hers with compassion, especially her need for acceptance and friendship. Adopting this path would lead me to real love again – love that knew to forgive. Thinking on these lines I calmed down. I understood that as a result of my revealing to Sairama the previous night's incident, I had ended up hurting her. Perhaps, at some level, she knew of her spouse's character but didn't have the courage to acknowledge it. It must have been too painful for her. May be, before blurting out the sordid truth, I should have gauged whether my dear friend was ready to hear it.

It was difficult to genuinely love, to spiritually grow. Hence, Baba had to take the trouble to come and tell me to go to their house. He wanted me to extend my limits through love; to do so by reaching out, so to speak, towards the other person, whose growth I wished to nurture.

If Ramu and his wife, Sairama had acted unkindly against me, why did I feel I had to do something about it instead of leaving this painful episode at His feet and forget about it? The trouble was with me. I could not let go of my vengeful and angry feelings. To love Sairama completely, it was not enough if I cared for her deeply; I had to be also able to accept her with her imperfections and be able to forgive her.

Counting the endless number of times that my guru had forgiven me for my own shortcomings, by now it should have been easy for me to accept that imperfection was part of being human. To be His image

I'd have to be brave enough to love and strong enough to forgive. This called for action, for love towards my dear friend. He made me understand that I had no right to be so uncharitable towards her.

Baba was teaching me to have a forgiving heart. Instantly, I put aside all my hurt feelings, forgave them and decided to join Glad. Sairama, was pleasantly surprised at my sight. She apologised for her hasty speech of the day before. As for Rama, with tears streaming down her cheeks, she begged my forgiveness on behalf of her brother and her sister-in-law. Ramu too apologised and seemed contrite. I forgave all of them. I moved away not from them but definitely from my own struggle. The discovery that this man and his wife whom I had demonised were feeling human beings, gave me the release I'd been looking for. My anger at them was slowly replaced by the earlier friendship with that family.

As I sat in their house, my silent prayer to my guru was, "Baba, what role do you see me playing in the lives of these friends of mine?" All of a sudden (as though in answer to my prayer), Sairama broke into my thoughts, by saying, "You know what I dreamt today? All three of us, i.e. Ramu, Rama and I together managed to drag the milk-white Kamdhenu cow into our house." (According to the Hindu mythology the Kamdhenu cow is supposed to be the one to bring about prosperity wherever she goes.)

A Birthday Gift from Baba

In a dream at 6 a.m. on 27th September '93, my Divine Parent surprised me by expressing His affection towards me by planting a feather-light kiss on my cheek, a birthday gift from my divine parent. (According to our Parsi calendar, this time my birthday happened to fall on that day.) As my Lord gazed deep into my eyes, His own eyes were full of compassion and I sat in a state of bliss. "Baba, when are you leaving for Parthi? Can you give me the exact date?" He seemed to ponder over my question for a while and then said, "6th, 7th, 8th, or rather the 9th." He sounded as if He found it difficult to make up His mind.

After thanking Him for His affection expressed by way of celebrating my birthday with me, by blessing me with a birthday kiss, I began a thorough introspection. The Lord was teaching me to face life with a smile, never worrying. This one year in His presence I learned that renunciation was more difficult than action. In the path of renunciation I was required to give up ego. And I promised to do so. In the path of action I was expected to give up expectations of any fruit of action. I resolved to do that as well. While living with my family and in the world I could renounce my likes, dislikes or ego. I'd be fit to serve God only when I learned to serve humanity. I need not dream of serving the masses in a large way. Even a small beginning would be enough. My seva could be words of sympathy, sharing sorrows, instilling optimistic thoughts in defeated souls.

The latter part of the dream was equally significant. Of late, He had been identifying Himself with me and vice versa! So I could never understand whether He was talking about Himself or me. When He mentioned the dates from the 6th onwards and stopped at the 9th, saying that He'd rather go on that day to Parthi, it did puzzle me because in one of Nagu's recent dreams He had already answered the same question, but with a different answer! She had asked Him for the exact date of His departure from Brindawan, Whitefield so that I could book a room for myself at Parthi from that very day and not a day in advance which would save me some money! To that He had answered in English whereupon Nagu had requested Him to talk to her in a language she could understand better. In response to that, He had asked her for a paper and pen and jotted down some numbers on it saying that He was sure she could at least understand the numbers. He had started from the 1st and written up to the 5th. and then told her that He was tired and would not stay a day longer than the 5th of October!

Of course He kept His word to Nagu. No one in the ashram knew the exact date of His departure so much in advance but we did. Glad and I would have loved to follow Him on the 6th itself when He left for Parthi, but could not do so. Both of us had taken ill, and had to visit the city doctor on the 7th. After sufficient rest, by the 9th, Glad and I were fit to travel to Parthi.

Reassurances from My Guru Regarding the Rest of My Stay in Parthi

When I was still at Whitefield with my Lord, on 30.9.93, in a dream Baba stood looking at the crowd gathered around Him. Then turning to me, He asked, "When did you come, my child?" Instead of joy that I should have felt, His question startled me. And I started having misgivings. Had I not left my loved ones at His command months back? Then, how was it that He was not aware as to when I had arrived? The thought of my guru being unaware of my date of arrival was anything but comforting. Not realizing that He was asking this question at a much deeper level, at a soul level, I responded in a sullen voice, "I arrived in May and have been in your presence since then." He continued to feign surprise and said, "O you have been here since then?" Not being able to fathom His strange words, I thought it wise to confirm if He still wanted me around or not. "Baba, I am here since the month of May and as per what you have said I intend to go to Mumbai not before March '94. Will the 1st of March be OK?" He nodded in the affirmative and then said, "Yes, you may go then." Once again my mind was filled with doubts, this time about Nargish Aunty's health for which I wanted some assurance. "Baba, everything will go well. Won't it be so when Nargish Aunty comes from Mumbai in order to give me company?" Understanding my anxiety, He reassured me in gentle tones, "Yes, my child." The moment I bent low to touch His feet, He too bent low and placed His palms (upturned) on His feet. Hence, ultimately, instead of being able to touch His feet my hands were placed into His hands.

I Needed to Use My Discretion on whom to Share His Messages with

My Lord constantly provided me with opportunities to explore myself. I had to be made aware of the impact I had on others by sharing my experiences (of Baba) with them. He assisted me in doing so by letting me take advantage of the insights He blessed me with.

Glad was a friend, someone dear to me and a person in whom I confided some of my dreams and visions. One night as I went on talking to her and she sat listening to me, she suddenly started with a volley of questions that shook me up. Though they were not by way of criticism, her words struck me with great force, "Khurshid, have you ever asked yourself why you talk so much of Swami?" And then she added more gently, "Do you realize what a great responsibility you shoulder? And also how blessed you are to have Swami come to you so often! With me it is fine and you can trust me but I feel you have to be discerning in the friends you choose or you may land yourself into trouble. So ask Him to let you know of your own motive behind trusting and confiding in people instead of keeping quiet about dreams and visions that you should hold dear to you and keep to yourself. If I speak to you in this manner, believe me, it is not with the intention of hurting your feelings because I hold you in high esteem and feel blessed to have known you for I think of Swami and you as equal partners."

"If it's my ego that is the reason behind sharing my experiences, then I don't deserve His grace any more." This feeling continued to grow upon me and became such a torment that I could not sleep. My Lord had always been telling me to keep quiet and I was the one who went on talking. The very idea of the possibility of my motive behind this disobedience being one to gain publicity among friends and acquaintances was repelling.

Yet, deep down in my heart I was sure that my devotion had always been for God alone and not to impress others. But the issue was that if I was deeply sincere, then outward fervour did not have to exist. In its place there should have been a deep inner state of consciousness. Had it been my subconscious wish to impress Glad? Analysing myself honestly, I believed it not to be so. My devotion had always been deep, sincere, withdrawn from public gaze and inward. Then why had it occasionally taken an outward turn in the form of sharing my divine experiences with friends like Nargish Aunty, Yasmin Aunty and now Glad? Baba knew it was with the sole intention to share my joy, the bliss I experienced. Yet, if He'd let me know His opinion in the matter as to whether I could continue to share my divine experiences with others or not, it would make things clear and I'd go by His command.

His answer in a dream early next morning set my mind to rest. It was a very symbolic dream, clear and informative. At the same time, it was not the answer I had expected. The dream was as follows:

For a long time I was caught up in the kitchen, busy preparing a variety of dishes for a little girl whom I intended to feed till her hunger was appeased. I served the dishes one after the other and she seemed pleased with all that was being offered to her. I didn't take the trouble to find out if she had had enough until the whole floor was laden with the number of dishes. Encouraged by her praises that the food was very delicious, I disregarded an important factor – her age and the digestion capacity that went with it. Considering her actual appetite and not merely her appeal for more food, I should have offered her only enough for her to digest and no more. The dream continued, with the child requesting for one more helping and I, believing it my duty to appease her hunger, acceding to her request. All of a sudden I could cook no more. The handle of the frying pan turned burning hot and I ended up scorching my fingers.

The message in the dream was quite clear. At least one burden was off my mind, now that I knew that I was not as bad as the opinion I had formed of myself. I was merely being foolish in feeding people with my tales of the Lord without gauging their digestion capacity! In His unique way He thus taught me to learn to be discreet. Though He had hinted that by sharing too much I might burn my fingers, He had also indirectly given permission to share with others, keeping in mind their capacity to absorb and assimilate.

I was Blessed with the Master Key to Divine Knowledge

In a dream on 4th October '93 a crowd of distressed people stood around me. Each of them held a lock in his/her hand that would not unlock despite their efforts. This crowd comprised of people young and old, people from different parts of the world. To my great surprise I happened to be in possession of the master key that could unlock each and every lock on earth! Hence, I decided not to disappoint the masses who approached me one after the other for help. Very patiently I went about serving them. As I unlocked one lock after the other, their faces beamed in joy. This work was never-ending.

The above dream was easy to interpret. Baba had, by way of innumerable lessons imparted to me over the years, blessed me with the precious possession of the master key which had the capacity to unlock the numerous problems faced by human beings. This master key, in the form of His teachings (via these volumes) would provide seekers with solutions to at least some of their unanswered queries.

At this level of awareness the external world was far, far away. He had made me travel to this depth, and I knew that this world to which I had descended was much more real, and what I understood at this depth was much more valid than what I saw on the surface. Yes, in the form of His teachings I held the master key to success – spiritual success.

In His simple way, my dear guru had provided me with insights to understand spiritualism as the relationship between my soul and other souls. Therefore, the master key I possessed was the key to happiness through self-knowledge, knowledge of the divine and the knowledge of the path that would guide human beings to become His image. It was the key to end the delusion.

3

The Divine Assures Me of His Company at All Times

In Sai's Divine Institute, I had to Undergo the Refresher's Course

Every single day now I was the recipient of some beautiful message or the other. On 5th October '93, it was one more of such dreams.

A group of people were running at top speed, all in one direction, and I joined them - not knowing where to or what for I was running. On the way I stumbled quite a few times but didn't give up. Upon inquiring with the person running by my side, I was told that we all were heading for the new institute where the world's best Professor would be delivering lectures! They were in such great haste because no one wanted to be late for the admission. That sounded logical and I also increased my speed to as fast as my feet could carry me, and was happy to find myself among the first few in the long queue of thousands of people waiting for admission! My turn came and I handed over my application to Baba who sat at the counter. On scrutinising my form, He seemed puzzled and said, "Sorry, but we can't grant you admission in this institute." "May I know why? Is it because my qualifications do not meet the institute's requirements?" I asked. In a gentle tone He replied, "You have already finished learning all that is being taught at this institute. And let me give you an example to illustrate my point. For instance, if this were to be a shorthand and typing institute, you as our student, have already completed the course, learning from the very beginning of the alphabets, to words, sentences and finally speed lessons in shorthand, all of it successfully. All these students would be starting with kindergarten studies. You would, I am sure, not want to start learning afresh from lesson number one. So, take my advice, my child. All that you need to do from now onwards is to keep in touch with everything that you have learnt here, by continuously being on your guard. That's like attending a refresher's course, the one you are attending since the past few months. Success depends solely on your own effort. Don't expect me as the Professor here to take on that responsibility." With that the dream came to an end.

He wanted me to become His image. But as long as I was full of myself, my own small desires and self-centred thoughts, I left no room whatsoever for Him to work in my life. If I had to live in harmony with the Divine will, my petty, selfish personal will had to go.

My dear Professor's answer had intrigued me but not for long. What He had said made absolute sense. From that moment, I resolved not to trouble my Divine Professor but to do as He bid. It would be a shame if I behaved as though I had unlearned all that He had taught me over the years and expect Him to start training me up all over again with the basics of living a life worthy of offering at the Lord's feet.

I took the message in the above dream as a compliment from my guru who felt I needn't join the new batch all over again but instead just join the refresher's batch in order to freshen up the memory of the divine within me and all around me.

He had already taught me the basics of spiritual living. The refresher's course was to bring me around to see clearly what I had lost and therefore, what I needed to rediscover. Why was it at all necessary for me to attend the refresher's course? Perhaps it was because, oftentimes I still fell into a life centred on fleeting pleasures of worldly ties, thus building a house on sand. Of late, I had resolved to lead an abundant and rewarding life. Hence, my 10 months long stay in Parthi / Whitefield attending the refresher's course, once again having the privilege of studying under the kind supervision of the world's best Professor, my dearest guru.

The education He was imparting was value-based education influencing the heart. He was helping us all achieve moral and ethical literacy. Education that built fundamental traits of character – such as compassion for others, honesty, unconditional love and every such thing that took His children closer to their goal – experiencing themselves and others as the spark of the Divine.

Mother Saraswati Rejoices at My Awakening

As steps in my awakening, Baba inspired me to discover and experience my oneness with all mankind. God was shining in all human beings equally as the immortal soul.

My attachment to Baba's form was such that I was like one obsessed and made a big hue and cry of it if He didn't visit me for a few days. Such was my condition on the 7th October '93. In a childish manner I was sobbing my heart out feeling abandoned by Him. I prayed that He come and let me know where I had gone wrong so that I could endeavour to rectify myself. Poor Glad tried her level best to pacify me and make me see sense but to no avail. A number of logical questions she asked me, "Are you not having symbolic dreams almost daily? Are you not guided about the future? Can you not learn to broaden your outlook and visualise Him in all? Has He not been giving you enough grace by coming to you so often? Is it not time that you take the leap in His direction by going from the form to the formless?" Knowing fully well that she was absolutely right in what she said, yet, I persisted in my foolish obstinacy that He Himself come and tell me so. And He did! The dream in answer to my prayer was as follows:

In a dream that I had on 8th October '93, Nagu ran to me and in an excited voice said, "Khurshid, Khurshid! Do you know something? I had been blessed to get a chance to feed Baba for so long, almost for a period of two months or more! I fed Him day after day with meals cooked by my own hands. How lucky I am to have received that grace, that chance of a lifetime!"

O what a dream, a world of meaning lay in those simple words of hers. Didn't it clearly imply that He was not limited to His own form but dwelled in each of us? "Baba, I beg your forgiveness. Today, once again you have expressed your omnipresent nature and I think I see light." No sooner had I said these words, in a clear wakeful state that I was then, I had a dazzling vision of Lord Sathya Sai in the kitchen with an apron on. He was cooking for me! Via this vision He was saying that as much as Nagu had to see Him in those whom she served, I had to equally see Him in those who served me! This vision was now followed by another dazzling vision – that of Mother Saraswati, with the expression of absolute delight on Her face!

After these wonderful experiences, I beheld my surroundings with a new perception. I could perceive God in the form of joy and goodness of humanity all around me.

With these beautiful experiences as live examples, Baba had provided me with the required conviction that enabled me to perceive Him in everyone, and behold everyone in Him. In the years to follow, I confess, there were times when my mind wavered and I lost sight of Him but He never lost sight of me. He continued to bless me with the divine insights.

It was easier for me to strive to realise Him as the personal God. In fact, approaching Him through the visible, through a form was more tangible to me. God incarnates again and again to guide and inspire His children. I had always confined Him to some form or the other, be it Krishna, Christ or Sai. But my Sai did not wish me to become attached to or dependent on His limited human form. He wanted me to see God all around me in every human being.

To go from the form to the formless God would be the ultimate step on my part. The nature of the unchangeable Brahman was such that He could not be seen. Yet, He was the absolute – all creation radiated from Him. To know Him I had to only turn the consciousness away from the objective world. To know Him it was imperative that I cleanse my intellect of all attachment, hatred, egoism, anger and the sense of possession. Each of us, every soul was a part of that Infinite God, we all were reflections of Him. The intense longing for realising God initially in the form of my guru, then in each of us and now in the formless – to experience Him all over was a big transformation gradually taking place within my heart.

And my attempts bore fruit – in the form of divine experiences that I was blessed with in abundance in the days and months to follow.

Divine Visions – One Followed by the Other

Love for the Lord had taken up residence in my soul. In a world marred by hurt and anguish, I felt profoundly grateful that the Lord was there to walk with me. I could feel love flowing from Him to me and back to Him again, complete, everlasting divine love.

Meditation on Him brought results that confirmed that I was not alone. For me, my guru opened worlds of Divine beauty, visions that brought about bliss in which I've remained mesmerised for long spells of time.

On 9th October '93, Glad and I left for Parthi by car. But I was not too happy since I had insisted and paid my share, which according to me was an extravagant expenditure on my part when I could have very well travelled by bus. But I could not let her spend on me, unless Baba permitted me to do so.

The room booked in my name by Mr. Bala Krishna was in the Sai Colony, Opposite State Bank of India, 3-461, on the first floor. It was a very bright, airy room with wall cabinets, a kitchen platform, attached western bathroom, and round the clock water and electricity supply. Thus, it had all the basic necessities, and yes – a proper bed as well. So I need not worry about comforts for Nargish Aunty. The owners, Mr. Hanumant Rao and his wife were Sai devotees, a very co-operative, humane and friendly couple who lived in their own house nearby. I was really grateful to Glad for the gas cylinder that she bought (a small one along with the stove) which we could use for our meals now, and which she later left with me. This made it easier for Nargish Aunty in preparing the meals for the two of us in the months to follow.

Whitefield and Parthi could not be compared in any respect as far as darshans were concerned. At Whitefield, after the dream in which my Lord had promised to come to receive me at the gate, every single day after that, till He left on the 6th, He came out for darshan the same minute as I reached the hall and was passing through the security check gate! And I will in no way attribute it to mere coincidence because there was no fixed time that I maintained for attending darshan, so there was no possibility of timing my arrival with His either. Every day it gave me great pleasure to walk in myself and take a place while watching Him walk towards us the same time! But now at Parthi I felt lost. All that play of ours had come to an abrupt end, or so I felt, and complained to Him about the same one evening as I was passing by the ashram shops facing the auditorium where He presently stayed. For the bhajans I went and sat under one of the arches so that I could sit in some shade and not in the terrible heat.

He seemed far away and I felt dejected. Seated in the Prashanti grounds, I went on praying and crying for Him. When I refused to give up until He responded, He answered by blessing me with the most wonderful, and one of the lengthiest vision I had ever had in my life which lasted almost throughout the bhajans i.e. for almost 20 minutes. Let me share with you my prayer to Him before I describe the vision at length. "Baba though I understand that it's impossible for us to continue playing our hide and seek game at Parthi, I am sure it's not too difficult for you to hear my cry for attention. Does it reach you or not? Can you hear my voice? You have to respond!" This prayer was followed by a series of visions while in a wakeful state. Each one seen individually made no sense, but put together, it was as though my Lord was having a conversation with me! Visions confirming our love for each other and also visions imparting knowledge about the role I was supposed to play in this lifetime.

The first vision: An arrow with burning flames came tearing through the air. Where was it heading to? This vision of the flying, burning arrow lasted for almost a few minutes! And I repeatedly asked the Lord to clarify its import, which He did by showing me the next vision – that of a red burning heart, a very large heart with flames emanating from it that seemed to cover the whole of the universe. "O Lord, give me simple visions, those that I can easily interpret." And the next moment the arrow of my first vision came and pierced itself into the heart! The moment it hit the heart, a sort of lightning took place and both of them shone forth even brighter than before. After this kind of vision there was no need for me to ask for further proof. My cry had pierced Him and we were one. At this beautiful vision I lost awareness of this world. In ecstasy I beheld the presence of God in the form of divine love.

The next vision: The Lord's divine hands were pouring grain, vibhuti, kumkum, milk, and so on into a golden bowl held by me. He was pouring His divine grace into my life. The bowl was oval in shape and a deep one. He filled it to the brim and then disappeared from sight. Now my hands and the bowl it held grew in size a million-fold. From all sides there appeared thousands of hands craving for some of the contents of it. All hands simultaneously dipped into it and took from it whatever they desired and each one seemed satisfied to have got their need met. This vision was perhaps indicative of the grace that the Lord showers upon me and one day people all over the world were to receive in the form of the teachings in the books.

It's a real joy for me to know that Baba wanted me to pass along to others the accumulated knowledge and inspiration that I had received throughout my life. The joy I felt was lasting because it was based on the knowledge of the Divine. The desire arose to selflessly serve mankind. I could perceive the great ocean of love that lay within me. As I sat doing japa, chanting my dear guru's name, my consciousness became absorbed in Him.

Learn to Recognise Me in all of Humanity

Time sped by quickly at the feet of my guru. Although I was deeply happy, the months of training were not without struggle. My Lord was firmly engaged in transforming His erring child to an exemplary disciple. His divine messages became the guiding light of my life. I'm proud of the fact that I've never been one to be afraid of criticism. I made no effort to hide my shortcomings and was always ready to challenge and re-examine the values that I held out to myself and to others.

2.45 a.m. dream on 10th October '93: Baba was obviously displeased at the manner in which I, breaking the rules of the ashram, ran forward and took my seat in the front row so that I could get better darshan! And in trying to touch His feet I made Him even angrier, because that was another form of disobeying Him! Now that I had brought His wrath upon myself, I had no option but to listen to the lecture He gave me on how to learn to maintain discipline. All I did was sit and shed tears as He went on and on for a long time. To others, though His words were not distinct, what was clear to them was that Baba was admonishing me. To find that He didn't allow me to sit in the front row was enough reason for them to come to the conclusion that I was unloved by Him. Baba was about to walk away when I got up, and in order to detain Him until He had forgiven me, I held His hand and pleaded, "Baba, please forgive me. Please, O please Baba." And I went on imploring Him till He said in a stern voice, "Yes, you better learn to go according to what I say to you." (To my mind, He meant not wasting my time sitting in token queues or praying for front rows but to use my time in more fruitful purposes such as completing my writing work.) And with that He walked away briskly, leaving me very repentant.

The dream continued. People in the crowd who had watched that Baba hardly paid any heed to my entreaties, looked at me with indifference. To my horror, the minute Baba left my side, some of the devotees from the crowd, both men and women dressed in white, turned to pounce upon me. And I took to my heels. They did not give up and I called out to Him. "Baba, Baba, Baba..." While I was calling out His name, I kept looking back to see how close they had reached to where I was. My Lord was not to be seen anywhere but the moment these people reached close enough to hold me in their clutches, His invisible hand lifted me by the hair! And I found myself rising in the air. The devotees dressed in spotless white clothes, stood in a daze and watched me being drifted outside the ashram walls and put safely on the ground into the village of Parthi by His divine hand! It was such a relief to note that none of them could follow me there. Upon receiving a gentle touch on my shoulder, I found a man in white looking into my eyes. I screamed in fright, "O Baba, how did this person follow me here when the rest of them were left behind?" Just as I was about to flee, my Lord's gentle, reassuring voice rang out clear. I stopped to listen to His advice given in a soft and tender voice, "He is not one of those who wants to harm you. Can't you recognise me if I come to you in this form? Come, don't be afraid, my child. Place your hand on me, feel me, and you shall know who I am." Though it was definitely my Lord's voice I could see Him nowhere around me. But mustering up enough courage I obeyed Him and placed my hand over that man's head only to feel the soft crown of hair of my Lord! And the dream ended.

The few ashramites I had come across were busy in their daily rituals, attending bhajans and darshans and also doing seva in His hospital or the shopping complex, yet, insensitive to the human needs that surrounded them, contradicting the very precepts they professed to believe in. In contrast, the attitude of devotees like Mr. Bala Krishna who lived in Parthi village outside the ashram, reflected more compassion and love for their fellow human beings. For some of the ashramites, the image or appearance had become a dominant consideration, leading to insensitivity and limiting their love to Him. Whether a devotee was an ashramite or not, what was important was that he / she live out the principles and values taught by our guru. Seeking permanent accommodation (or otherwise) within the ashram premises as a must undermined my sense of balance. The divine power had to be channelized into my nature regardless of where I lived.

As shown in the dream, my experiences with those living outside the ashram turned out to be wonderful. Yes, I was now actually in the company of those in whom it was easy to visualise Him. Bala Krishna uncle and others living in Parthi, were very friendly, helpful people and so were my foreigner friends, Glad and Kirsten. (Kirsten was a young Australian woman in her early 30's. Once in a while, we spent time sharing our respective experiences of Baba.) Now, outside the ashram where He had placed me, I felt happy and at peace with myself. I could now carry on with my writing work without disturbance of any kind.

Expressing His Approval at My Writing Assignment

I underwent numerous different emotions as I leafed through my hand-written notes in diaries. They contained memories I had penned down spanning over a decade. He wanted me to write these Volumes. I, however, felt very differently about my ability of writing His books. I felt very inadequate but only till such time that I changed my attitude.

I knew it as the Divine will. I had a duty to this world which I could not escape and which no one else could take for me. In fulfilling my duty, my attitude had to be such that I understood Him as the doer and myself as His willing instrument. Becoming His instrument freed me of all worries; my defects and weaknesses did not essentially matter. It was Baba working through me.

Serving Baba as I did in carrying on with His writing work – was a rare privilege. And I filled every moment with humble gratitude for the blessing of being able to serve Him. To my astonishment in the dream to follow, He indicated that He was aware of the book's progress and my effort to write it to the best of my ability.

On 12th October '93, when He appeared in my dream, He could sense my fear to run to Him; fear of inviting His wrath for breaking the discipline. This time I found myself waiting along with the other people for His darshan as His car was expected to pass by any moment. He stepped out of the car and came walking towards me. We were just two of us, a lady volunteer and I, who had moved ourselves to a solitary spot. He stood in front of us, talking to the volunteer in a very enthusiastic manner, but as it was in a language I couldn't follow, it didn't bring me any joy, though His presence did. Feeling ignored by the indifferent attitude towards me, I stood longing for a sign of pardon from Him. And while talking to that lady, my Lord touched my hand lightly. Then to my great joy, in order to reassure me that He could never ignore or forsake me, He held my hands in His own. Still remembering the last time when I had angered Him by trying to touch His feet, I dared not to do so now. He seemed to be in a very happy mood giving me lots of information, not a word of which I understood since He was all the while talking in Telugu! And I implored Him in English, "Baba, please talk to me in Hindi, which is a language I understand well." He immediately switched over to Hindi, "O I was talking to you about..." My next question to Him before He could complete the sentence was, "Baba, are you glad that I am here? Is my writing work going on well? Shall I be able to..." (He never let me complete the sentence which would have been to say 'finish my work by March?') He responded softly, "It's OK, it's OK, O yes, O yes." These were His exact words now in English. And then He added in Hindi, "But you need to be very much on the alert as regards your work!" With that He left and the dream ended.

After His above message, with my fresh set of resolutions, I decided to carry on with my writing assignment.

Sought my Guru's Permission to Attend my Brother's Engagement

On the 15th, Glad and I had gone to bed, as usual, by about 9 p.m. A rude knock on the door woke us up and a quick look at the watch showed it to be one o'clock! Who could that be knocking at our door in the middle of the night? The voice seemed to be that of the owner who stayed downstairs. So I opened the window to talk to him. He said he had received the news of a likely earthquake between one and six in the morning. The news had already spread around the village like wild fire and people rushed out of their homes before they could be buried alive if the information they had received was correct. (He claimed, the news was from a reliable source.) All sorts of fears invaded my mind and I packed my books in a big handbag while the landlord continued to frantically call out to us to leave the house. Poor Glad draped a saree over her nightdress and in a hurry just took her visa and passport, and we were out in the village, where we saw many other Sai devotees, Indians and foreigners, all making a bee-line for the ashram. But the man at the ashram gate was supposed to do his duty and did not open the gate to let us in and we sat at the entrance for about an hour or so, when suddenly police jeeps were on the rounds telling people to go back to their homes, that there was no earthquake likely to take place, and that it was only a rumour spread by a mischief monger.

After all that excitement, I could not sleep for another hour or so. Finally, when I did fall asleep, it was only to wake up with the memory of the dream I had just had at 3.30 a.m. on 16.10.93. "Baba, are you happy that Glad is staying with me?" I asked my Lord. "Nothing to worry about," He replied in a tone as though to say there was absolutely no need for me to even raise such a question and that if she was with me it was His will. "Baba, can she come with me to Bhopal?" was my next question. He looked incredulous as He asked in great surprise as if He was hearing something unheard of. "To Bhopal!" He exclaimed in a questioning tone. "Yes Baba," I repeated, "can she accompany me to Bhopal?" "Not now," He replied quietly, and I implored Him to let me know the reason for saying so. "Why, Baba, why can't she come?" "Because the boys are on wheels," and with that strange statement that made no sense to me, He walked away. Running after Him, I said, "Baba, please clarify what you mean since I can't understand it at all!" To my pleadings, all He said was, "Only time will tell." With that He vanished from my sight and I woke up.

The dream left me in tears. My brother was currently posted at Bhopal. And his engagement was to take place. Baba had not permitted me to return to Mumbai before March '94, which meant that I would not be attending his wedding. Hence, I made sure to at least attend his engagement. With no course left open, I knew I'd be travelling to Bhopal all alone.

My dear friend Glad felt upset that she could not accompany me to Bhopal as per His wish because she said that she was an opportunist and would have loved to see different places and meet my family. The only part of the dream that was some consolation to us was that the Lord was happy at our staying together. And, by saying, 'nothing to worry about', He had given me an indirect indication that she was certainly one to be trusted with my treasure – the books, if need be. Glad kept the books safely in her custody until my return from Bhopal.

But before I go on with my life, let me put in a word for Glad who had been extremely patient with me, and never did I think twice before approaching her or calling out to her in the middle of the night, 'Glad, are you awake? You know I am worried about ... Now what do I do? Swami just told me......' Each time she patiently sat up and heard me out, consoled me. Not once did she get irritated or lose her temper on me.

Glad, if you ever happen to lay hands on this book, I want you to know that I have always cherished the memories of our stay together. Thanks for all your consistent support and love. Thanks for keeping in touch with me via your letters and emails. I always think of you with fondness. (Readers, today, when I do a re-edit of this Volume in May '09, I'm happy beyond words to state that Glad and I are again in regular touch with each other.)

Peshotan's Prayers for an Improvement in My Physical Vision

In one of his letters to me, Peshotan had written, "Khurshid, today for the first time in my life I prayed to Baba and asked Him to give you a permanent cure for your failing vision so that you may have perfect sight once and for all." My brother looked upon me as entirely dependant on Baba's kindness and sympathised with my condition. And another letter that he had written in the same vein, asking if his prayers had been heard, was still on its way to me (it reached me on 17th October '93 in the afternoon), when on the 17th morning I had a positive reply from Baba!

"Baba, what do you have to say about my eyesight?" I inquired when He appeared in a dream on 17th October '93. And I pressed His hands on to my eyes after removing my glasses. He examined my left eye very carefully and blessed it! And then He started checking my right eye. And I cried out in anguish, "I am blind in the right eye!" "No, no, not gone blind, it's just..." I could not follow the medical terms He used to describe the problem but His soothing voice lessened my anguish. Leaving me in a daze, He walked towards the others. And one of the lady devotees remarked sarcastically, "How fortunate this girl is. She seldom goes for darshan and if at all she does, she makes no attempt to go in for token lines. Yet, amongst all of Swami's devotees, she is the one who has the maximum contact with Him!" In reply to that my Lord merely smiled sweetly. The dream ended.

Upon my return from Bhopal, Glad offered to join me on my one day trip to Mysore. We had stayed overnight at Nagu's place and it was a pleasure to have Nagu and Krishnabai also join us on our trip.

On finding myself alone in the room for a few moments, I presently mastered my strong emotion which made me long to tell Glad how much her company had meant to me during these past few months. Especially so, because she had been one of the few individuals to prove herself faithful to the spirit of a friendship in which the status in life had no part to play. And I left it to my Lord to thank her on my behalf for I could think of no adequate way of expressing my feelings of gratitude to her.

An Eventful Trip to Bhopal for My Brother's Engagement

Peshotan was there at the Bhopal station to receive me. Looking at his beautiful house, a lovely two storey bungalow, made me wonder if I was awake or dreaming! It was certainly like a palace to me who had all my life stayed in the small, cramped little place of 300 sq. feet., with five of us in it. It is either on the terrace or on the first floor balcony that I spent some moments of peace and quiet. Occasionally, a motor cycle or a car sped swiftly along that road, or a hawker could be heard advertising his wares, but the general atmosphere of the place was expressive of solitude.

The luxurious, spacious, well-furnished house seemed strange to me after my hard life in Parthi / Whitefield. The next morning when I woke up, I rubbed my eyes when I saw a young boy (around 18 to 20 years of age) with a tray of cups of tea in his hands! Peshotan introduced him as his cook. My brother never had any superiority complex and treated those working under him with great respect. He made sure that Daddoo, the cook, had meals with him at the same table except in the presence of the guests who might have objected to that kind gesture.

The first day i.e. the 20th of October, Peshotan and I were all by ourselves in that big house. Mum, dad and Jasmine were to arrive the next morning, while Nandini (my to-be sister in law) and her family were expected on the 22nd, which was the day of the engagement. Soon the day came to an end. We had a lot to share with each other and then went on a shopping spree. As I sat at his dining table, it was like a feast after the months of deprivation.

The days to follow too were filled with joy. Nandini and her family came to Bhopal on the 22nd. And I loved that girl the moment my eyes fell on her sweet, child-like face. Yes, she would certainly make my brother and the rest of my family members happy and proud of her presence in our family. The same morning even before she had arrived, in the dream when I requested Baba to bless Peshotan and Nandini, He responded by saying in a very grave voice, "They have to work for the community that is going from bad to worse." "Baba, bless Jasmine," I said. In response to that He placed His divine hand upon her head. What blessings the Lord had showered on us on the day of engagement! He not only approved of my sweet sister-in-law, but in the dream He had said that they should be working for the betterment of the world!

Baba wished that my dear brother and his wife be concerned with practical welfare activities for the community. I'm sure this yearning of His extends towards each of us. With the pure motive of love for humanity, which was equivalent to love for God, He was blessing Peshotan and Nandini with the motivation for the humanitarian work He expected them to take on. Whether it is Peshotan or any of His other children, He wanted none of us to invest all our time and effort only in pursuing our careers and climbing the professional ladder. Worldly success, at the cost of spiritual progress, would not be worth the toil. Baba was perhaps conveying that alongside career goals if Peshotan also focussed on the upliftment of the downtrodden, the underprivileged masses, it would make Him extremely happy. I believe, He wants each of us to spend time also on self-reflection, meditation and prayer.

The engagement party went off very well. The next evening my parents and Jasmine left for Mumbai.

Once when I had asked Baba whom He loved most from among us at home, (of course the Lord loves all equally but what I meant was who was the one most worthy of Him) He had immediately given Peshotan's name! Baba knows best.

The final day of my stay in Bhopal which was the 24th of October, once again found us i.e. Peshotan and myself all to ourselves, now with Nandini's family gone. We had friendly chats and he assured me that he would make it a point to help dad financially. And he kept his word.

On the 25th morning, he came to leave me at the station. The next day I was back at Whitefield at Nagu's place – in the company of Glad.

Sai Taking Me under His Umbrella of Love and Protection

"Baba, Glad will soon be leaving for Australia and it will be a few days before Nargish Aunty can come to stay with me at Parthi. Then who will give me company in the interim period?" The same morning, i.e. at 6 a.m. on the 20th I had a beautiful vision of the Lord in response to this appeal to Him.

It was a vision of my Lord Sathya Sai who patiently waited for me to come under His umbrella. There was a heavy downpour and He wanted to save me from being drowned in a deluge of rain. By gestures, He told me to come under His umbrella and then patiently waited for me to accept His invitation.

With genuine caring, my dear guru encouraged me to open the gate of change and self-growth. He took me under His umbrella and taught me that real success is not in having a successful materialistic life, but in having mastery, having victory over self. With His guidance I became self-aware and therefore, able to examine my deepest values. This one year stay at Parthi / Whitefield, filled with divine insights, only confirmed that God had a direct, perpetual, loving relationship with each human being.

Giving yet one more Proof of His Omnipresence and Omniscience

Baba provided me with indisputable proof of His omnipresence. Every prayer of mine reached Him. He never hesitated to let me know that He was sensitively receptive to them. No sooner had He become aware of my yearning that He gave messages to confirm that He had heard my prayer and was willing to gratify it. This time He did so by appearing in Nagmani's dream at Whitefield.

It was a joy to see my dear girl, Nagmani (Nagu), who had had a few dreams in the past and went about disclosing them to me. One of it in particular, remains imprinted in my mind for the love He expressed therein – His immense love towards me! In her own words, "Khurshid, in the dream I saw Baba carrying a heavy load of bricks on His head. He was dressed as a construction worker and was serving in that capacity. Seeing Him in the form of a labourer shocked me and made me ask Him about the reason for it. He merely smiled and told me that He was in the process of building new houses for His devotees. Hearing this I immediately thought of you and asked Him, 'What about Khurshid, Baba?' And dear Swami promised that He would build a room for you as well!"

Could it be that it was a room in His heart He was referring to? I feel so. But this dream held much more importance to me for the simple reason that it was in response to one of my prayers, a silent prayer that I had made a few weeks ago while I was at Parthi and then completely forgotten about it. But He was not one to forget and so that I may be sure of His love, He answered it through Nagmani in Bangalore! A few weeks ago when I had seen some construction workers going about their work at the floor above the Poornachandra auditorium where our guru now resided (He had shifted from the temple premises to this place), I felt envious of the workers. To me, they at least had the chance to reach up to His house and I had said, "Baba, only if someone were to permit me to do so, I would gladly carry bricks on my head. Even if I were allowed to place one single brick, it would give me immense joy, the very thought that I too had a hand in the construction of the house where my Lord dwells! But, I suppose, I shall never be fortunate enough to fulfil my dream." I feel He could not have responded to my cry in a better way than He did by appearing in Nagu's dream in the form of a construction labourer.

The next day we were off to Srirangapatnam and Mysore on a day's trip from Whitefield, Bangalore. Glad and I shared the expense between ourselves. Nagu, her niece, and Krishnabai (Nagu's mother) joined us and we had a lovely time together. The places we visited were Halagappa's temple, mother Durga's temple on Chamundi hills, the Maharaja's palace at Mysore, and then the Mysore gardens. As Glad was feeling too tired, I stayed back in the car to give her company when the others along with the driver went to the gardens. Then came to an end the joyous months spent in Glad's company at Whitefield and Parthi.

To My Delight, My Guru Sings a Bhajan for Me

The first day when I reached Parthi late in the evening I felt strange to be on my own with no one to talk to. I also missed Glad a lot. At length, I lay down on my mat and, trusting the guidance of the Lord, soon freed myself from all anxieties and fell asleep. And in the days that followed I was astonished at actually experiencing bliss at being alone – nay, in the company of my Lord whose presence I could feel all around me. No longer did I crave for human company. Yet, it will not be the complete truth to say that my father and Nargish Aunty's arrival on the 1st of November did not give me some relief. It was indeed a moment of immense joy to see them at my doorstep. The first few days seemed to fly at a great speed and it was time for dad to leave for Mumbai. This time dad's departure to Mumbai did not make me feel heartbroken. Hadn't my Divine parent promised to respond to each and every prayer of mine? And wasn't Nargish Aunty going to be with me till the last day of my stay in Parthi?

My dreams and visions continued as before. On 2nd November '93 at around 9 p.m. – vision of Lord Christ on the cross, on His face the lines of pain clearly visible as He spent His last moments on earth. Though this vision had barely lasted for a few seconds, for days afterwards the face full of pain kept appearing to my mind's eye. Every time I thought of the suffering He had undergone for mankind I thanked Him for thus giving me the courage to bear with my own cross bravely.

To me, personally, the best form of prayer was music in the form of bhajans that I attended daily. As I listened to the devotees sing the devotional songs, I was convinced that music was a melodious medium of expression of an inner spiritual fulfilment. Today, on November 5th, I was doubly blessed. This time it was not as if the Lord appeared in my dream or even in a vision, He was in my room not to be seen but I could hear His melodious voice singing the song, "Krishnaya Sharanam, Krishnaya Sharanam, Krishnaya Sharanam, Namo, Namo. Sri Sai Sharanam, Sri Sai Sharanam, Sri Sai Sharanam, Namo, Namo." Ah what a blessing to hear my dear guru sing specially for me. I listened to the enthralling music, the bhajan on Krishna sung by my dear guru in His divine melodious voice.

This was the first experience of its kind and suddenly 1 began doubting the same. "Baba, did I actually hear your voice? Were you singing in my room? If so, enlighten me on it." With this prayer I went to bed only to have Him come in my dream not once but twice!

6th November '93 – 4 a.m. – Hand in hand, my Lord and I walked and stood watching the public. All of a sudden He brought His face closer to mine and whispered into my ears, "Khurshid, before the storm comes let me sing for you." So saying, He once again sang the song He had sung for me the day before! His voice rang out loud and clear, drifting me to a fairy-land where none but the two of us existed. (A few days after this dream, when I had gone to hear His public discourse, because of a heavy downpour, I had left for home before He could end the discourse with a song in His melodious voice. As He had known I was to miss out on that beautiful blessing of hearing Him sing, He had blessed me in advance!)

Brahma Muhurat – As explained by Sai

It is true that there are periods, times in which communion with God is best achieved. Nargish Aunty insisted that the right time was only in the early morning hours before the break of dawn, preferably as early as 3 a.m. onwards – that Brahma Muhurat was between 3 a.m. to 5 a.m. In all probability, she could have been correct in her guidance but for me it was impossible to wake up so early and meditate. Besides, in my opinion, for someone who wanted to be in commune with God had to be in tune with God any time of the day, to be receptive to His grace every minute of the day. Yet, I thought it best to check it out with Him.

In less than two hours of the above dream, He once again appeared to me in yet another dream, this time to give me divine wisdom! Besides obeying Him and trusting Him implicitly, He wished that I have the knowledge of the simple spiritual truths in order to put them into practice in my daily life. Hence, my Lord now day after day toiled to make me a fit recipient of the perfect truth.

5.30 a.m. – 6th November '93 – He provided me with clarifications on another important matter about which I was still in the dark. Never having undergone any spiritual practices or austerities, I was in no way capable of guiding others on that. To wake up early in the morning was something beyond me. Moreover, there was no point in getting up and starting prayers or meditation at 4 a.m. just because others advised me to do so. It had to come from within.

In this dream, I was surprised to find our Lord clicking photographs of a lady sitting next to me. It was a camera that instantly popped out photos. My guru knelt before me and like a child happy at what the photos revealed; He carefully explained to her what He saw in her photos. I inched forward to get closer to Him until my head touched His! This tempted me to be yet closer. As usual the desire to be in the arms of my Divine Parent sprung up. With a mischievous smile playing on His lips, looking at nobody in particular, He took hold of the situation and in a sing song way remarked, "Aye, there should be no hugging. No hugging." His words sounded so funny and were uttered in such a childlike tone, that I was not hurt at having been refused the chance of holding Him in my arms. As He now moved away to others, I ran behind Him. Finally I asked, "Baba, when do I have to put the medicines into my eyes?" He feigned surprise as though it was such a simple matter that I ought to have known the answer. "Didn't anyone guide you regarding the same?" Then as if realising the futility of His question, He remarked in an understanding tone, "Ah! But none knows." And the next moment becoming very serious, He continued, "Put the drops into your eyes at Brahma Muharat." Brahma Muharat in the literal sense meant 'auspicious time'. Not knowing what He meant by that and accepting my state of ignorance, I asked, "And when is Brahma Muharat?" To this He very lovingly explained in a soft melodious voice, "Brahma Muharat is the time I come to you almost every day and soon after which you find yourself awake."

I was fundamentally divine in nature just as every human being is. However, my divinity was veiled by my endless chain of thoughts and desires that had to be eliminated. But my dear guru chose to focus only on the spark of the divine in me and hence, knelt before me, leaving me richer with a lesson in true humility.

As for His message on Brahma Muharat, it was clear that each time my Lord Brahma in the form of Sai appeared to me, it was Brahma Muharat. Taken in the literal sense also it meant any time of the day and night because He appeared to me not just in the early morning hours but also in the middle of the night; even blessed me with His vision in the afternoons or evenings as well. If this message were to be taken at a deeper level, then the eye medicine was the wisdom He was pouring into my being in order to improve my inner vision. And Brahma Muharat was each time I woke up to the spiritual truths after His counsel. What a simple way to explain the meaning of Brahma Muharat.

Baba Declared that I had the Best Vision Among All

Expressed compliments were very rare in my life. But Baba expressed them freely and on a very regular basis. Initially I ended up feeling embarrassed and felt unworthy of the compliments but eventually learned to receive them with joy and the conviction that I actually deserved them. Coming from my guru they could never be exaggerated. Actually I emerged from such experiences feeling approved and more confident to tread the path He had chosen for me.

By giving out compliments whenever I deserved them, He taught me not to miss out on any opportunity to give sincere compliments to others. He also taught me to accept compliments graciously, with humility.

One of the many lessons I had learned in the past few months was that I could choose my attitude even though I could not always choose my circumstances. Even though I could not always control all the events that happened in my life, I could at least control how to deal with them. My guru was there to appreciate my efforts at my own development.

On 7th November '93, I woke up at 2.45 a.m. with tears rolling down my cheeks. Over and over again I reminded myself of what He had just said and done in the dream. He had gently pulled me closer to Him, held my hand and then spoke to a lady, by pointing out to me with His free hand, "She has the best vision among all." It is needless to say that with this statement of His which I considered as one of the greatest rewards of my lifetime, there arose a special need for trying to live up to it for the rest of my life. A little reflection, a bit of introspection was enough to bring to light my failings, and our merciful Lord who said I had the best vision perhaps said so because He overlooked my failings and saw in me only His reflection.

Unknown to Others, Baba's Guidance at Every Step Continues

With great care my guru had guided my steps since the past so many years. Yet, He did not deem the time right for establishing openly the never severed link. His seeming indifference to me (in public) for that one year long stay in His presence may have been to make me realise His presence at the soul level instead of meeting him merely on a physical plane. Moreover, He could perceive that I was not filled with ego and that I willingly and obediently took a backseat. Happy at my surrender to His will, He rewarded me by coming to meet me in private every now and then.

During this wonderful period, He taught me more than I could have ever learnt during my lifetime. Baba continued to grant me these private interviews behind the pillar, away from public gaze and poured divine wisdom over me. On my part, I resolved to put into practice all His teachings in life.

Dream – 3.30 a.m.– 8th November '93 – Hidden behind a huge pillar just outside the darshan grounds, I awaited my turn. The Lord was giving darshan to the multitude gathered there. In turns, He held the hand of each individual whom He chose for the special grace of love. Hidden from public view from where I stood, no one was aware of my presence, with the exception of the Lord of course. As He approached me, I stood with hands joined in reverence. Instead of rushing towards Him, this time I kept a respectful distance. Pleased at my disciplined behaviour, He granted me a private interview by Himself coming and taking a position behind the same pillar. Nobody knew of His whereabouts just then. Placing His hand gently under my chin, He lifted my face. As I looked at Him, His eyes shone with love, it had a glow of joy as He spoke to me. "Very good, I like that." He appreciated my resolution to go by His command and not let the masses know of my oneness with Him in spirit, our daily meetings behind the pillar – dreams and visions, away from public gaze!

But this was not all. Now a third person came on the scene as the dream continued. That stranger told me, "You better make a list of the qualifications, the credentials a devotee is required to have." I jotted down all the possible credentials that I could think of into my book. My dear guru stood by me, watched me carefully and every now and then nodded in agreement as if to say that I was noting it down all right! With that the dream came to an end.

If I did not possess qualities such as compassion, love for humanity and the desire to become His image combined with the effort required to let that dream become a reality, I could not claim being in possession of the credentials required to be a child of God aspiring self-realisation. With the Lord by my side guiding me at every step, I was sure that the possibility of becoming His image would one day turn into a reality.

Treading the spiritual path had never been so easy, at least, initially. To succeed on that path, as Baba claimed, I did have the capability. But I realised that capability alone was insufficient. In addition, I needed unwavering faith in myself besides faith in Baba. My dear guru wished me to have one pointed concentration on God and perseverance, necessary credentials for anyone to be accepted as a devotee aspiring realisation. Disappointments and failures could possibly come now and then, but it was important to make up my mind never to give up. With my guru ever holding my hand in a firm grasp, nothing was impossible; it was only my lack of tenacity that made it seem impossible.

Sai in My Mother's form Assisting Granny

Hearing the sad news of the bad fall that my maternal granny at Mumbai had had which had resulted in a broken hipbone and a surgery, I prayed to the Lord to give her some relief from pain and help her get back to her feet. The next morning i.e. on the 14th, I had a vision of my dear Lord with a large dot of kumkum on His forehead. He was assisting an old lady to the bathroom! This vision repeated itself a number of times. (Baba was seen with kumkum on His head because He was playing the role of my mother who had actually gone to stay at granny's place to take care of her. I got to know of it when I called her up some days later.)

My Guru Asking for the English Version of the Bhajans Composed by Me

On the 19th morning in a dream, I handed over a poem book of mine into His divine hands for His approval. After scanning through its pages, He said, "But it's the Hindi version. Where is the English translation of the same?" In a voice full of regret, I replied, "Baba that is not ready as yet." "Well then prepare that too and give both of them together to me." So saying He walked away and the dream ended.

A Glimpse into My Future that had Me Baffled

On the 22nd November '93, by way of an answer to my prayer of the previous night to give me a glimpse into my future, for the first time in my life, I dreamt of Mahatma Gandhi! Gandhi, who was the father of the nation, his frail little form with a stick in his hand used as support, walking slowly, leading the masses. Yes, a large crowd followed him. The venerable old saint did not once stop in his tracks. He went on walking as long as his feet could carry him, leading lakhs of people to their destination. This was all that I dreamt. The scene of Gandhi leading his fellowmen to their destination carried on for a long time.

In no way could I imagine my own future anywhere close to the life of the Mahatma. To me there appeared to be, till date, no resemblance in our lives whatsoever. Not being able to perceive myself as even worthy of the dust of the feet of that holy man, I considered it a sacrilege to ever compare myself with him.

I had always been my own harshest critic. My self-image until last year had largely reflected the image my family members had of me. Baba's consistent message of love taught me that they were wrong in perceiving me as unworthy. In the past, my entire potential as a spark of the divinity had been stunted by my self-defeating perceptions of myself. Hence my capacity to enrich the lives of others had all but been lost.

Via the above message, Baba seemed to claim that I had unlimited potential. It seemed like an impossible feat that He wanted me to achieve. Yet, it appeared as though my dear guru did not have a shadow of doubt that I could achieve what Gandhi had achieved during his lifetime, provided I put in the same effort. He wanted me to lead His children out of their shell of ignorance to eternal bliss – through love divine conveyed to them via my various contributions to mankind. Firstly, through these volumes and secondly, through whatever larger role He had in mind for me in order to reach out to my fellow human beings in need.

A Special Prayer to Baba being Answered via Nagmani

On 23rd November it was my beloved Lord's birthday. He gave me an extra darshan in a dream early in the morning. And I was delighted with it. It turned out to be a day of great joy for me. Twice during the day I had very close darshan as His car passed by. That evening after darshan at the stadium, before the aarti could come to an end, I decided to leave the grounds with Nargish Aunty. This was to avoid the rush later. This move on our part blessed us with close proximity with our guru. The moment the two of us moved away from the crowd, the volunteers made sure that nobody else left their place till His car left the stadium. Nargish Aunty and I were the only two people who therefore had the privilege to walk behind His car as it very slowly passed by the crowd, Baba blessing the thousands gathered there. All throughout my heart had been calling out to Him, "Baba, are you aware of my presence? Or am I just one among the thousands gathered here and should not be craving for special attention? You have to respond to me."

His response to my cry of anguish came in the form of a letter from Nagu, apparently written much before the Lord's birthday, long before the thought had even entered my mind, thus, clearly indicating His all knowing nature. Nagu had mentioned many of her dreams, but since this one related to my appeal, let me share it with you. In that dream she had seen herself along with me by her side, hand in hand, running behind the Lord's car. Our Lord out of love alighted from the car, came up to us and kissed our hands!

As Nagu related her dream (in the letter) to me, I was lost in contemplation, reminding myself of His recent promise to me that He was my father and mother; that I just had to call out and He'd surely respond. How my mind delighted in reading Nagu's dream, thrilled from the bliss I derived knowing that Baba had responded to my birthday wishes to Him in this unique manner. To all outward appearances, during the actual happening of the event, He might have seemed indifferent to my longing for closeness to Him as I walked behind His car. Yet, at a soul level not only had He sensed my yearning for acknowledgement but had moved out of His car and kissed my hand. My dear Lord's sweet sport of going to a third person in some other village to respond to my prayer was more than what I could have asked for and it intoxicated me with infinite joy.

Blessings in the Shirdi Sai form

On the 26th morning, most unexpectedly a clear vision of our Lord in His Shirdi Sai form sprung up before my eyes. Sai was sitting on a stone and then got up to walk in my direction. Visions such as these or that of any other form of the Lord that I often got while fully awake, took me into the higher realms of consciousness.

On days that He didn't bless me with special darshans in dreams or visions, I comforted myself with the memory of such beautiful visions in the past and daily darshans, even though from afar.

Sai Eases My Journey by Sending Help from an Unexpected Source

The message in the vision that I got on 28.11.93 at 3 a.m. was not quite clear. It left me puzzled at that time to see my Lord Sathya Sai accepting a car-ride from a devotee.

Later that day, Kirsten, our Australian friend, dropped in at our place most unexpectedly. She came up with the proposition that we travel with her to Whitefield, Bangalore whenever Baba left for that place. "Khurshid, I'd be glad if the two of you could give me company to Bangalore. It will be a pleasure to have you with me as I have already booked a car and am in any case not going to take any more devotees to share it."

Now I understood what the vision had foretold. Baba, with His usual care and meticulous attention to detail for the comfort of each of His devotees, had already made arrangements for a comfortable car ride from Parthi to Whitefield for Nargish Aunty and myself. Kirsten was sponsoring our trip.

My Consistent Efforts at Becoming His Image

And my next dream started with a scene in which I sat in the hot sun awaiting the Lord's darshan. Initially, Baba's form as He came on the scene was a blur, just a dot in the distance. I was feeling like an alien in the overcrowded ashram. So very small and lost in the crowd I was! Deciding to move closer to the Lord, I did so, one step at a time. And our guru took the exact number of steps in my direction!

As He came into focus and stood opposite me, I carefully examined His robe minutely. This minute inspection was so that I may dress in a similar fashion.

Gradually, I was discovering my nature and getting to know who I really was - a part of Him. That meant I had the potential within me to fulfil my dream of becoming His image – only if I observed Him and His divine life minutely and followed His footsteps.

He made me aware of my true self – the divinity inherent in me– and I could overcome my numerous fears, guilt and feelings of insecurity.

Baba Planting the Seed of Divine Consciousness

On 29th November '93, in a dream, our dear guru was seen busy ploughing the fields! Perhaps the dream was indicative of His wish to plant into the soil of my heart and in the hearts of all His devotees the seed of God's consciousness and make us realise our divinity. Thus He laboured for all of us who were under the delusion and identified ourselves with the body and not with the spirit of God.

Even the Smallest Detail Did Not Escape His Attention

On the 30th of November '93 in a dream, Baba gave me a handkerchief that was handed over to Him by someone else. It was white and blue in colour. The kerchief was all crumpled. Yet, I accepted it with gratitude because it was something that was touched by my Lord and given by Him.

The same afternoon when Kirsten offered me her blue and white Punjabi suit, I had half a mind to refuse her when I saw that she was giving it to me unwashed, crumpled all over. But on second thoughts, I changed my mind, accepting it as the Lord's gift as per the dream that morning. Besides, it would save me the expense of buying a new one when upon my return to Mumbai and rejoining CRY, I would require some reasonably good clothes. (Later on Kirsten left with me a few more of her dresses at our last meeting in January when she went back to her country.)

Receiving is another part of giving and it's not always the easiest thing to do with grace. Via this incident, He had taught me that the art of receiving with appreciation and sensitivity was every bit as important as the giving. She was giving me things in love and I was receiving them in the same spirit.

In the dream mentioned above, He had then moved on to a lady sitting to my left. Handing over a rose to her, He had said, "I do remember a Parsi's birthday!" (As if to say that even if others had forgotten about it, He hadn't.)

The birthday message was a reminder for me. My mum's birthday had been completely erased from my memory and hence I had not even called her up to wish her. But my Lord was not one to forget! I ran to the public telephone booth and called up home and wished her, apologising that I could not do so earlier. Her reply stunned me into silence. "Khurshid, thank you for calling up today to wish me, though, it's almost a week since then. Had you called even a day earlier, you would not have got me on the line. Since the past two weeks I had been at granny's place at Vasai, and just returned back home. She is totally bed-ridden and needs all the possible help. As they haven't kept a maid for her at home, I had stayed back to take care of her."

Well, now I understood why my Lord had reminded me of it now, and not earlier. And also what had made Him seem so grateful to her to give her the rose. Of course, it is not as if He had forgotten her birthday but today on her return after dedicated service to her sick mother, she deserved the appreciation in the form of a rose!

Apart from helping me see myself as a spark of the Divine, Baba also made me see myself in all my human imperfections. He gave me room to make mistakes and the strength to never give up my attempts at becoming His image. Each time I slipped, He was there to encourage me to start all over.

The love that we give and receive is all that matters and all that is remembered. Suffering disappears; love remains.

Sai – A Wish Fulfilling Tree

In my relationship with Baba I was the recipient of His consistent love regardless of my conduct in life. To repay that kindness, this is what I resolved to do in life: No matter what my relationship with others could be, I would not look on them as people who could give me love. Instead I would look on them as individuals I could give my love to; individuals to whom I could go on always giving. If they reciprocated my love, I'd accept it graciously as His reward. If they didn't love me, I'd not be hurt because that expectation was never there. I also understood that my love did not have to confine itself to just one person or one family. It had to envelop the entire creation.

The next few days, I was stuck to bed with a bout of flu and temperature. Every second day, I got beautiful visions of His but that didn't satisfy my thirst and one day my prayer to Him was, "Baba, in what form do you want me to visualise you?" The immediate vision was that of a tree, in the trunk of which my Lord stood with outstretched arms. Vibhuti, amrit, and a number of blessings continued to flow from His palms.

The amrit and vibhuti flowing from His palms took the form of divine experiences in my daily life. My Lord knew that unless I myself saw the divine visions and also experienced the oneness of all mankind, I would not be able to comprehend the same. No amount of reading religious books would have satisfied my agitated, confused and wavering mind as my practical experiences with Him in daily life did. Personally, I was convinced that attainment of God's wisdom was beyond verbal knowledge, and actually belonged to the realm of practical experience.

Baba's instructions followed by practical experiences truly confirmed the abstract truth that He sought to be taught. Simply knowing that the supreme spirit dwelled in all beings as the soul was not sufficient. It was the daily visions and experiences that followed to confirm the same that aroused the unflinching faith in me. Thus He blessed me with the amrit of Divine wisdom.

4

Recognising the Inherent Divinity in One and All

Experiencing Humanity in the form of Sparks of the Divine

On the evening of 7th December '93, as I sat among the crowd attending bhajans at Prashanti Nilayam, I entreated the Lord to tell me if I had made any progress during the period of my stay in His presence. The vision that followed the prayer was as follows: A curtain had been drawn over the stage. It gradually began lifting, revealing the stage that lay beyond. It was a very, very gradual process and took quite some time before it lifted itself off completely.

"Baba, give me a glimpse of what lies at the other end of the stage," was my next appeal to Him. Once again I was blessed with a divine vision. Thousands of people were assembled, each with a bright flame burning on their outstretched palms. They stood forming a large circle and started coming closer to each other, until their hands touched each others'. As a consequence, the little flames merged into each other. The millions of flames thus merged together took the form of a bright fire that lit up the entire stage.

The presence of my dear God in the form of light slowly vanished, leaving me in ecstasy. Love for God, and for God in all, was the eternal message He wanted me to live out every moment of my life. Baba, my Divine Mother, took the responsibility of lifting the veil of maya that covered my vision.

It is on realising the atma that He made me aware that my individual consciousness, though infinite, was manifested in the form of body and mind. My ultimate goal in life was to attain oneness with the infinite by getting over the body-mind consciousness.

I was the Blessed Recipient of His Compassionate Gaze during Darshan

On 8th Decemeber '93, with Kirsten we left for Whitefield, following Baba's car. I remember that day with great joy. He gave me a long, penetrating look at Whitefield where I was sitting right in the front enclosure with hardly a group of a hundred people in all. With no VIPs around, we were allowed to sit in the front. During the bhajans, as I sat before my guru, He gazed at me for long periods, lasting almost half a minute each time. I felt drawn to Him by an invisible string.

Sainath Waiting to be Let into Our Hearts

In the next dream that I had a few days later, I found myself lying peacefully on the floor of a palace. Thousands of people lay in deep slumber. The turmoil created in my mind and heart would not let me doze off even for a moment. How foolish we all were, I thought, to waste our lives in this manner instead of opening the gate for the Lord to enter. Why didn't anyone rise to do so? How long was our Lord to patiently await our arrival at the gate?

After a while I rebuked myself severely for being no better than the rest. Why couldn't I get up and open the gate myself to let Him in? It appeared such a herculean task since the gate was too large and that too an iron one, requiring tremendous strength and the combined effort on the part of His children. With His name on my lips I endeavoured to do it single-handed and succeeded. A mere feather touch on my part did the trick! The door opened by itself to reveal the most divine scene I had ever seen. It was dawn. The sun rose gradually and my Lord walked in that light. The glory and splendour of His beauty dazed me, yet I was still conscious of my good fortune and invited Him to enter my home. To my amazement, He changed His form to that of an ordinary man and I lost sight of Him in the crowd where He mingled. As I turned my eyes to my left, there among another lot of simple folk I found Him walking in all His majesty. But no sooner my eyes fell on Him, He once again took the form of someone else and was lost in the crowd, only to reappear in His own form somewhere least expected. This went on for a long while.

As the dream continued, I decided to visualise Him in all. As I went through the back gate, the scene was that of the Parthi ashram. The inmates therein were busy quarrelling and arguing over petty matters. Most of them did not seem to have the time or inclination to listen to my plea that the Lord was waiting at the gate to be let in and would they mind opening the gate.

Now I found myself face to face with someone who claimed to be the Police Commissioner and decided to try my luck with him. If my Lord did dwell in him just as He had claimed He dwelled in all, it shouldn't be difficult for me to visualise Him in the Commissioner. This man asked me, "Khurshid, how are you? Do you know of my achievements in life?" He went to describe his worldly achievements at length, not once mentioning God. Finding it difficult to visualise God in this man, I moved on to the next person. To my surprise, his behaviour was even stranger. No, he did not brag about his achievements. But neither did he do anything except keep his gaze fixed on a photo album. The minute he saw me, he was all excited and said, "Come, come let me show you my photos and there are lots of newspaper cuttings which I have preserved. Every time I excelled in sports, the media covered my achievements and my picture came in the news and I have treasured them all." Fear gripped me. What if these people asked me for an account of my achievements in life? I had none because I excelled neither in sports nor a business career. Nor was I famous for any other achievement. Moreover, this worldly talk did not interest me in the least, so why not move on to the next person who may, perhaps, be interested in spiritual matters? And all throughout the dream I tried in vain, never able to find a soul immersed in the Lord.

This dream convinced me that He was seeking us far more than we were seeking Him. Therefore, we did not have to remain indifferent to Him. Experience had taught me that He yearned for our love. He had given each of us the free will to seek Him or reject Him. It was left to us to wake up from the deep slumber of ignorance. The iron gate that we had closed on His face was the gate of delusion. Our dear guru stood at the door of our consciousness. We had to let Him in.

He had always emphasised the necessity for vigilance, utmost vigilance, every moment of my life. I could at least make the effort to open the doors of my heart, and not let the Divine Guest pass unnoticed by me. The Divine was manifesting itself to me so often, but that was His grace and not because I had put in any effort. I had to continue to aspire for better progress and pray to Him to let the Divine light illumine the many unlit corners of my being and make me a worthy instrument of His. For what I had achieved was very little compared to the much that remained to be learned from Him.

For those of His children who were too engrossed in their petty selves, I suspect I could understand some of their problems. They had not only set but even met their individual goals, career goals, etc. They were people who had achieved an incredible degree of outward success, but still struggled for control over their feelings and emotions. Their desire for fame and recognition seemed to have taken over their desire for spiritual success. Perhaps, they were not even aware of a life beyond the one they lived. But why was I so consumed with the desire that the spark of the divine should be visible in each of them? Why could I not tolerate the idea of accepting divinity dormant in those people for the time being? Instead of feeling impatient and giving up on them, why couldn't I be just as patient and compassionate as the Lord had been with me for over a decade now? Wasn't I the lucky recipient of His unconditional love despite my falling short of His expectations time and again?

If we could recognise each other at a soul level, we would be able to extend ourselves beyond our own self-centeredness instead of being completely engrossed only in our own worldly achievements. The above dream was an eye opener. Before I could expect others to change, I would have to begin with changing myself.

The dream also signified that what most of us were lacking in was humility. We had to stop expecting that our importance be consistently acknowledged.

To some people success meant receiving an opportunity to be ashramites, permanent residents of the ashram. To others it was wealth or fame. What this dream told me was that success was subjective. It could mean different things to different people. I had to determine my success in life not by how I was doing compared to others, but how I was doing compared to what Baba believed I was capable of doing.

Seek Me Not Outside of You for I Dwell in Your Heart

On 11th December '93 the evening bhajans were going on and I prayed to Him, "Baba, you want me to see you in one and all and I try my level best to do so. Yet, it would be a relief if you would permit me to worship any one specific form of yours. When I sit for my prayers or if I try to meditate, I'd love to keep your form before my eyes, but if you feel I am too attached to your present form, then I leave it to you to choose the form you want me to visualise you in." No sooner had I completed this prayer, the vision before my eyes was that of the Lord's hand holding a mirror, oval in shape. In it was my own reflection. Yes, He wished that I turn my gaze inward and seek that which is eternal.

Baba loved me for myself. He wanted perfection for me. He wanted me to know and experience that He and I were one. With the Lord thus becoming a part of my daily life, there came into my life such peace as I had never dreamt possible. When I saw the Lord within me face to face, I saw simultaneously that the Lord shone from every face around me.

An introspection revealed to me many unknown regions never thought of before. It gave me a new assessment of life's values. My limited vision changed for the unlimited, and a soothing calm descended on my being. Instead of leaving the responsibility of my progress to Him as a separate entity from me, He was training me to turn inward. My dear guru did not ever give me any mantra claiming that it would lead me to realization. I was aware that a mere desire for self-realization would produce no results. With the daily insights that He blessed me with, I'd have to work hard upon myself. The way to knowledge would be long and difficult. But, He wanted me to put in every effort and learn to tread the path confidently under His divine guidance.

You and I are One – He Re-emphasised

2.40 a.m.–12th December '93 – dream: Baba was seen having lunch and thoroughly relishing the dishes being offered to Him. Then the scene changed. I found myself standing at the doorstep of Rama's house waiting for His darshan. As His car passed by, He turned and looked directly at me.

Rama had called me for lunch the same day so it was easy to interpret the former part of the above dream. The Lord dwelling in me was going to enjoy the lunch being offered by Rama. And it was so. She had excelled in her cooking. No sooner did I think of the Lord's dream, Rama's voice full of excitement rang out clear, "Khurshid, today as Baba's car passed by our house and we waited for His darshan, He actually turned in our direction. Yes, He looked at us, whereas normally He does not do so."

Helping me Perceive all Human Beings Including Myself as Divine

Since the past two days I was being blessed with His darshan eight to ten times a day! Most of them were in a wakeful state; in the form of beautiful visions of the different forms of God. Quite often when I closed my eyes there appeared a Shiva Lingam before me! In all humility each time I bowed to it mentally.

A vision that I was blessed with that evening at the Shiva temple in Kadugodi village had shaken me up. Nagu had told me that it was their yearly festival and that everyone from the village would be going to that particular temple to do puja. When I reached the temple, Nagu astonished me by revealing that the exact one thousand lamps burning all around the temple, the electric lighting, the music, the feeding of the village folk; all of it was sponsored by her parents. They had themselves even cooked the food in large quantities with their own hands. Indeed, the sight of the temple in its village background, lit with those thousand lamps was breathtaking.

Now as I stood inside the temple with the aarti going on and closed my eyes, I got a clear vision of the Shiva Lingam. That in itself was fine. But the next moment I saw two human hands emerge from its sides and join in reverence, bowing to me in obeisance! It was something so unexpected and unnerving, that it was with great difficulty I controlled my tears. My Lord had once again acknowledged my presence and bowed to me, a mere human with innumerable failings. It was scary. To play the role of God meant that He'd expect me to be perfect like Him. I wanted my Lord to only treat me as His child and not as a part of Himself.

Once again by this beautiful vision, God had made me realise that just as He dwelled in each human being, He also lived within the temple of this perishable body of mine. As a result of this vision, the spark of the Divine within me awakened to the glorious realisation that it was a reflection of the all pervading spirit of God.

My Lord had extended His hand of friendship to me a decade ago. I had clasped it, never to let it go. This friendship had evolved from a guru disciple relationship and had gradually taken a completely different form – that of a parent and child. Now He was equipping me with the worship of the spirit. He was conferring on me the capacity to be able to perceive all human beings including myself as divine – as one. Lord Shiva had simply bowed to the inherent divinity in me. This supreme revelation left me spellbound.

This was just the beginning of my journey to God and I had to learn, in fact, to live two lives. One absorbed in the knowledge that He and I were one; the other to live in the world focussing on my duties and responsibilities towards my family and the society at large.

There at the Shiva temple I hesitated to share with Nagu the beautiful vision I had had, lest I disturb the tranquillity I was experiencing. Just then, she looked up and broke my reverie as she said softly, "Khurshid, come, light as many lamps as you like."

The Lord Inching His Way Towards Me as I Make An Attempt at Meditation

There were times when I did attempt at meditation, but in vain. The earthly ties deceived my consciousness. But the moment I was willing to make an attempt to come out of the darkness, He was instantly there – in visions.

Meditation on the Lord was something that I did not succeed at. As I sat feeling helpless and frustrated that I could see nothing but darkness when I closed my eyes, I was showered with grace by the most startling vision. In front of me was a huge, dark wall that blocked my vision. Suddenly my dear guru appeared on the scene and created a gap in it enough to make His entry through it by crawling to me from the other end! The darkness disappeared. In the brilliance of the inner light, I saw the form of my guru as it emerged from the space created in the wall of darkness. Oh, what joy I felt, such ecstasy! I experienced love and oneness with Him.

The next question that rose to my lips was, "How do I break the wall of darkness that separates us, O Lord?" Now it was a vision of a lotus in its full bloom, with its stem in the muddy water, but the flower itself coolly floating above it!

From then onwards, the joy I found in my efforts at meditation or at writing was something more valuable than anything else on earth. It was simply the thrill of doing my best. Not measured by anybody else but my guru Himself who acknowledged every little effort of mine.

As Greedy as ever for His Special Attention

On 14th December '93 during morning darshan, for once I had taken my place in the token queues and was fortunate to be in the front row. Hence, I made a silent prayer that He bless me by giving me three sweets. He immediately responded by doing so while passing by me! He must have been really exasperated with my silly behaviour and must have felt sad that all His attempts to change this girl into realising her Godhood were in vain!

These little gestures on His part, not in dreams or visions but in reality, reconfirmed my faith in His concern and love for me.

My Guru Acknowledged that Some of His Volunteers Lacked Sensitivity

On 18th December '93, at 6.30 a.m., I had a vision that had me puzzled. But only for an hour or so after which it became quite clear. In that vision Baba assumed a gigantic form. As He walked towards the devotees (including myself) seated under a tree near the steps of South Prashanti behind the temple, we tried to move away from His path in order to avoid ourselves getting trampled under His feet. As He got closer to us, He changed His form to a ferocious looking stout lady. All of a sudden, from the skies above, my dear guru's voice rang out loud and clear, that this ferocious looking lady who tried to play His role was simply one of His robots who had gone out of control and was moving about trying to exhibit her might by terrorising the harmless devotees! Personally, I decided to keep away from that robot.

Hardly an hour had passed after this strange vision. Among a hundred devotees or so (the latecomers for morning darshan) I took my seat. It was my usual place outside the darshan grounds, near the South Wing of the ashram. As per our daily habit, without coming in anyone's way or breaking any rule of the ashram, I sat there waiting to catch a glimpse of Him as He would walk into the grounds.

Baba had already come on the scene when one of the prominent lady volunteers actually ran up to us and ordered us to move away from there as ashram rules did not permit her to allow latecomers like me to have His darshan even from that far a distance. Then she turned away from me to address the Seva Dal workers and fired them for having allowed people like us to have darshan.

For once, instead of feeling angry or upset, I was actually amused at her behaviour. It was as if my vision of the morning had just repeated itself. And I recalled His message in which He had claimed that it was simply one of His robots out of control. If only His ashram had more volunteers with heart that knew to love, a heart that could recognise Him dwelling in others, it would have made life for simple devotees like me so much easier.

I knew that the Divine was manifest in others too. The awakening of the Divine within me had opened the eye to recognise the Divine in others whether visible or not. Once I awoke to the fact of the Divine presence in others as well, a new tone of regard, of consideration for them entered into my relation with them.

Mother Mary's Appearance to Me

Each time that I closed my eyes to meditate on God, I was blessed with beautiful visions of His in His multiple forms. Thus meditation for whatever little time that I did, any time of the day, helped me establish a relationship with God that in turn gave meaning to everything else in life.

19th December '93 at 6.40 a.m., I had a vision of Mother Mary in all Her heavenly beauty and splendour, dressed in a sky blue coloured robe. A cream coloured veil covered Her head. What drew my attention was also the shining star just above Her head. This vision lasted not for a second or two but much longer, almost for a quarter of a minute or so.

Baba's Explanation on the Different Perceptions on Spirituality

We tend to adopt fixed attitudes in certain matters. We cling to the rightness of views and in the process confine ourselves to the limits of our own experience.

I wanted to tread the path of God in the full freedom of my choice. I simply couldn't follow the rigid ideas and beliefs that Nargish Aunty did. In my spiritual quest, I did not wish to conform and settle to standards that were right at one time but were no longer relevant now or at least impractical in my daily life. For instance, it was beyond me to have a cold water bath and start meditating by 4 a.m. I felt I'd be doing an injustice to myself as my weak constitution could not take that kind of a strain. What had attracted me to this dear lady was the selfless spirit in which she loved me. She was a wonderful friend. In almost every way she was a delight, but I'd never known her bend any of the rigid rules she applied in her daily life beginning with getting up at 4 a.m. every morning. The outstanding impression I had of her was that of saintliness. She was deeply religious. She often took the hardest vows and kept them without flinching. For the past 40 years she had had one meal daily, ate only once in 24 hours. Illness was never a reason for relaxing any of her vows.

Despite having one thing in common – our love for God, it was during debates on one's way of expressing his devotion to God that our viewpoints did not match. Here, she tried to impose her views on me. The problem with her was that at times she attempted to fit me into a particular category and expected me to act accordingly. On such occasions, she tried to prevent me from being myself.

Perhaps she was never able to understand that I worked for Him from morning till late evening without a break – even for darshans of my guru I didn't sit in token queues but entered the grounds at the last moment, being content with a glimpse of His from afar. I believed that I deserved my quota of rest and need not wake up before 6 a.m.

as long as I did not miss out on His darshan. And I made sure to reach a few minutes before He could make His appearance to the devotees gathered for His darshan.

Instead of elaborate rituals of the olden days, I was of the considered view that it was easier to reach the Lord merely by chanting His name, singing His glories and serving humanity. No doubt, Baba Himself gives the ritual its due importance but He understood that I personally found namasmaran and surrender to His will the easiest and the surest way to reach Him.

His message in one of the dreams clarified the issue – both for aunty and me. In the dream, the two of us, i.e. Nargish Aunty and I were attending a class in one of the colleges, and seated among the back-benchers. From the way aunty repeatedly kept calling out to Baba (who was then playing the role of the Professor) in order to draw His attention, it was apparent that something was on her mind which she wanted to come out with. Ultimately in exasperation, He gave her an opportunity to speak out her mind. In response, she protested that He had changed the syllabus and that the problems He had put before this new batch of students were comparatively easier than the ones she had had to solve during her time of examination! He in turn told her by pointing his finger at me, "With students like her, I have had to change the syllabus to an easier onc since the past one and a half year. Don't grumble about it. You are bound to find this problem easy compared to the ones you were faced with and expected to solve during your days." One look at the black-board, where He had drawn out the designs like those in a horoscope, and I decided there was no need to break my head over the problem. It was beyond me to solve it. Why not instead leave it to the Professor to do so and focus my full attention on Him instead. Now hand in hand, aunty and I left the classroom. Both of us had decided that this class was not meant for students like us; aunty because she found the studies too easy, and I in turn had left it to Him to solve the problems mentioned in my horoscope.

Fortunately, after sharing the above dream with her, her rebellious mood receded. And it was a relief for me, since I didn't want to create further tension just to prove a point. She very gracefully grew out of her judgmental attitude, allowing some of her basic perceptions to change. And I grew wiser from the experience, full of gratitude that she had the humility to accept the Lord's word.

With the above insight, my exasperation evaporated. I saw such problems now from her perspective, and instead of wishing she were different, my attention went to getting to know her and understand her.

All Paths Ultimately Lead to Him

I did not know what religion meant. To me it was simply anything that helped my internal evolution and gave assistance to attain transformation.

As I sat thinking about the Lord, I had a sudden unexpected vision. A vision of dad balancing himself on a narrow wooden plank laid across a large lake. I was travelling to the same destination but via a proper road, making an easier journey. Both of us were walking in the direction of our guru. We both met at the end of the road and dad said, "Khurshid, if the Lord were to will it so, I wouldn't mind walking your way either."

The lesson was that all paths led to Him. But each has to be left to his own way of treading the path to God. One need not necessarily walk exactly in the manner of another. The Divine would certainly guide the steps in the way most suited to each person. But on the seeker's part total reliance on the Divine guidance was a requirement because very often his own judgement could be inadequate. But the Divine guidance on the path that suited each individual's needs could be relied upon.

Yes, all paths led to Him. What was required was mutual respect for each other's path. If I listened to another with respect, it would usually be a short time before that person would listen with respect to me. Once this attitude was established, each of us would begin to see the positives of the path the others had resolved to tread.

"Baba, both the paths ultimately lead to you. Am I right in my interpretation of the vision I have just had?" As if in response to my question, I was immediately blessed with another clear vision. This time it was of our Sai with His back turned to me. He parted His thick crown of hair right at the centre, making it into two halves. Then as suddenly, He took the two lots and mixed them up and the partition could be seen no more, the two had merged into one.

The Lord in His Multiple Forms Continued to Manifest Before Me

One morning I decided to maintain complete silence for a day and also to abstain from food though I did take a cup of milk twice a day. Sooner or later I had to master all the senses, why not begin with the job that I found impossible – to master my tongue both ways, by way of gaining control over speech and taste. My guru approved of my attempt at gaining control over my senses. And made sure to let me know how much He appreciated it by appearing to me almost five times in less than an hour's time! Twice in a dream and thrice in visions.

In the first dream I sat at the computer but not being aware of the name of the document, I pressed any key at random with the result that I got Lord Sai in His Shirdi form on the screen! He was seated at Dwarkamai in all His majesty with devotees gathered around Him singing bhajans. The next key I pressed brought the divine Mother Mary on the screen and devotees singing her praises! Then I said to myself, "Let me find out other forms of the Lord the data in my file can provide." The scene on the computer screen changed to that of a tree that gave not only shade, but water gushed forth from its trunk and roots in great torrents! The dream ended and as I woke up, the immediate vision that I was blessed with (that lasted for a few seconds) was of my dear guru, Sri Sathya Sai distributing these volumes of 'A Glimpse of Joy' to the devotees.

Since it was still very early in the morning, once again I went to sleep. He blessed me with one more darshan, this time in a dream. He let me hold Him in a tight embrace, making me feel quite secure to be in the arms of my beloved parent. And I thus remained entwined in His arms for a long, long time. He had all the while placed His hands on my head, instead of embracing me in return. By that kind gesture of His, He was conveying how pleased He was at my conduct. As I placed my arms around His neck and kept staring at His face, all I could find in those lovely eyes was a mother's love. Next I addressed Him as 'my little child'. He allowed me to enjoy the feeling of holding my little baby in my arms though it was in His own form that He appeared throughout the dream.

On waking up He appeared twice to me in visions in the next 10 minutes, the first time just standing before me and the second time with His hands raised in blessing!

To Overcome My Anger was what Baba Wished of Me

Anger was something over which I still had no control. I either stifled my anger or let it explode. In either case it wasn't healthy or correct on my part to do so. If the cause of anger was relatively unimportant and there was nothing I could do to change the outcome, I had to let it go.

11.30 p.m.– 21st December '93 – dream: After all the love He had showered me with, His sudden, absolute strictness and chiding came as a rude shock to me. Following the example of some naughty children, I too ran and took my seat in the front row, very close to His chair. As I sat gazing at His face, it assumed a very formidable look and His eyes full of anger now turned upon me. Pointing out to me with His forefinger, He called me to Him. I ran in great joy thinking of telling Him that Nargish Aunty too had come with me and if He permitted, I'd bring her along. But no such opportunity presented itself, as He straightaway took to scolding me very severely. "How dare you lose your temper and fight?" "Baba, I don't lose my temper any more," I said in a pathetic voice, close to tears. That made Him even angrier and He said, "What about the other day when you argued for so long? Do you think I am not present in the room to know what you do every moment of your life? Don't dare fight with anyone. This is the last warning I am giving you. Is that clear?" In the same tone, He then asked, "What has happened to your poetry book?" "Baba, you said you wanted the English translations as well. Though I have started on it, I have not got the poetic talent to write in a rhythmic form." He was not one to relent and said, "Well, there are other devotees who are good at it. You could have certainly given it to them!" But once again He changed His mind and the next moment said, "Never mind, it will do without the English translation. Just give me the Hindi poems." Then after a pause, He added in a tone of authority, "14, 24, whatever they are. Now you may go." Like a little child who had displeased her Lord by not coming up to His expectations, I felt as though I was being banished from His kingdom by way of punishment.

Patience was the mark of love and courage. I would resolve disagreements through patience. The above situation in which we had found ourselves out of control and Baba had to intervene was because I had been impatient and started retaliating and so had Nargish Aunty. From then on, both of us valued and nurtured our friendship.

My relationship with aunty was an extremely loving one. But we had many disagreements. After Baba's firing, I made every attempt to ensure that she and I could coexist in love. Of course we kept the dialogue going. If she saw something as white and I saw it as black or vice versa, there was a meeting point, a grey area, upon which we began to agree. Though she and I never fully agreed, we both at least came to understand that there were many ways of seeing things. I didn't get into arguments as before. And even if I did, I wouldn't get into it with a closed mind but with the clear understanding that the other person could be possibly right. It made it easier to understand from another's point of view. I liked to be straightforward in my dealings with others but it's only now that I realised that honesty required a measure of kindness.

That night I wept for a long time. Foolish as I was, I did not pause to consider why He had adopted such a stern attitude towards me; moreover, I was neither willing to consider that it was His love for me that led Him to scold me the way He had done. Presently putting aside all other considerations, I only pondered on one thing – how to become as dear to Him as I had been till this fateful day. When I had argued with aunty I had had no intentions of hurting her sentiments but that is what I had eventually ended up doing. The only way out for me was not just to beg His forgiveness but hers as well. And that is what I did, promising her never again to fight or argue with her on any issue.

I sobbed at the very thought of what He might have tried to convey when He had said that it was the final warning He had given me. Did He imply that He would stop coming to me? If so, was life worth living any more? Till 1.30 a.m. I was lost in painful musings, very much uncertain of what to do in order to gain back the love that seemed lost forever.

When I tended to judge myself too harshly – and consequently suffer a great deal – because I felt I was not living up to His expectations, He again gave me the right perspective. He forgave easily and helped me forgive myself. The unintentional wrong that I had done did not matter. What was important was what I became as a result of His chiding. Sensing my need to know that I was forgiven, He appeared in my dream at 4.30 a.m. and let me kiss His hand. I was profoundly thankful that I'd won back His trust that I'd so thoughtlessly lost.

At 4.30 a.m. I woke up in high spirits and related to aunty the dream I had just had a few minutes ago. That dear lady had prayed that He come to me before I open my eyes in the morning and He had evidently heard her prayer. This time He stood before me with a mischievous smile playing on His lips but since I didn't dare to run to Him as I usually did, He extended His hand towards me. "Baba!" I cried sobbingly, "O Baba!" With a smothered cry of ecstasy, I sprang to seize the outstretched hand of my beloved Lord, and covered it with kisses. My Lord smiled compassionately and let me kiss His hand to my heart's content.

Now in the same dream, His attention turned to a lady standing next to me with outstretched hands, cupped together, and she complained to the Lord that He wasn't paying any heed to her request. For a while He appeared to be meditative. At length, He said, "It is not my fault if you can't retain the vibhuti blessing that I am pouring out into your cupped palms. How can you expect to retain my gifts if you let a gap remain between your hands and allow the vibhuti to flow out?"

I was conscious of the presence of Grace in my life but I too, like the lady in the above dream, had to be ready to receive it. My cooperation was required for the descent of the Grace. The effort on my part that the Lord expected was to keep myself quietly receptive, awaiting and vigilant in assimilation.

Baba Touched My Feet as Obeisance to a Mother

Even on Christmas, I didn't wake up early but only at 5.30 a.m. which meant missing out on the early morning special darshan of Christmas. I closed my eyes to beg His forgiveness and the very next moment His face appeared before me, so clear and at such close quarters that I felt His face was hardly inches away from my own. He had given me instant darshan, special darshan and hence, I had not missed out on the early morning darshan after all.

By loving me unconditionally, Baba sparked in me the hope that I could dedicate myself to the process of learning to love one and all.

The next morning in a dream my Lord walked up to where I sat and knelt before me. Then, most unexpectedly, with childlike humility, He bent low and touched my feet as obeisance towards a mother. After that He laboriously smoothened out the creases on the mat on which I sat, ensuring my comfort. Too overcome to say a word, I sat lost in Him. I gazed at Him in reverence – and saw motherly love on His face as He gently cupped my face in His hands and kissed me on the forehead.

My heart was completely free from loneliness; the radiant force newly generated within me after the above dream conveyed an assurance of an undying divine love of which I was sure of being the privileged recipient till the end of my life and thereafter.

Before meeting and experiencing sincere friendship from individuals like Nargish Aunty or Nagu, I had been a sceptic, constantly on my guard, unwilling to accept the possibility that there are friends all around, or that acts of kindness and goodness happen all the time.

I was a product of my past experience. Today my viewpoint had changed. Life was full of wonderful people whom I seemed to be attracting all the time.

Each of us is Divinity in Disguise

The next few days He gave me darshan in the visions I got immediately after waking up every morning. These visions were simply the extra darshans, and with no message in particular. On the 31st of December, 1993 I had a beautiful dream of Baba sitting through bhajans and myself in the front row, lost in Him. On waking up, I thanked Him for His constant love. "Baba, I am a mere human with innumerable failings. Yet, you seem to be finding some good quality in me to draw you to me so often. Give me a glimpse of whatever good exists in me."

His reply left me wonderstruck. He blessed me with a sudden vision of Himself. There emerged from His body an exact replica of Himself! The two gazed at each other lovingly. The Lord was looking at His own reflection (!), while I, utterly unprepared for such a vision, was for a moment taken aback and at a loss for words. This vision went on for a few seconds only but left a lasting impression on my mind.

Baba was unfolding the divinity within me. Being infinite and unbounded was pure joy. He had cut me off from worldly ties in order that I discover my higher self and also experience the same God dwelling in others. Baba, via this message of His, had let me know that each of us were divinity in disguise and that the God within us was seeking to be fully materialised.

He always emphasised that I was perfect just as each person was perfect, but He insisted that I had to work hard to reflect that perfection. Once I experienced the power of my inner self, fear vanished and there was no struggle for approval either. I recognised everyone as my own self, the same spark of God in different forms.

My guru's conviction about my divinity was such that I felt lifted to another plane of consciousness. If He claimed that I was made in His image, it was for me to strive to the best of my ability to manifest that goodness and purity that lay within me.

His Simple Remedies for Ordinary Ailments

I complained to my dear guru about the severe headache that I suffered from every now and then. On 1st January '94, He blessed me with a vision of Himself wearing a hat and He was smiling mischievously.

My heart warmed by His loving concern over my welfare. The solution He had provided was quite simple. To avoid sunstroke, I should be keeping my head covered, with a shawl or a hat.

5

The Gradual Awakening

One More of His Dream Messages

The dream on 2nd January '94 was as follows: There was a huge circular hall with thousands of gates. On each gate, just inside the hall, stood an individual, young or old, male or female, Indian or foreigner. Each one was left to choose his or her respective gate. To my surprise, our Lord entered through my gate and blessed me. The minute He left me, Mrs. Jasawala ran up to me and asked, "How come you chose the right gate when we all missed out on His darshan?"

Our Guru Intimating Me of Nargish Aunty's Impending Accident

On 4th January '94 in the dream Nargish Aunty and I were seated in the very back rows among the crowd gathered for darshan. Baba made His way through the thick crowd and stood before us. "Baba, Nargish Aunty desires to touch your feet," I said. "Well, she may have my knee for that is as good as having touched my feet. Will that do?" So saying, He sat cross-legged on the floor right opposite her. Aunty was too stunned to say a word. So once again hurriedly I spoke on her behalf lest He change His mind and she be deprived of even having the knee! "But of course. Whatever you give is fine with her and she will accept it." As she bent forward to touch Him, He put His hand at the back of her head and with a sudden jerk, with great force, pulled her towards Him. She was flat on the ground, with her head buried in His lap!

I had intuitively understood what the Divine was telling me through this dream. It foretold a serious fall and Nargish Aunty injuring her kneecap. The dream also indicated that Baba would at least save her face from being crushed. (This is exactly what took place a few days later.)

Some Visions of the Lord

On 7th January '94 I had three visions of the Lord:

1. Our guru as a teenager, not in His usual robe but in a suit with tie.
2. Vision of Lord Christ on His knees. He was atop a hill.
3. I see myself standing before a mirror expecting to see my own reflection. Instead, what met my eyes was the smiling face of my Lord reflected in the mirror!

On the Day of Silence, the Mind should Stay Equally Calm

Once I resolved to maintain complete silence for a day and checked it out with my guru if that was something that He appreciated.

At 2.30 a.m. on 11th January '94, my Lord appeared in my dream to express His joy at my obedience and at the effort that I was putting in to improve myself. A middle-aged lady and I stood facing our Lord Sathya Sai just at the porch of His mandir where people who are called in for an interview were seated. His eyes had an imploring look as He addressed her, "Chattering, chattering, chattering, chattering, chattering." I even lost count of how many times He repeated the word but I felt so very sad when I realized how patient He was being with her. Thereafter, my beloved guru turned His eyes upon me. He looked at me tenderly, then seemed to be in raptures as He continued to gaze at me with a smile of satisfaction and delight! For the first time I didn't feel the need to run to Him or say a word. So I prayed inwardly, "Baba, are you so very happy to see me?" The next moment He changed His form to that of my dear, dear, Maiji (my parents' guru) who now stood smiling at me. And she seemed to be enjoying my presence. Soon He was back to His own form. In this dream there had been no verbal communication but in the silence our hearts had been communicating Divine love. The Mother in Him was happy to note the difference in me, even if it was a mere attempt on my part to maintain silence.

But later He also expressed His displeasure when I carried on with my silence for almost a week, driving Nargish Aunty crazy with my sign language or by writing things out for her into a note-book. Any exaggerated course such as 'complete silence for a week' was also discouraged. On at least one occasion He made this very clear. He pointed out that it is better to control speech than to renounce it. The real silence is in the heart and it is possible to remain silent in the midst of speech.

When I went on a week's silence, initially my internal dialogue became even more turbulent. Gradually, internal dialogue began to quieten and I began to experience His presence within me, around me, all over in every human being. Of course, let me confess that this blissful experience happened only for short spells of time. Yet, thereafter, in the midst of movement and activity, I carried with me the stillness within that He had blessed me with.

Only if Sherry would Learn to Forgive, Her Own Wounds would Heal

Happiness is largely in our control. I've been fortunate to spend my life under His guidance, and one of the most significant conclusions I've drawn is this: there is little correlation between the circumstances of people's lives and how happy they are. The secret of happiness is gratitude.

On the 14th January '94 Baba once again appeared in my dream. He was sitting on the steps of the Western canteen at Brindavan. Sitting quite close to Him, I looked at His face intently, but He had turned it to the other side. As I shifted my gaze to His feet, He pulled His robe a bit to reveal His feet up to the ankles. Suddenly the feet were no longer His own. They were those of Sherry (name changed), swollen and very fair. But the next moment they were full of open wounds. To my uneasiness, He kept on digging into those wounds. The sores grew worse. How sick I felt looking at that scene. Why was He causing Himself so much trouble and then wincing in pain? But I had to keep quiet instead of telling Him that nobody but Himself was to be blamed for the pain He now underwent. Why did He have to dig into the old, dried up wounds and make them bleed once again and then cry out that He was in pain?

The dream was symbolic. Sherry had an unfailing memory of the wounds others, especially her family members, had inflicted on her. She needed to learn to forgive others. It was time she liberated herself from anger. Love was not about opening old wounds but moving forward and getting on with life. She often lived inside her own private world. The walls between her and the events of the past were so low that her attention was often drawn to the past instead of the present, leaving her in pain.

Doctors and Staff at Parthi General Hospital Treat Nargish Aunty with Great Care

Monday morning Nargish Aunty and I decided to go in for token lines henceforth. And we hurried along to be there in time. It was about 5.30 a.m. As we were walking past the back entrance of the temple, from the ladies side, Nargish Aunty didn't notice a water pipe in the way. She tripped over it and fell headlong on her face! For a few seconds as she lay there unmoving, my heart seemed to stop in fright. Finally, when she did get up, she was feeling quite fine except for a little pain in the knee and insisted that we go for token numbers. Now it began to drizzle and there was no chance of getting token numbers and we found place amongst the latecomers. Hence, we decided to get back to our old original place outside the grounds under a tree close to South Prashanti blocks. All of a sudden, there was a heavy downpour for almost an hour, with people running helter-skelter, but a few still sat where they were in spite of getting drenched to the skin.

As for the two of us, we had to take an auto straight to the hospital since the pain in her knee had become intense and she could not put her foot down. With the Lord's grace the X-rays revealed no broken bones. But the ligaments had torn and the pain was severe. The doctor who treated her at Baba's General Hospital, Dr. Krishnamurthy, was a gem of a devotee, so gentle and caring, very different from the other lady doctors whom we had earlier experienced a few months ago during aunty's hospitalisation. Mr. Reddy, the nursing man who put the bandage over her foot and who was also in charge of the X-ray department, was another good man, full of humility and dedication. I'd also like to mention two lady Seva Dal workers belonging to the group from Kerala who were on duty then. They were full of love and affection for the patients and went out of their way to assist them and give them a few words of consolation, besides giving them the courage that the Lord was there to take care of them. The two ladies were Lata Ramchandran and Rajamma Vijayar. The purpose of mentioning these details is so that I don't make the error of conveying a wrong picture of Baba's hospital or staff. Our earlier bad experience had to be followed by this extremely humane one to make aunty and I understand that not all devotees (permanent ashramites or staff at His general hospital) were full of themselves. The majority of them were humane to the core. If I were to mention only those who were insensitive, I'd be giving the readers a biased picture of the ashramites and the General hospital staff. Hence, I'm mentioning this information on aunt's second experience at the hospital which was a very positive one.

On How to Fast Without Health Getting Affected

In the past month I had given up on dinner. Initially it had been out of choice, the Lord had never compelled me to have only one meal a day, but later when I sought His opinion, in dreams and visions, He expressed His desire that I continue with the practice. I believed that eating spicy food at the South Indian canteen in the ashram upset my stomach. Others felt I had to accept it as prasad. Accepting that I should stop making a fuss, I resolved to have my meals at the South Indian canteen at least once a week. (In contrast, the food at the Western canteen was much to my liking, never spicy. Even though the rates were extremely reasonable, it cost me more to have a meal there as compared to the South Indian canteen, so I had been avoiding going there.)

In the dream to follow, I was moving about in the ashram and then proceeded to the canteen with a plate in my hand waiting to be served. None of the ladies served me with what I asked for, saying that the pungent food was not the food meant for me. An unseen hand offered me two cups of curds, an apple and a pomegranate. Everyone's eyes turned upwards when a voice from above addressed me thus: "This is the ashram food you should have once a week." Again the voice repeated, "This is the ashram food you should have once a week." On waking up immediately after this dream, I asked the Lord if that is what He desired – that I fast once a week, consuming only curds and the specified fruits. Immediately I had a vision of Lord Krishna bending over something and as I turned my gaze lower, I found Him making an offering of something into a fire. Now I accepted my fasting with joy, as it would give me an opportunity to demonstrate the power of spirit over material objects of the world.

In my path to God, my attitude towards petty desires (food in my case) did not have to be one of forceful suppression, but of detachment. Because, according to me, forceful suppression stood on the same level as free indulgence.

Strengthening the will by defying the strong desire for dinner (or anything to eat between lunch and the breakfast next morning) required a long, gruelling fight. But then there came a turning point. I discovered that there was more satisfaction in defying a desire than in yielding to it. Thus Baba trained me to gain self-mastery.

Habits, I learned, could not be given up by suppression, but could be easily uprooted by understanding. Baba helped uproot my habits and eliminate unnecessary desires. (I followed His instructions very strictly only for a few years. Later, on days that I didn't have a proper lunch or when I felt tempted to have dinner, I did so. From the year 2000, I regularly took a light meal for dinner. To conclude that I was forever able to uproot and eliminate the desire for food completely would not be correct.)

My dear guru wanted to teach me that during a fast, I had to hold to the consciousness that I was not starving myself, that cosmic energy was sustaining me. I had to cater less to the demands of the body, knowing that I was not the body but the soul.

The first time I began my fast, at the end of the day, I felt the master of myself. The same morning I had also been blessed with a vision of Lord Shiva.

Sai did not Permit Me to Attend My Brother's Wedding

On the 20th afternoon (20th January '94), I went to the Parthi airport to receive dad, Yasmin Aunty and Aban. It was a great joy to see them all. While Yasmin Aunty and dad had made their respective bookings in lodges close to the ashram, Aban came over to our place.

During the very first darshan during bhajan time, dad was blessed with an opportunity to touch Baba's feet and place his head on them. The next morning Baba even accepted my brother Peshotan's wedding reception card from dad's hand. When dad told Him that He was invited to attend the wedding and the reception, my Lord smiled and nodded His head in the affirmative!

Dad had brought letters addressed to me by Peshotan and Jasmine, both of them requesting me to ask Baba at least one more time if it was permissible for me to attend Peshotan's wedding in February. Jasmine had also mentioned another problem which she faced in her office and wanted me to seek Baba's advice as to whether it would be correct on her part to ask for a transfer to another division or not.

A day before dad left for Mumbai, at 2.15 a.m. I found myself scribbling down the message I had just received from the Lord. The dream: "Baba, earlier you had said that I may return to Mumbai not before March '94, but now that my brother's wedding is fixed for the 15th of February, do you think I should be attending it? Or do you still want me to stay back till March?" He became very serious though not angry, and said, "No, as such there is no need to go because I can see..." After a pause and looking very grave He scanned the space as though searching for what lay in the future and then added, "Because I can see 'Shankh' (a Hindi word for 'conch'). "Baba," I continued, "what about Jasmine's job? Can she ask for a transfer to another department in her office?" He pretended not to have heard me and made me repeat my query, actually looking puzzled as if the question was one that baffled Him and then said, "O, I myself don't know what to say, yes, or no!" Then with a mischievous smile, He added, "Why don't you ask those pages that provide you with instant answers to let you know if it's yes or no this time?" As per His instructions in the dream itself, I opened a book at random for an answer but was scared to read anything therein because I knew that Jasmine would not believe me if I were to tell her that it was an answer I had received from the book. She would be more inclined to go by His command given to me in a dream. I turned to Him for help whereupon He gave me a very kind look and said, "Yes, she may do so."

One might wonder what pages He was referring to. Well, it had so happened that a few months ago, my prayer to Him had been as follows: "Baba, you come in my dream to often solve my problems. But if I need an immediate answer and cannot wait till you appear in my dream the next morning, in such a case how do I seek your help, your presence and your guidance?" Thereupon, my dear guru had responded in a dream by telling me to open any book at random and added that I'd find my answers therein. I did go by His advice and never once did He fail me. But I am desisting from writing in these books any of those experiences. (In these Volumes I have only shared my dreams and visions of His.)

Because Aban requested that I sit in token queues for one day, along with her, I too was blessed with token no. 1 both during morning and evening darshan. Aban's joy knew no bounds to be at His feet each time. Baba, who is our Divine Parent, had taken her close to Him because He was aware of her anguish at having lost her father recently. Because our Lord did not want me to touch His feet, I obeyed Him for once, though with great reluctance. The next afternoon, dad and Aban left for Mumbai.

Poonam Saroj Kumar in whom He Dwelled

I was grateful to Him for His constant guidance. One afternoon, as I closed my eyes to thank Him, He blessed me with a beautiful vision of Himself sitting on one of the swings in the primary school playground.

Within hours when I was at the Sathya Sai Primary school, in the company of my dear child, Poonam, the vision materialised itself. My dear girl ran and sat on a swing. In the vision Baba had expressed as much enthusiasm and joy as He had soared high over my head. (With Poonam's parents away, I was her guardian upon her mother's request.)

Once again Baba had blessed me with the shining gift of understanding divinity, visualising Him in all; a gift I had respect for and lived out in the months and years to follow. The challenge was to break out of my limitations, self-imposed or otherwise, and accept the fact of my limitless self. As the days passed I was sure that by the end of my stay, Baba would make me understand self-knowledge and personal growth as things attainable in many ways.

Let the Lord Alone be Seated in the Pupil of Your Eye

On 24th January '94 at 9 p.m. before going to bed my prayer to the Lord was as follows: "Dear God, help me improve in order to become worthy of you. Guide me, O Lord, to know your will. Oftentimes you have said that you're working on improving my vision. Is it physical sight or the spiritual vision that you have been referring to? To grow spiritually, what do you expect of me? Just let me know and I'll not fail to obey you."

His response, as usual, was immediate. He blessed me with a beautiful vision. It was a vision of an eye. In the pupil of the eye, Lord Krishna stood playing the flute.

In order to convince myself that I had not imagined it all but that Krishna had just appeared to me, I prayed that He bless me once more. Upon closing my eyes, the same enchanting form of my Lord Krishna in the pupil of the eye appeared before me. The message seemed very simple and easy to follow. He wanted me to focus on Him alone, to have Him and no one else seated in the pupil of my eye.

My dear guru did not allow inattentiveness. Whenever my mind had a tendency to move away from divinity, He came to remind me of my goal. Meditation, as He made me understand, was the ability to take the mind away from every object of distraction and put it upon God.

Even if I meditated only for a few minutes, those few minutes had to be one hundred percent concentration upon God. Each time my mind thought of anything external, His clear vision sprung up as though to remind me that I needed to focus on Him alone. He helped me go deeper within until I felt at complete peace and the divine love began to well up within my consciousness.

Baba wished me to acquire equanimity under all circumstances. And I began making the effort to arrive at that state. He wished me to meditate with undivided attention. In the months and years to follow, I did make attempts at meditation, but could never do so for more than a few minutes. Besides, personally, I believed that I was always doing 24 hours meditation. Doing His will, whether writing His books or later, when I received an opportunity to serve the underprivileged sections of society, was meditation on Him.

HE Intimated that at Times I didn't Keep My Heart Open for Him to Enter

On 28th January '94 – between 5.30 p.m. and 5.45 p.m. as the bhajans were going on I was blessed with a vision of Lord Sathya Sai waiting at the doorstep of my house. Despite His attempts, He could not enter since the door was very slightly ajar and not open completely to leave enough space for Him to enter.

Instead of shutting Him out of any of my activities I had to include Him in everything I did. He was there in the form of light waiting to be received. All I needed to do was open the doors and windows of my heart to let Him in. I need not deny the existence of light by sitting in the dark, keeping the doors and windows of my heart closed to the light of wisdom waiting to be let in.

"The Writing Work Requires Utmost Care and Attention," said Baba

The dream of 30th January '94: In this dream, my dear guru was playing the role of a Professor who seemed to be quite lenient with the other students but rather strict towards me. My complaint to Him was, "Why are you so particular as far as my writing work is concerned that you keep on finding fault with it, pointing out to errors so very insignificant according to me?" "To you these mistakes may seem very small and insignificant in nature but your writing one letter wrong shall change the meaning of what you actually wish to say and shall therefore convey an altogether different meaning." I looked at Him speechless. "Besides, not a single flaw should remain in your work," He added gently. On waking up after this dream, I had a vision of His for as long a period as a few minutes!

I could never sense the mystery of His divine sport. I failed to understand it. With that deluding human form, Baba had been with me as my friend, mother, father and child. I had so often let myself get carried away only in that kind of a loving relationship, forgetting the millions of devotees who looked upon Him with reverence due to a guru and God. Hence, it required vigilance on my part while writing these books; I had to be careful and sure of what I was putting down on paper in His name. His warning was a timely one; that my writing one letter wrong could change the meaning of what I actually wished to say and could convey an altogether different meaning. He was actually referring to the way in which I shared His messages in these Volumes.

His Attempt at Transforming Devotees – An Uphill Task

Once again Baba blessed me with a vision that left me speechless and full of remorse. This is what I saw: The ashram grounds were packed to the full. A lady in front of me stood up and blocked my view, thereby depriving me of the Lord's darshan. Very politely, I told her to be seated. Again and again I repeated the request until I finally lost my temper and gave her a push that sent her rolling on the floor. There, right in front of us, stood our Lord who immediately turned His face and walked away in the opposite direction. But I could not forget the expression on His face before He walked away. How sad He had appeared to be at my unacceptable behaviour. The crowd around me was unruly, no one caring to maintain discipline, each one eager to have His darshan at any cost, regardless of the inconvenience they put others to. Making it a point not to lose sight of Him, I followed Him. The scene that met my eyes puzzled me and I could just not comprehend His strange behaviour. He stood at the doorstep of a large hall with a jug of water in His hands. Scanning the room with a very sad face and a lost look in His eyes, bending low, He started pouring the water over all the pots spread out in the room. But alas, His attempts were in vain. Not a single pot could retain even a drop of water. Why? Because they were turned upside down! My Lord was not one to lose hope and carried on with His laborious task, but with the same sad result. Though He was disappointed, He did not give up. His perseverance made me feel ashamed and I told myself that if not the others, at least I needn't ignore His counsel, the Divine knowledge He was giving out to one and all in order to make them lead disciplined, divine lives.

This particular vision overwhelmed me. One of the overturned pots had to be myself. I was aware that my dear guru in all humility would continue to bend, pouring over me the Divine wisdom. His success depended not just on His efforts but my receptivity. I prayed that by my efforts I'd make Him feel proud of me. I also prayed that I be able to take the necessary steps and be in a state to not only receive but retain His blessings that He continued to pour on me as much as on all of us. The above dream had made me resolve that the least I could do to help Him succeed in His mission was to co-operate with Him in His effort to make me gain self-realisation by being a receptive child.

We should be prepared to assimilate the knowledge He is so eager to share with all of us. The flow of His grace in our direction is never ending and so is His patience with us. Hence, instead of giving up on any of us, He'll do everything in His capacity to help us become happy individuals reflecting divinity. Baba wants all of us to reach that ultimate state of divinity of experiencing God as the formless, all pervading spirit and thereafter to experience ourselves as a part of the self-same spirit of God.

Guru in the Garb of a Friend whom I couldn't Recognise

Baba's way of disciplining me was such that I understood that discipline meant teaching and not punishing. Next to love, a sense of discipline was my dear parent's second most important gift to me. He implemented discipline with firmness and kindness; hence it did not feel like a threat. He always gave me prompt and specific instructions for any inappropriate behaviour on my part, but in a calm way without shouting, nagging or criticising.

On my part I learnt to not only be disciplined but I also resolved that if, in the future, an opportunity arose to discipline any child of His, I'd adopt the same humane manner to do so.

On 31st January '94 at 4 a.m., I was in tears because the Lord had scolded me once again. In the dream I climbed down the steps of my building at top speed with the result I was making too much noise. But then I was unaware of my Lord's presence at the end of the steps, where to the right He was sleeping on the mattress spread out on the floor. My irresponsible, childish behaviour disturbed Him and He woke up. His one angry stare at me was enough to make my heart skip a beat. As He slowly took steps in my direction, I knelt before Him and joined my hands, begging His forgiveness. Thereupon He asked me, "Are you the girl who stays here?" "Baba, I stay upstairs with my aunt," I said shakily. "How dare you make so much noise?" As He uttered these words I felt the years roll back; once again I felt I was His young child, quietened by His rebuke. He continued to scold me for a long time – now in a language I couldn't understand. It could have been Telugu. All the time while chiding me He was pointing His index finger at me. It was as if I were a child who had gone astray and had to be reprimanded severely. Once again I asked for His pardon. And with that the dream came to an end.

My guru came to me garbed in the guise of friends. Today He had opened my eyes to the fact that He had been living so close to me in yet one more form – Narayan – who served the residents of the apartments where I lived – Narayan who fetched us drinking water during times of water shortage. Narayan slept in the passage just below the steps of our house. The night prior to the above dream, as per my daily habit, I had called out to Narayan. Everyday he came to collect his share of food that Nargish Aunty had to offer to him. But that night, unknown to me, he had gone to bed early. Only when he reached our doorstep did I realise that I had actually woken him up from sleep. I could have easily gone down the steps to check first whether he was awake or not and not simply call out to him from the top. Hence, in the dream, my guru had merely appealed to me to recognise, respect and love Him unconditionally in His multifarious roles – in a friend who cooked for me and also in another friend who carried drinking water to my home. My dear guru thus forbid me to seek Him in only select forms of my choosing lest I failed to recognise Him in all human beings.

Discriminate between the Voice of the Divine vis a vis the Subtle Ego

Yasmin Aunty (who hailed from Singapore and had earlier on as well spent a month with Nargish Aunty and me at Whitefield / Parthi) paid attention to what she believed were her inner voices. She claimed that on a daily basis God spoke to her through such voices and that she had been blessed to hear that voice of God throughout the day.

We need to count on our inner voice to guide us at all times. This inner voice would always be gentle and clear, vibrating in a peace of its own. Each of us have to learn, however, that every voice that we hear may not necessarily be the inner voice. We need to learn to discriminate between the voice of the divine and the voice of the subtle ego. If we'd remain sufficiently vigilant there would be little difficulty in recognising the true nature of the different voices. What is required at all times is sincerity.

All along I had easily believed this dear aunt of mine when she claimed that Baba had just appeared to her and she was going by His instructions. To me it had never sounded strange that He should appear to somebody on a daily basis. It's only much later when ego came in her way and her attitude towards me, towards seva, completely changed that I understood that now she went by the voice of the ego and not the voice of her conscience that she could have been referring to as His voice.

One day she claimed that it was Baba's message that I eat stale food since she had prepared enough to last for two days. (There was no refrigerator where we stayed on rent.) For the first time I started having my doubts that she could have been possibly mistaken into believing that it was Baba's voice that spoke to her day in and day out. On one or two more occasions, she behaved in a pompous manner and would order me in front of her very well-to-do friends to tell them in detail about her good deeds towards me when I had needed someone to take care of me. "Khurshid, how can you be so careless? How did you forget to tell them about the new clothes that I had presented you with?"

(Dear reader, you might wonder what caused me to be at the receiving end of such behaviour. It was my total economic dependence on her as much as on Nargish Aunty for my basic necessities in life such as food, clothing and shelter. Since I'm on the topic, I'd like to mention here that at least Nargish Aunty never made me feel obliged for her support to me.)

When Yasmin Aunty tried to produce feelings of guilt in me when I refused to eat stale food or when I resolved not to repeat her so-called story of good deeds again and again to a different audience each time, I knew it was necessary to let her know how I was feeling. I believed that pointing it out in a kind manner that I was feeling insulted and manipulated would be enough to get her to reconsider her behaviour if she truly cared about me.

The whole idea that she expected me to behave in a prescribed manner or conform to a preset image, especially when she snatched away my dignity, no longer made me feel like accepting her support any more. Just then, I felt so damaged and broken.

Didn't I still feel the pain of labels that had devastated me long ago, even if nowadays it were only occasionally? Then why was I being so small and judging her by this one event? Why was I completely rejecting and excluding her from my life? I had to discard such inappropriate behaviour and enlarge my love, certainly not narrow it down to loving people only if they were flawless. Baba helped me reach a point when I could look beyond the hurt rather than backward in anger and resentment.

In a very gentle manner, I explained the following things to her: What gives significance to a charitable act is the purpose for which it is done, the spirit in which it is carried out. It is the intention behind your giving and receiving that is most important.

Baba wanted me to apply love to all life situations. By my act of forgiving her I released myself from bondage. It then became possible for me to move forward and love her again. True forgiveness required that I not only stop taking personally any harsh thing said or done to me, but that I make an all-out effort to understand the other person. When this happened, I knew that resentment couldn't stand a chance. Through caring communication, we forgot about all the things that separated us and were soon friends as before.

Whenever confronted by the good as well as the not so good experiences with Jasawala Aunty, Yasmin Aunty, Dolly, Ramu or Nagu's mother, I had reminded myself that the experiences with them were as they should be. Whatever relationships I had attracted now or previously in my life were precisely those I needed in my life at that moment. There was a hidden meaning behind all events, one that served my own evolution.

What I learned from the above incident was this: In future if God ever chose to put me in a position to serve the less privileged I'd be extremely sincere and sensitive in my attitude towards them, grateful for the opportunity to serve God through them. If I had suffered anguish at the way Yasmin Aunty had treated me, it was a small price I had paid for such an important lesson in life.

My Lord taught me not only to forgive others but to follow up this forgiving with genuine acts of kindness so that the other person may not feel like repeating his / her harsh actions. The transformation that Baba brought about in me did not completely wipe away anger from my system. Yet, what it did for me was that it became easier for me to make more of an effort to be patient with others and when anger did come up, it wasn't as bad as before to make me say hurtful things in order to hit back.

All are Equal to Him

My dear guru's daily revelations made my life more meaningful. From the incident that was to follow, I learned how profoundly disappointing unfulfilled expectations could be, especially when the expectation was of concrete proof of love and attention from our Lord. The lesson has stayed with me. Who could understand Yasmin Aunty's feelings better than I? If He didn't appear in my dreams or visions for a week or two, didn't I experience a sense of abandonment by my guru?

One morning she was not to be seen in the darshan grounds at her usual place among the VVIPs. After darshan, as we reached her guesthouse, she seemed to be without her usual glow and bounce. Her gaze was distant and the sparkle was gone. It was very painful to see her in that condition and it made me very sad and anxious. Almost in tears she told us, "I have resolved to leave Parthi with immediate effect. I have booked my tickets to Mumbai and from there to Singapore." She had to make an effort to throw off the cloud that had fallen upon her but in vain. There was surely something she was not telling us; for nothing had happened to our knowledge that could make her go so far as to refuse to stay in Parthi even a day longer. Upon insisting that she share her sorrow with us, she said, "Baba does not care for me, never once appears to guide me as He comes to you. I feel neglected by Him and can't take that kind of pain any longer. Yesterday night when I felt utterly sick and called out to Him, He didn't respond to my cry. No, He never responds! Imagine the condition of people like me who follow each and every instruction of His, and try their very best to please Him by being good to everyone, and, yet, He ignores us. Now that I am leaving for Mumbai, I have told Him that He is going to lose out on a very good devotee. You at least have Him come to you and guide you through dreams and visions. As for me, I have no guidance. He never, never comes to me or talks to me."

Until the previous day, Yasmin Aunty had incessantly chattered about the frequent visions and live appearances of Baba that she witnessed in her house. To me, it wasn't surprising. If He could visit me so often, He could certainly be visiting her the way she claimed. But all this, as I understood it now, was a façade to cover up an inner emptiness, a need for His presence in her life. Today, she said with tears rolling down her cheeks that she'd be the happiest person if He'd ever appear to her to guide her. The harsh reality must, I felt, have been just a little too much for her to accept.

Yet, Baba could not allow her to leave Parthi on so wrong a ground. Hence, He had taken upon Himself to clear the misunderstanding in her mind via the 'boss' dream that I had had the same morning. (This was some time in January '94.)

Right before my eyes rolled the scenes of the beautiful dream I had had early that morning, a dream in which Yasmin Aunty and I had been presumably employed by the same company and worked for the same person, Baba, who was supposedly our boss! And she said in distress, "Khurshid, throughout our lives, we have worked for the same organisation under the supervision of the same person. Yet, there is a vast difference in our lives. You have always had easy access to Him, always had an opportunity to be with Him daily inside His cabin, whereas the rest of us are left out, totally ignored by Him." "Aunty, your question seems justified. Please wait a minute. I'll personally go and check out with our boss, I'll demand an explanation from Him." With this reassurance to her, I entered our Lord's cabin. On coming out of the cabin, I shared with her Baba's message to me. "Aunty, our boss has told me to give you the message that people like you have been given outdoor duties which He expects all of you to continue to discharge to the best of your ability. He wants you to do so without grudging the fact that He calls me into His cabin so very often. He's just told me that if He does so, it's because He has to dictate so many things to me. The boss has also told me to convey to you and the others working in their individual capacity to know that at the end of it all, each one shall be given a reward according to the manner in which they discharged their duties. He has also instructed me to inform you all that He never ignores a single individual but that He keeps an eye on each one. Aunty, He also showed me a recording machine that was fitted in His office and told me that the machine took down a detailed account of each one's deeds during his/her lifetime!" With that the dream came to an end.

After hearing my dream she appeared a bit relieved. Sensing her loneliness and the need for warmth of loving friends, Nargish Aunty and I took her along to stay with us.

I had been given privileges of close, regular personal contact – via dreams of His which Yasmin Aunty rarely experienced but would have been only too glad to have. It was not because I had a greater claim on our guru than her. If it were a matter of claim based on the devotees' spiritual status, there were many who'd have preceded me. This privilege had been given to me because He had made me His instrument through whose life, the life of a lay person, He had resolved to pass on simple messages of good and godly life to mankind. Via my experiences, He wanted to let the masses know that if someone like me who had made such grave errors in life could be pardoned and shown the path to light and spirituality, there was definitely hope for every human being on earth to be blessed by His constant presence in life the way I was. The sunlight of our guru's love shines on all. He could never be partial. He had also never decided on making me His instrument out of personal preference, but according to the necessities of the work. By telling me to write these Volumes, Baba was inviting me more to share my experiences than to strive to be a teacher.

The innumerable dreams, visions and divine experiences I'd been blessed with, did not confer on me any superiority over others. To the Divine eye, we were all equal, whatever our individual role in life. In all humility, I understood that the slightest sense of self-importance was a signal for re-appraisal.

No doubt, our dear Boss called me to His cabin (at a spiritual level, via dreams and visions) more often than He called the rest of His employees. But He had now clarified that His purpose in doing so was not that I was more loved than the rest as much as for the benefit of my fellow human beings who'd be reading these Volumes. My Lord was using me as His instrument to assist Him in His designs for the welfare of the masses. I had no desire whatsoever to mislead anybody into believing that I had easier access to the Lord and could win His grace for others. I was myself still a student eager to learn all that I could to become a worthy child of His.

By Clearing My Vision He Made Me Focus on the Divine Consciousness

On 7th February '94 in a dream, Nargish Aunty and I looked out of our window to the side terrace where our Lord stood inspecting the clothes on the clothes line which had been just washed by me. Not my clothes alone, but also that of Yasmin and Nargish Aunty. I leaped in joy that Baba was busy inspecting my work and from the looks of Him, He seemed to be very pleased at the result of my effort. But every now and then, a whiff of air blew Nargish Aunty's gown and it would get crumpled, but the Lord gently smothered those creases and tried to make it straight. Seeing that, I hugged aunty in joy and cried out, "See how much He cares for you. How lucky you are that He is so concerned to make your dress without creases." Now our Lord turned and walked up to our window. Not losing any time, I immediately told Him, "Baba, we are leaving on the 28th (actually it would be 1st March '94 since we had to board the train after midnight)." He seemed not to understand and I repeated my words asking Him if that was OK. This time I had repeated my question not in English but in Hindi. Yet, He appeared not to have comprehended and kept on talking in a language I didn't follow. I pleaded with Him that as I hailed from Mumbai, I was conver-sant only with four languages, English, Gujarati, Hindi and Marathi! It was futile to make Him understand because He was bent upon talking in, what I supposed was Telugu.

The latter part of the above-mentioned dream (7th February '94) was as follows: He held a long hollow pipe of about an inch in diameter and a few feet in length. He placed one end of that pipe – or rather somehow managed to fix it on my eye and by placing the other end of the same pipe into His own mouth, He began to blow out all the impurities from my eye!

By blowing away the impurities from my eyes, impurities that blocked the vision of the divine, He ensured that I was in constant, unbroken awareness of the 'atma'

Baba wanted me to attain perfection. He wanted my individual consciousness to become one with universal consciousness. Therefore, He was blessing me with the knowledge of the spirit, helping me on the path of self-realisation, to live oblivious of the body and mind consciousness that bound me to this earth.

Every single day I was receiving so much love from Baba that I decided to give something to everyone I came in contact with. It took the form not of material things (since I had no material wealth to distribute to others), but words of love, appreciation, gratitude, compliments or a small prayer to God for their well-being. I gave them the gifts of caring, affection and selfless love. And in giving I was receiving love and friendship all the time.

The Role He Wished Me to Play in Life

Baba did not want me to underestimate myself, but to have faith and confidence in myself. My divine parent believed that I had tremendous capabilities. Not using these capabilities would not only be a waste for me, but a waste for the society as well.

That evening during bhajans I insisted that He bless me with a glimpse of the kind of role He expected me to play in the future. The vision that sprung up before my eyes was that of a parachute opening high up in the air and on its way down to earth. "O Lord, as a parachute what do you feel I should be doing?" An immediate answer to my prayer came in the form of another vision wherein now I saw so many people hanging on to the one and only parachute then in sight, the one that helped them have a safe landing!

Basking in the sunshine of my guru's love – unspoken but keenly felt, I banished from my conscious mind the fact that the day to bid Him farewell was drawing nearer. Baba's trust in me plunged me into the depths of my being, where I made a decision that took a few years to bear fruit: to live my life for a worthy cause and lead others by example to do so.

I Resolve to Live out All My Learnings in Life

Baba always filled the void in my life with His surprise gifts on an almost daily basis. These took the form of divine visions and dreams, immediately in response to each appeal of mine to Him. He consistently blessed me with visions that provided insights into my potential future. These blessings were just a sign that my guru was all the time thinking of enhancing my vision, my self-esteem, my love for humanity, my self-confidence in writing His books.

My endless writings about God, about my experiences with Him were not, in themselves enough. If I were to actually pay heed to His words then I'd have to live out those learnings in my daily life: henceforth and unto my last breath.

The next evening during bhajans my prayer was, "Baba, what I want to know today is your expectations of me. What do you wish to see in me? What form of mine shall please you most?" So saying, I lifted my eyes towards the sky. There was a sudden blinding flash of light, and in that light I saw a huge cloud taking the form of Lord Hanuman flying with the Sanjeevani peak in His hand.

This Divine vision thrilled me with joy indescribable. I realised anew how blessed and privileged I was to behold Lord Hanuman in His beautiful form.

Also, this vision that I had had with open eyes, left me perturbed. He expected me to achieve the impossible. How could I even dream of reaching the height of Lord Hanuman who was the greatest devotee of the Lord and who was Himself worshipped by many as God?

Whenever Necessary, it's OK to Oppose – but with Love and Understanding

Learning to love all of mankind was the most daring of disciplines. The real measure of love according to Baba was to love all regardless of the fact that they did not share my views or reciprocated my love. It also meant doing good to those who disliked me.

Yet, to remain calm did not mean that I always smile and bear in silence the pain others put me through. Agreeing with others all the time because I was afraid to speak the truth, lest I displease them or hurt their sentiments was wrong attitude on my part. I had to learn to speak when necessary and never compromise on my own inner peace.

Every day that dawned brought more and more messages from my Lord, each one of them pointing out to yet another failing of mine and also the way in which I could overcome them. Early morning on

9th February '94, I had a feeling that Baba wanted to contact me and pass on a message to me. The minute I closed my eyes, (and even before I could fall asleep), He blessed me with a vision of Himself seated on a chair, smiling at me, and, by gestures of the hand telling me to look at something He wished me to see. Almost immediately after this vision I went to sleep and had the following dream:

Very unintentionally, on and often Meena (name changed), pricked me with a rusty needle that she always held in her hand. At one point in time the needle pricked the vein leading to my heart. Not wanting to let her know of my pain, I put a band-aid tape over each of the wounds, telling myself, "Haven't I been doing so all my life? Why let anyone know of my wounds?" Suddenly, Sai, the Divine Doctor came on the scene and told me it was foolish on my part to simply keep applying band-aids that didn't serve any purpose. Later, losing His temper with me, He said, "Khurshid, don't make the mistake of thinking that you are doing her a favour by keeping quiet. If you care for her spiritual progress you would understand that your silence in such matters can do more harm than good to her. Only if you had brought it to her notice earlier, she would have realised her mistake a long time ago and not repeated it." The dream ended.

Whenever one person has higher standards in a certain area than the other person, nagging comes naturally. Meena, however, didn't recognize nagging for what it was: a veiled way of criticising. Her standards of tidiness or prayers / meditation at fixed hours weren't the same as mine. She believed I was sloppy, lazy and showed disrespect to Baba. Her constant question was that why did He, in spite of my laziness, appear to me so often.

The band-aids applied over the wounds caused by the needle pricks (her words that cut through my heart), was certainly not good for my well-being. It solved the problem temporarily, but left the underlying chronic problems untouched to fester and resurface again and again.

Of course, my goal was to never think ill of others. But that did not mean I should not oppose other people lovingly when necessary. When someone was making a mistake or acting unkindly, putting up with tender opposition would be often a demonstration of just how much I cared. But it was essential to oppose kindly, without offending the person or making him / her experience guilt. In the above case, after the initial displeasure at having been opposed, Meena was sensitive enough to understand that it was because I cared for her so much that I had dared to share with her my feelings. In the years to follow, this incident and the way we both handled it, added respect and depth to our relationship.

To His Dismay, some of His Students Lacked Focus

On 10th February' 94, at 5 p.m. my prayer to the Lord was, "Baba, help me that my mind steadfastly dwell on you. And I shall endeavour to drive away all distracting thoughts. Let me have no body consciousness. O Lord, increase my capacity to endure whatever pain is in store for me. Go on revealing to me the pitfalls on the spiritual path so that I may avoid them."

The same night at 11.30 p.m., He appeared in my dream. He was sitting on the stage with students to His left singing bhajans. Suddenly mid-way through, they started giggling away, forgetting that they were supposed to be singing bhajans. Our Lord in a very sad tone, said, "Don't do that, or else poor Dabdi will think that none of my students came up to the level of devotion that she has reached."

One More Attempt of His to Help Me Overcome My Anger

The dream of our guru that I had at 1 a.m. on 12th February '94: He suddenly asked me an unexpected question, "Shall I tell you the story of Vamana? This is how it goes." "Baba," I entreated with tears streaming down my eyes, "No, please do not tell me any story. I have limited intelligence and hardly anything goes into my brain." So saying, I fell at His feet and was about to touch them.

All of a sudden, He was roaring like a lion and He placed His foot on my back and crushed me, crying out angrily, "Krodha?" I let Him place His full weight on me, without emitting a single cry myself though the pain due to the heavy weight was intense. And the dream came to an end.

For the benefit of those not familiar with the term 'Krodha', let me translate it into English. Krodha in the literal sense means anger. Let me clarify further. He was crushing the anger that I often found difficult to keep under control.

He was my constant Divine companion with whom I could freely share my feelings. He was still in the process of crushing to naught my innumerable defects and limitations. I knew that the day I sat satisfied with my limited progress, I would cease to grow spiritually. I resolved never to do anything that would drag my consciousness down from my goal – God realisation.

I had yet to reach a stage when the windows of all my senses would close down completely and I'd be able to meditate for long periods at a stretch with one pointed attention on God. By my own mode of living and behaviour I had to show others how one could progress towards self-realisation. If I lived by my convictions, there would be complete unity between what I said and how I lived.

Making His Omniscience Known Once Again

After the Vamana dream, I was scared of Him. Did He still love me as before? Or was He planning to move away from me? My dear guru never wanted me to harbour a fear of Him. I was His child on whom He would never give up. To make me overcome my sudden fear of Him, He gave me a glimpse of His sense of humour.

On the 13th February '94, at 6 a.m. in the dream He appeared to be in a very jovial and mischievous mood. He was moving about in the darshan grounds, waving out a hanky, and saying, "Where is the lady who used to bring this hanky here everyday? Tell her to come and claim it and I give guarantee of returning it to her." Then He placed His feet on the seva dal scarves of both the gents and the ladies Seva Dals.

Actually, Nargish Aunty had been bringing along a handkerchief to be blessed by Baba. That day she was feeling indisposed so she had decided to miss out on His darshan. Keeping in mind the dream message I had received the same morning, I went for darshan and even sat in the token queues in the hope of getting her hanky blessed by Him. How happy aunty would feel to have her wish fulfilled as she had been bringing the hanky during bhajan time every evening in the hope that He would look her way while going back to the auditorium after the bhajans. With the Lord's grace, I was in the third row during darshan time, and to my great joy found Paula, a foreigner friend of mine, in the front row and she agreed to hand over my hanky to Baba. When she did so, my Lord took it in His hand and placed it among the letters He had received. For a moment, I thought He would walk away with it, and my heart gave an indignant cry, "Didn't you guarantee to return it?" He had already taken a few steps but He turned and walked up to us. Then He handed over the hanky once again to Paula, while giving me a mischievous look and a sweet smile before moving on to the other devotees..

My Literal View on becoming His Mother not Acceptable to Him

At 10.30 a.m. on 14th February '94, He once again appeared in my dream to set my vision right. This is how it all began. At the top of a hillock stood my Lord, Sathya Sai, watching over the people gathered down below to have His darshan. Most of the devotees were either busy talking amongst themselves, or focussing their camera lens on to others in an endeavour to click their photos. One westerner who was too engrossed in focussing her camera on to me was taken unawares by the Lord who all of a sudden came sliding down the hill to come and sit right next to her. Before she could click my photo, He turned her camera to face her own self and pressed the button. She was startled at Baba's action. My dear Lord was busy teaching us to do introspection.

As I tried to reach out to Him, in very loving tones, He said softly, (in Hindi – 'Mangal ho, Khush Raho, Mangal Ho, Khush Raho'). "May everything good and auspicious happen, May you remain happy. May everything good and auspicious happen, May you remain happy." Yes, He said it twice. And all of a sudden I asked, "Baba in which year am I going to be your mother?" His stern look followed by words said with a note of exasperation in them struck me as a thunderbolt. "This view of yours is not correct." (His exact words uttered in Hindi were 'yeh tera view theek nahi hai!') In desperation I cried out, "Then is it that I shall never be your mother?" To that He simply replied, "After 11-12, Baba shall summon you and after that He'll call out to you in that manner." (His words spoken in Hindi were – gyara bara ke baad jub Baba bulaenge tow tumhe aise pukarenge'.) With that message of His, the dream ended.

Currently, my vision was so limited that I still chose to interpret His promise of arrival in my life in the literal sense. Hence, I was devastated. Since the past one decade hadn't He Himself made me consider myself His mother first, any other relationship with Him second? Did He expect me to give up my dream without undergoing pain? It was an emotional blow I felt I wouldn't survive.

It is many years after the above mentioned dream, i.e. almost 6 to 8 months after I gave birth to my brainchild 'Sunbeam' that I understood the implications of His statement that my perspective of imagining myself as His mother in the literal sense had not been without flaw. Sunbeam got registered as a Public Charitable Trust on 10th December '99. It was as late as in the year mid 2000 that I realised that motherhood went beyond a physical or reproductive function. It had to do with unconditional love, compassion, selflessness and support.

Could it be that after a decade or two, or on completion of these Volumes much later, He would be calling me to Parthi? And at that point in time, would He be addressing me as 'Mother'? By saying, 'after 11 or 12', had He meant after the calendar year 2011 or 2012? Only time would tell.

He Clarified He was Working upon Improving My Spiritual Vision

The very next morning i.e. on 15th February '94, I sat in bed jotting down a dream that I had just had. The dream was as follows:

"Baba, shall I begin my work on the computer?" And in response He just said the word, "computer." My next question was, "Baba, as per your wish I will come to you again in the month of May. Please tell me how long you want me to stay then. When can I return home?" After pondering a while, He said, "June." This answer came as a great relief. Finally, I broached the topic of my failing vision, "My vision has not improved much." To that complaint He responded in a stern voice, "No, you shall not have normal vision if it is the physical sight you mean because that is certainly not what I had in mind when I said that I'm working upon improving your vision." "Then you will not cure me, Baba, so that I can see properly with the right eye?" Once again in a serious tone, He replied, "No, I shall not."

After the above dream, I didn't feel sad at all though my right eye had almost lost its vision. It had only enough vision for me to be able to see a person at a distance of a few feet, but not be able to identify him her. Now the vision in the left eye too had begun to deteriorate, though very gradually.

My dear guru no longer wanted me to be under the delusion of maya. That is why He didn't pay much attention to physical healing as much as to the healing of my soul's ignorance. Each time that He blessed me with inner vision, I realised the body as nothing but a shell in which my soul temporarily resided.

Baba had always been referring to the spiritual sight. That was a lesson in itself. Yes, I had been asking for inner vision and He had consistently been blessing me with glimpses of the same each time I was able to efface the 'I' in me. Gradually, He was succeeding in making me aware of my relationship with the larger family, His entire creation.

My prayer was the longing of my heart to break free from the narrow confines of the individual self to find the universal. It was a journey that led one from isolation to an encounter with the divine in every bit of God's creation. My Lord was there to guide me to that supreme vision. Baba had indeed blessed me with the divine eye to make me see Him in His innumerable divine forms of the different avatars of His. Also He blessed me with the vision that enabled me to see Him as the indweller of all.

There was no Parting from Him Ever

On 19th February '94, I prayed to Him to bless me that a period of six hours of sleep be sufficient for me to spend my day in good health so that I could, with His help, get up and pray for an hour or so in the morning. To my surprise, by 3.40 a.m., I found myself wide awake, feeling quite fresh! For once I sat and meditated for almost 45 minutes, meditated on His lotus feet. But I confess, more often than not, my mind wandered home. I continued with my prayer only in the hope that I'd be able to concentrate better with daily practice. Now as I sat praying the Gayatri Mantra, He, as usual, did give me His darshan by blessing me with a vision of His form.

The love of a mother shone in the eyes that locked me in a divine embrace. This vision was one more proof that upon my return to Mumbai, there was to be no parting from Him. The grief I had been experiencing since the past few days at the prospect of leaving His divine company, now no longer existed. Going back to Mumbai, to my family and job was going to be different. This time, I'd not be going alone, but taking Him along with me in my heart.

Each Time that My Concentration on Him Broke, He Appeared to Me!

One morning I sat chanting the Gayatri Mantra. For a moment I had a fleeting vision of the Lord and then, once again another vision. This time it lasted longer.

During meditation I did strive to empty the mind of all physical and mental burdens and restlessness. Surprisingly, each time that my concentration on Him broke, He was there to bless me with a vision of His and a stern look. Baba was always tender, warm and affectionate. Yet, if I erred He could be firm with me. The look that came over Him when He was disappointed or angry over my behaviour was a dreaded punishment. The most unbearable form of His punishment though was temporarily withdrawing His blessings of special darshans in my dreams and visions.

Through meditation He wanted me to learn to experience pure awareness. But I just could not experience stillness and each time my mind wavered to my family or any worldly desire, He blessed me with a vision of His. The stern look He gave me was enough to bring my mind back on Him. Once again I felt connected to Him, the innermost essence of my being.

His Deep Concern Regarding Matters Relating to My Nourishment

22nd February '94, during the evening bhajans, I had a vision of a flame, a bright, steady flame right before my eyes. This vision lasted for a few minutes unlike most other visions that lasted merely for a second to a few seconds.

At 3 a.m. the next day my Lord appeared in a dream. I stood where I was, waiting for Him to come closer. With folded hands, I bowed to Him mentally. Now He stopped in front of me and quietly said, "Put your hands down." He blessed me by placing His hand on my head. Coming closer to me once again, He almost whispered into my ears, "Khurshid, now listen carefully to what I have to say." People gathered around to hear Him. I too was all attention, thinking a great spiritual message was to be imparted. What He said into my ears was something that made me wonder if I had heard right! "Khurshid," He said softly, "have a little bit of pure ghee on a daily basis." Still not sure if I had heard right I made Him repeat the entire message! And the next moment He was gone from my sight.

This message may seem a very silly one, but not so in my case, because perhaps according to Him, pure ghee, was necessary for my health to improve. On 25th February '94, He blessed me with a vision of Himself early in the morning the minute I woke up. As a result of this vision, I sat up in bed and started praying. People pray in order to receive grace and visions of the Lord, whereas, I'd begin my prayers mostly upon receiving the Lord's vision.

26th April '94 – during evening bhajan, the vision was of a bright, steady flame for more than a minute.

The Lord in Narayan who had Served us Dutifully

The Lord adopts endless forms, to manifest Himself in the world. His manifestation for me was always in conformity with the need of the time. Though unreachable in His form of Sathya Sai on a physical plane, He was within reach in the multiple forms He assumed (via dreams and visions).

Time and again He was passing on the message that it is not correct to limit God to any form. The dream I was blessed with on the last day of my 10 months stay in His presence and the actual experience to follow (i.e. on 28th February '94), was also indicative of the same. In the dream Baba appeared to me and said something to me twice but I was unable to grasp its meaning. This was because He was speaking to me in a language which, I suppose, was Telugu.

Within seconds of opening my eyes, I found Narayan, waiting at the door. He was the same man who fetched us not only drinking water but also bucketfuls of water whenever the water pump was out of order. Now he stood talking to me in Telugu so I couldn't understand a single word of his. Today, for the first time in the past few months since we knew him, he walked away after getting five buckets of water – without charging us for his services. Baba dwelled in him as much as He dwelled in others. This man had served us with devotion and today being our last day, perhaps he had wanted to do free seva for us. God bless him.

My Return to Mumbai did not Imply Separation from My Guru

My journey was coming to an end and I was returning home with the clear awareness that I had a special gift of God – the faith and conviction that every human being is a spark of the divine. I prayed to Baba to help me spread His light and love by way of service to humanity.

On 28th February '94, leaving Parthi and going back to the world where He was sending me, was something that didn't bring tears of separation. Wherever He placed me, I knew I would draw Him there by selfless acts of love towards one and all. My dear guru had trained me to adopt the path of karma yoga; taught me to offer the fruits of all my actions at the feet of God.

In the years to follow, in the midst of all my actions towards fulfilling my duties and responsibilities, I continued to experience bliss, joy and oneness with divinity.

My life lay amid the city crowds, not in Parthi / Whitefield ashrams. During this long stay in His presence, I had learned that if I discharged my responsibilities without personal motive or attachment, I would be treading the sure path of enlightenment. I had to lead a balanced life and conscientiously fulfil my family and spiritual duties.

It had taken so much effort on His part to make me realise that I didn't need to be loved by everyone, and that the world didn't end if I was ever to be rejected by family and friends. Instead, it was my duty to love everyone, see the spark of the Divine in each human being I came across.

It was certainly going to be different being back in Mumbai with my family and rejoining my services at CRY. However, I would look back with fondness at what I had experienced here in His heavenly abode, as also in gratitude for where it had led me. I believed that these Divine teachings imparted to me over the past one year would be invaluable in my relationships with others and also how I viewed myself.

Seeking God meant also to serve Him in mankind. Baba had made me aware that I could not be wholly immersed in Divine consciousness until I had learned how to balance my life with meditation and service to mankind. Wholly immersed in God, I could still be engrossed in selfless dedication to God's work whatever He chose to assign to me. Hence, I resolved to continue to put to use all His teachings even after my return to Mumbai. While performing my duties, I would constantly keep my attention on God awareness. I would be back in the world fulfilling – not shirking my duties in life. I would offer all my acts to Him.

From Him in the multiple individuals who had helped me during my stay in Parthi / Whitefield, I had learnt so much. I learnt the power of a kind word and the smallest act of caring. It made my life so full of love and warmth.

Back in Mumbai, Baba continued to nurture as before, my capacity to love, and hence my will to grow. (Today while I am at a re-edit of this Volume on 7th June '09, it's overwhelming to recall the innumerable opportunities He blessed me with over the years to pass on that selfless love to others.)

To be aware of His grace, to personally experience its constant presence, to know my nearness to God, was to know and continually experience an inner tranquillity and peace that was a direct result of His love divine. Today, I can say with conviction that had it not been for His tireless effort towards moulding me into His image, I'd never have understood the purpose of my life – the evolution of my soul.

On 3rd March '94, within days of reaching Mumbai, Baba blessed me with a beautiful vision, that of Himself dancing in joy!

Baba had been holding my hand for over a decade now, yet He had not considered it wise to begin imparting spiritual knowledge to me until only a year ago. He had awakened the disciple within me. Though it had been a very gradual process, it was certainly measurable. Eventually, when I had reached a stage where I was ready to surrender to His will, He had called me to His abode to impart Divine wisdom. Whenever He had taken it upon Himself to teach me a new lesson, as you must have already noticed in this Volume, He made sure that it was followed by a live experience to prove its authenticity and validity. With day to day simple experiences in life, He had succeeded in teaching me such profound truths. Everything in the whole wide world had become my guru in the past one year and continues to be so even now. If all these experiences had made me realise my limitations and even helped me in overcoming them to a large extent, it's only because I had cultivated and adopted the humility required to be able to completely surrender myself to His will.

Today was a day for rejoicing. Because my dear guru was rejoicing at my consistent effort; rejoicing at the inner transformation coming about in me. He was celebrating my rebirth. The vision of my dear guru dancing in joy reflected also the joy surging within me, surrounding my very being.

That the progress of a devotee mattered to Him so much was a lesson in humility. Waves of rapture engulfed me as I recalled the divine spectacle I had just beheld. It was overwhelming to know that a devotee's surrender to His will was the food on which our guru thrived. As I sat up in bed and made a small thanksgiving prayer, I was full of joy. I sincerely hope that I continue to succeed in making Him experience the satisfaction of reading with pride the results of my progress card each time I appear for the tests that come my way. I have stumbled and may continue to once in a while, but I trust that He will focus only on my effort and never give up on me. Under the shade of my guru's everlasting grace and unconditional love I am carrying on with my efforts at becoming His image.

6

On My Return to Mumbai, I Rejoined CRY

My Resolution to Live Out the Values Taught by My Guru
After a year-long stay in the ashram of my guru, Sri Sathya Sainath, I was back with my family in March '94. The reunion with my parents, my brother Peshotan and my sister Jasmine was filled with happy tears and embraces. But even as my heart warmed to the family getting together once again, and I acknowledged that my experiences in life had begun to take shape in the form of writing these Volumes, there was so much more to be done. I'd now have to take that extra step and translate His teachings into actions in my daily life. I had not been made to live in His presence for so long simply to bathe in momentary bliss of His Divine company on a physical plane, but learn to carry this security, this inner peace with me to my home.

By now it was quite clear to me that according to my guru, spiritualism for me was not to be equated with going into forests or ashrams. It was practising the presence of divinity while living actively in this world and carrying out my duties. Friends, from Volume II onwards, I've attempted to convey how I have known God closely and be able to talk to Him at all times. I have always believed in direct communion with God. God wants to be known and loved by all of us. Divine Union is possible through self-effort. I've been able to achieve what I had earlier believed to be an impossible goal. All it required was a desire to know Him and an equally strong desire and effort in the direction of moving out of the sensory world of delusion.

He had taught me that I was neither the body nor the mind: but the immortal soul. Being interested in spiritual matters did not mean losing interest in everything else. I could be interested in the world, but without any attachment. I did not have to ascribe undue importance to psychic experiences; I had to look at how I actually lived. If I felt united with God, I had to be united with mankind.

What I could aim for was not to have mystical experiences, but making my life a gift to my immediate family and also to the society just as it had been given as a gift to me. If spiritual experiences did come my way, they would serve to inspire me and further assist me in my efforts to be of use to mankind. His children would learn by what I was and what I did more than by what I wrote in the books. I resolved to live out the values taught by Him; not merely write about them.

Experience proved that staying away from each other made a heart grow fonder. Surprisingly, for the first time in life, my family members actually expressed their immense love for me in ways that touched me deeply. Moreover, now there was a mutual understanding and respect between us. They didn't interfere in my matters and I left them to their beliefs and practices. On the 3rd of March '94, I received the computer at home. (Aban's sister had been kind enough to let me use one of her computers for a few months. In the next two to three months I keyed in Volume I and part of Volume II before rejoining CRY.)

My Dear Friend Rippan Breathing his Last

In a dream on 10th March' 94, my Lord expressed a wish that I go to Delhi and Gaziabad!! Why, how and with whom? In the same dream, when I asked Him if I could get in touch with the CRY office or call at Rippan's place and talk to him once about my rejoining the organisation in case a suitable vacancy existed, He advised me to wait till I came back from Delhi.

Within days, my guru's command made sense. On 23rd of March '94, I had to suddenly leave for Delhi with Nandini (my sister in law). Till the last day my brother had hoped to be able to go with her but was not granted leave from office. In order not to break the hearts of her family members who expected her to be with them on the auspicious occasion of Holi, I accompanied her, which I knew was in submission to His will.

The festival of Holi is associated with colours. But I, in particular, didn't look forward to being smeared with colours to be pasted on me in a moment of joviality. My happiness lay in being with Nandini and her family, in having given her company and in having obeyed my Lord.

Within a few days, we were on our way back to Mumbai. To my great surprise one of the ladies in our coupe turned out to be Rippan's aunt. She was conversing with Nandini through whom she came to know that I worked for CRY, and asked me if I had heard of Rippan Kapur, who was her nephew. She said he was ill and had expressed a wish to see her, hence she was making a long-distance journey all the way to Mumbai. Though she didn't inform me that he was in the hospital breathing his last, I could guess as much. I had to be utterly realistic; it had been a long, hard struggle for him and this time if his relatives had been called for, in all probability the end was drawing closer.

The same afternoon I received a call from Aban. Our conversation was predominantly about my Delhi trip and recent Baba experiences, but at one point she did mention that Rippan was very ill and in the hospital. And she asked if I'd like to go to visit him along with her the same evening.

I approached my dear friend's hospital bed with trepidation, unsure of what to say or do. Not wanting to confront the feelings that his impending death raised, I kept my overwhelming sadness at bay. When I saw him in the condition that he was, for a split second I was paralysed by doubt. Would he recover this time as he had done so many times in the past few years? O Lord, how many days more was he going to live? Doubts by the dozen. He smiled with an effort, had no strength to even lift his head. He was nothing but a bag of bones lying on the bed, looking so frail that I had to fight the urge to cry. It was visible that he would not survive for long. He looked at me for a while and said, "So Khurshid, you have come back." There was a sort of a questioning look in his eyes. He may have felt relieved to know that I had not decided to live in an ashram for all my life but would instead adopt the path of karma and take care of my family. We spoke for a while. Before leaving, he inquired what I was doing presently. On telling him that my writing work had finished and that I had got a computer at home from where I worked, he said, "You will keep on coming to see me, won't you?" I gave a positive reply, but alas, never kept my word.

In the recent past I had had two dreams of his impending death. The first one I had in Parthi itself. A dream in which I saw him sitting across the table, both of us at work. But the place of work was not an office. We were simply sitting in a flower garden, and all around us pleasing to the sight were lovely peaks. Rippan was in ecstasy as he exclaimed, "Khurshid, now I can see the trees, the mountains, the beauty around me that I had always failed to see in spite of your attempts at making me do so. Now I can visualise what you always spoke about but, for years, something that I had found difficulty in experiencing." He ran about in the garden in a joyous mood. I expressed my surprise by saying, "Rippan, now that I am back, what sort of an office is this? Where are the walls that make the structure of an office?" "O Khurshid, this time when you have rejoined CRY, there are no walls now. This time when we work together there won't be any walls around!" he added.

The next dream had been in mid-March '94. Here I saw myself going to visit a dying plant and blowing over the drooping leaves. All of a sudden life came back in that plant and instead of the old, worn-out yellow leaves, the plant was now covered with fresh, new, green leaves!

Instead of understanding its clear message, of shedding the old body for a new one, I took it to be a miraculous recovery for the dying plant! Thus, I kept fooling myself till the very end. I kept telling myself that I'd visit him the next day, but never mustered up enough courage to do so. Why? Because I couldn't bear to see him breathe his last. A week later he was discharged from the hospital, so that he could spend his last days in the company of his near and dear ones – his family. He breathed his last a week later.

Twice Baba appeared in my dreams to instruct me to visit Rippan before it was too late. Yet, after the dreams, I had just remained at home, paralysed. Then I had tried to figure out what I needed to do. Visit him at his house? But there was nothing I could have accomplished there, I convinced myself. My dear friend was dying and nothing I could do or say would affect the outcome. Be there for moral support? Well, maybe. But he'd be surrounded by family and CRY members who would provide more than enough comfort.

In the dream on 7th April '94, I found myself at Whitefield with my Lord giving darshan to the devotees who had gathered in large numbers. As I was not seated among them inside the hall, but stood with the few individuals outside the gate, He, my Lord walked right up to the end of the hall. He did not travel beyond the gate, but by gestures called me to Him very urgently. Thinking that He was calling the person to my right, I nudged that man, but when he mentioned that I should myself go to the Lord, I turned to the person on my left and told her that perhaps it was her whom the Lord was calling. That lady really got annoyed and said in furious tones, "O Khurshid, He may not be calling out your name in this crowd but can't you see that He is calling you and no one else? You fail to see that His eyes are searching for you in the crowd, no, you can't see that since you haven't worn the glasses that would have made you see it. Go, go to Him, He is calling out to you."

Now in the dream itself, I ran to the inner room, to my Lord. Something puzzling took place. Initially, as He started walking in my direction, it was certainly Baba in His own form, but later on He took the form of another person upon whose face I didn't bother to look, but I saw that it was a white kurta-pyjama He was dressed in now. When He gave me His hand with that white sleeve, I held it reverentially, taking it still to be the Lord Himself. With this the dream ended. (Since the time I had known Rippan, I had always seen him in a white kurta pyjama, at least at CRY.)

Was it the Lord Himself who had put a veil of maya before my eyes so as not to be able to understand that He, my Lord, was referring to Rippan?

On Sunday morning, i.e. on 10th April, my Lord once again appeared in my dream. This time as before, He spoke not a word but only by gestures conveyed His messages. Today, His eyes searched about the room frantically. Once again, I wasn't sure if He was calling out to me. And by the time I realised it to be so, it was already too late. He had entered a small temple, the gates of which were now locked by the gate-keeper. Since the temple gate was made of iron bars, I could still see my Lord within. But He was no more in flesh and blood. He had changed to the form of a mere photo-frame with His photo within! With that the dream came to an end.

It was about 4.30 p.m. the same evening when I received a call from Aban to say that Rippan was no more! She informed me that she would come to pick me up at my residence and then we could proceed to his house (his mother's place) from where the body was to be taken to the crematorium.

When I reached his home, I was directed to a room where his body lay. I stood in pained, stunned silence. The experience had taught me a few lessons. Even if I was powerless to change someone's destiny, even if it meant I'd have just stood by and watched him die, it was critical that I just do that – just be there when someone needed me. The other lesson I learnt was that the opposite of love was not hate – but indifference. And I resolved that at least henceforth I wouldn't be indifferent to someone else's need of my company in their time of trial.

My dear friend's funeral took place. In my mind I thanked him for coming into my world – rather for his invitation to me to experience his world – CRY Child Relief and You, and thereby renewing my life with a strong conviction that each of us have the potential to do something to bring about laughter and sunshine in another's life. My regret for his death at such a young age remained, but alongside it was gratitude. He had taught me to understand life more profoundly and to never be content with any little act of generosity or hard work but to do my best for those in need. The opportunity I had got to work so closely with Rippan, I believe, had not come by chance, but by design, the Lord's plan. Forever I would carry indelible memories with me of his friendship and of his concern for the underprivileged children, his convictions in life, his down to earth mannerisms, his contribution to the children whom CRY reached out to.

In the days to follow, the newspapers wrote the longest pieces about his achievements as the founder of CRY who had brought it from a one man organisation to what it was now, reaching out to those in need. Being a friend, I didn't think of him as just the head of CRY or as the man for whom they sang praises for all that he had done in his lifetime. I remembered him as a friend who had so often while dictating letters, stopped half-way to ask me if he would live long. I remembered the days when he'd begin to weep and tell me that he wanted to live, and also remembered how often he had told me to ask Baba about his life-span.

But what did I feel on the 10th, upon hearing of his passing away and putting away the receiver? I'm trying to recollect my emotions, to comprehend my mixed feelings even as I pen them down for you. I just didn't want to believe what I had heard! But I knew that another chapter of my life had closed forever. My stomach had churned several times over with fear, at the loss I felt. My Lord had made me come in contact with two men in my life in whose company I had spent three individual years – each man an extreme opposite of the other! The first one, an evil man in the disguise of a saint, and, the second one, a sincere human being who had throughout shunned publicity while dedicating his life to the service of humanity. For the one steeped in worldly pleasures, Baba had said he would be dying soon, – yes, he was out of my life, and dead to me forever, though he must have lived in his mortal frame much longer. And here was this simple, good soul for whom the Lord's mother had once promised a life of a hundred years (after saying that he was to live just a little while physically). Yes, in the form of his brainchild, CRY – Child Relief and You, he would continue to live a hundred years and beyond.

Now at his mother's house where Rippan's body lay, just one look at it and the turmoil going on within me was terrible. Today, I had lost someone who cared for me, and, I knew there were very few whom I could call friends and now the number was less by one. Crying is an expression of helplessness and that's what I felt when I thought of the number of times Rippan had told me, "Khurshid, I want to live. By giving me such short time God has cheated me." And I thought of the past two weeks in which I had not gone to visit him even once! The guilt! The helplessness! I could only cry! From his house, along with the others I went to the crematorium. On my return home, I felt as though a part of me was missing.

I Rejoined CRY and Made Several Lasting Friendships

Vanita Malhotra, All India Admin. Head, CRY, was in need of a secretary and had wanted to know if I'd like to rejoin CRY. I took up the offer, saying that I would be in a position to rejoin services w.e.f. 20th of June '94. This was the third time I was to serve the same organisation. The second time when I had done so, Baba had given the message that I should rejoin CRY where I'd be on my father's lap – Rippan's lap. And for the two years that I worked there, it had indeed been so. Now that father and friend of mine was no more.

A few days later when I called up Vanita at CRY, she informed me that there was a slight change in my reappointment. It was a decision taken by the Managing Committee of CRY that I be appointed in the Head Office to assist V. S. Srinivasan, the Distribution Manager. (Srini and I had no issues working together. It had always been a great working relationship.)

I was happy at the prospect of once again working in CRY – the only place where I always felt at home (after Mazda Services), regardless of the working conditions.

Naturally, Rippan's death left me feeling sad and worried at rejoining CRY without having him around. But fortunately, I found remarkable colleagues and bosses to work with. For the next decade that I worked with CRY, I made many wonderful friends – Leela Alvares, Sangeeta Kapila, Pervin Varma, Puja Marwaha and Sandeep Donde – and my interaction with all of them became lasting friendships. My stay at CRY became one full of happy experiences.

The Lord Removing the Husk of Maya from My Very Being

The day after my friend's passing away, I decided to attend the bhajans at Pushpa Kunj at Churchgate where Sathya Sai bhajans were held every Monday. What a blissful state I found myself in during the bhajans, particularly so, when my Lord answered my plea to let me know how to have my mind under control and remain unruffled in all situations in life. In response He blessed me with a vision of Himself taking upon the job of cleaning a plateful of wheat, by carefully removing the husk that still lay stuck on some of the grains as also the little pebbles that were present among the grains! Yes, all that I had to do was to clean my mind of all maya – of worldly ties and attachments to make it a worthy offering to the Lord.

This vision was an eye opener and I was my own self once again, the happy joyous person who carried on with her work with a smile on her face and looked forward to the forthcoming short trip to my Lord in the month of May, prior to rejoining CRY.

Media Reports on Rippan's Contribution to the Society

On 14th April '94, a prayer meeting was held at the CRY office in Rippan's memory. And, I knew I had to attend it out of respect for the departed soul. Each of the speakers had something nice to say, and whatever we all heard was not without the moistening of the eye and the swelling of the heart. But very often my mind was diverted to the dream I had had that morning, a dream in which Rippan had appeared to me for the first time after his passing away. I found myself being escorted by Rippan into a cab. On our way I enquired about our destination, whereupon he simply replied that each one's destination solely depended on the driver! The cab came to a sudden halt at a railway station. He alighted from it and so did I, after collecting my luggage, which was just a small plastic bag. To my surprise, Rippan had assumed a huge form! How tall he looked beside me as he firmly grasped my hand and walked with me! And he requested me to let him carry my luggage. After allowing him to do so for a little while, my heart would not permit me to let him carry my luggage. Because, to my amazement I saw that tall man bend completely under the weight of my little bag that contained my Volumes of the series of 'A Glimpse of Joy'. The same bag, the minute I forcibly took back and carried it myself, appeared very light to me. Very quietly and with ease I bore the weight. Now we came to a huge hall which he said was the waiting room for all the passengers who wanted to travel. Leaving me all alone in the waiting room, he went into the inner chambers where I was not permitted to follow him. But I could still see him from afar as, unlike the others, I could at least walk up to the gate of the inner chambers and peep in whenever I liked. From where he now stood, Rippan comforted me by saying, "You need not fear of having been left alone. While you spend your time in the waiting room, there shall be someone or the other to hold your hand and be with you till such time that you enter the inner chambers, which is possible only at the opportune time." With that the dream ended.

One night, almost a month after his passing away, when he had once again appeared to me in a dream, he told me, "Khurshid, if you wish to visit me, the only one who seems to be in possession of my visiting card with my own signature on it is Rajashree Bansiwar. Hence, if you wish to have a glimpse of me, you may go and see what she is doing." "Rippan, it's nice of you to come to me on and often but just in case I wish to contact you, how do I go about it?" I asked. (In the dream I was well aware of his having passed away and my talking to his soul.) He simply replied, "O for me to get in touch with you or anybody else for that matter is very easy but if you wish to contact me, you can do so only by burning your cloth." Understanding the implications of his words fully well, I was taken aback and told him in a shocked voice, "But I don't wish to burn the cloth (my body) just yet even if it means not being able to reach out to you. Why, it's so simple instead to call out to my Baba who immediately responds to my call. I'd prefer to continue to do that. You may as and when you like, come to me to guide me." The next moment he was out of sight – and the dream ended.

Friends, Rajashri Bansiwar whom Rippan had referred to in the above dream was an ex-employee of CRY. While at CRY she had been the Head of Development Support Division. Now she had started a project of her own which directly worked with the underprivileged children.

That morning the prayer meeting that I attended at the office was one of the best prayer meetings I had attended till then. Hundreds had gathered at the office and many expressed their feelings beautifully. And before I end the chapter of my life that concerns my dear friend who is no more, I'd like to pen down one of the beautiful articles that came in the news. The Indian Express dated 15th April '94, carried the article mentioned below:

Quote:

'Rippan's 'magic' worked wonders for CRY'

All that it needed was just Rs. 50 and a strong initiative that worked as the driving force in setting up CRY – Child Relief and You – and helping the underprivileged children see a ray of hope. And the man who took this initiative to make people aware of the injustice of poverty, to suggest ways in which to remove it, and to encourage concrete action was Rippan Kapur. He died on Sunday in Mumbai at the young age of 40 and the poor children have lost a friend.

"What I want to do, I must do," he used to say. And he used to respond to every cry in the dark. He was a man who shunned publicity when he was alive. He used to say that this helped him to focus on the betterment of children. He wanted to live a long life so that he would be able to help more and more needy children but the untimely death has left his life's mission unfulfilled.

Raising funds is no child's play, and that too for a noble cause needed real talent. Rippan Kapur had this inborn talent and he had a soft corner for the helpless. This was quite evident even from his school days when he used to read to the blind children and teach slum-dwellers.

From day one he faced paucity of funds. Just the will power to help the needy is not sufficient, it should be backed up by monetary resources, he used to feel. He soon realised that the work of the welfare agencies was constantly hampered for lack of funds and this forced him to think, "Why not raise funds?" And once the thought struck him, there was no looking back.

In 1978 he got six of his friends together at his Mumbai home and collected Rs. 50 and started CRY. And now among the countless human beings in whose lives he made a profound difference with his dreams and actions, are also 5,00,000 children all over India.

Fifteen years ago when he was setting up CRY, Rippan said, "We recognise that on one hand, there are many people who have the means and the skills to help less fortunate children, but feel overwhelmed by the magnitude of the problem, by the feeling that they cannot do very much as individuals. And on the other hand are the many agencies doing things to help children, but who are constantly strapped for man-power, funds and infrastructure.

CRY responded to the cry for help from the needy and channelized money and skilled personnel for agencies and projects that needed them in their work for the children. And they banked on those who had the resources.

Rallying people for a cause was Rippan's ambition and he had the knack for inspiring sincerity and selflessness among others. Thanks to Rippan, CRY today draws the selfless commitment and skills of innumerable professionals from fields as diverse as architecture, art and music.

But it was not devoid of heart-burns. When CRY was started Rippan's dining table at home served as an office. But things were not the same in the coming years. Rippan used to say that the biggest problem he faced was not funds but space. Since its inception the employees in CRY had been leading a bohemian existence. They had to move to more than a dozen places, working in people's homes, garages, terraces and warehouses, trying somehow to keep the outfit alive.

It is only in December 1993, when he was prodded about the future of CRY that Rippan hesitantly said, 'In the coming years a few more thousands would be brought into its fold and, against all odds, it will continue to respond to the thought that there was a child somewhere crying for help'. Rippan has left behind a dream with wings to fly. And it is left for the others to take the cue.

Unquote

Yes, dear friends, after reading the above mentioned article on Rippan and CRY, I prayed to the Lord that his soul rest in peace, and that many more of us carry on with the work he has begun and contribute to the cause according to our fullest capacity.

7

Sai's Efforts at Improving My Spiritual Vision

Some Visions and a Dream Conveying My Guru's Proximity to Me

The joy I felt at the divine visions of the Lord (in His different forms) that continued, though not as frequently as in Parthi and Bangalore, was calm and sustaining. Mostly they were momentary visions in the early hours of the morning just after waking up and sitting with eyes closed for a minute or so, trying to concentrate on the Lord as I couldn't dream of sitting still for longer than that period!

For instance, on the 28th April '94 before going to bed at night, I had a vision of Lord Krishna with Radha at His side.

On 2nd May '94 I had the Lord's vision not once but twice, within minutes of opening my eyes to greet the new day that dawned. The first time He smiled at me and seemed very pleased with me. In the second vision, His face appeared grave as He gave me a deep penetrating look. On 5th May '94 at 5 a.m., He appeared in my dream to bless me.

On 17th May '94, a day prior to my short trip to Whitefield, once again in a dream He let me know what it was to be like on this trip of mine. In the dream, I went and took a seat among Baba's college students so that I could be very close to the stage on which He sat majestically on His chair. When a volunteer rudely made me get up and go at the back, I was glad to do so because the raised platform of the stage completely blocked the view of the Lord seated there. (Perhaps the true meaning of the above incident was that those who seemed to be physically closest to the Lord need not have necessarily gained the opportunity to experience His divinity.) To my surprise, the same volunteer forced me to leave my next seat as well and ordered me to sit further away, right at the back. Without a word, accepting it all as the Lord's Will, I took my seat. Now I had a clear view of my Lord but it didn't satisfy me since I was too far away to be able to make out the expression on His face or to know whether He could see me or not. The very next moment He turned His face in my direction and as time ticked by, it began to grow larger in size. It appeared as if I were looking through a magnifying glass and found Him getting closer and closer to me until He had assumed a form huge enough to cover the universe and I saw nothing but Him wherever my eyes turned!

Verena Huber's Expression of Selfless Love

Unfortunately, my dear Nargish Aunty could not accompany me on this trip. On my way to Bangalore, Jyoti joined me. (She was Nargish Aunty's acquaintance who lived in Sholapur.) She had a desire to have Baba's darshan but could not afford the expense. Hence Yasmin Aunty (who always went out of her way to help others in need) had sponsored her trip. This time I received a warm welcome from Krishnabai, Nagmani's mother and the rest of her family. (Friends, for those of you who may not recollect who Namani is, let me introduce her to you. It was at Nagmani's house at Whitefield that I had earlier stayed for months on end, at an extremely nominal rent that I could afford to pay. At that point in time, Krishnabai had resented the idea of my inability to pay a more decent rent.) Today, it felt like I was home again though it was not the same without my dear, innocent Nagmani who now stayed with her in-laws. Now, Krishnabai was very cooperative and allowed Jyoti and me to use her kitchen to cook our own meals.

Once in a while I invited my dear friend Verena Huber (the German lady who permanently stayed in the ashram) to lunch. It made me so happy to talk to her, to accept her priceless gifts of beautiful photos of Baba, photos of my choice. One incident that is still etched in my memory I now share with you.

Once I made the mistake of adding salt twice to the meal that I had prepared. It had clearly become unpalatable. Since Verena preferred to eat early and I wasn't hungry as yet, I had not joined her for lunch. Much later when I got to know of my error and was myself unable to eat beyond the first morsel, I was full of remorse and apologised to her the next day. "You are a good cook. So what if by error you put extra salt? You had prepared it with so much love and I would never dream of ever wasting the food. I come to you not for lunch but to hear you talk about the teachings the Lord imparts to you via dreams. And let me tell you that I love you a lot."

Dear Verena, if you happen to read this book, I'd like you to know that I've always had the highest respect and regard for you. Thank you for your friendship.

A Vision of Mother Earth being Held by Baba

As before, I was still as lazy and meditated on Him for not more than a minute or two. Yet, in His mercy He continued to bless me with beautiful visions during that short span of time while I sat still, not so much trying to meditate on Him as to wait for Him to appear to me with a message!

The vision I had then was of devotees, one at a time, offering an empty plate to the Lord. Feeling sad for Him and knowing that being His child I owed Him whatever was within my capacity, I offered Him a tray full of sweets, from which He in turn picked out one with a yellow wrapper (a mango sweet) and placed it into my hand as prasad. He distributed the rest of the sweets to the large gathering of devotees.

There was no way I could interpret the above vision but one thing that made me very happy was that within hours of the vision, the multitude gathered there after darshan were given a mango each as prasad from Baba!

For the next two days the Lord ignored me completely as He walked past me during darshan, without even so much as a glance in my direction. Well, He made up for the seeming indifference by blessing me with a beautiful vision during bhajans. Baba holding a miniature form of mother earth (continuously rotating) between His forefinger and thumb.

Pleas from Friends to Intercede to Baba on their Behalf

On 24th May '94 as I opened my eyes at 5 a.m. I remembered the dream that I had just had and I shivered. In the dream, I had seen myself floating about in the air over places such as Bangalore, Mumbai and even other unknown places, where I came across a number of people calling out my name. I heard their pleas but was too scared to go any nearer because among them I saw my Kainaz Aunty (name changed), who time and again called out to me piteously. Perhaps she was in trouble and wanted to contact me, but I, somehow knew for sure that I would be in no position to lessen her pain and hence just moved on, ignoring her pleas.

A few days after this dream, when dad called me up at Nagmani's place, he informed me that Kainaz Aunty's husband was struggling between life and death and that it was Aunty's wish that I pray to Baba for his recovery. It was only then that I understood why in the dream, she had been trying to contact me. It was sheer torture for her to see her husband suffer so. The very fact that in the dream I had been desperate to get away from her instead of hurting her sentiments by saying that in no way would I be able to help her, meant that he would be dying shortly.

For instance, a dear friend of mine appeared to me so often not merely in dreams, but in visions as well, in order to complain about the problems in her marriage. She turned to me for help and the trust in her eyes was overpowering. In visions, she kept repeating that she would ring the bell in the Lord's temple without intermission until He heard her cry. How very unbelievable I found these dreams and visions to be (that she herself was unaware of), considering the fact that whenever I met her in person, she always said that all was well between her husband and herself. Almost a month or two later I did come to know from the couple (each one individually) that what I had seen in the dreams and visions was right.

Baba's Indication about His Prema Sai Avatar

On 28th May '94 at 1.30 a.m., I woke up immediately after the following dream: Baba was expected to appear before the devotees to grant them darshan. As He passed by, without as much as a glance in my direction, I cried out in sheer agony before He could move out of sight, "Baba, don't go away." My Lord turned to look straight into my eyes, His own eyes red and swollen and brimming with tears as though expressing His helplessness and feeling compelled to ignore me in public. He walked up to me and lay down on the bare ground right before me. I held on to His lotus feet and He addressed me very softly in sad tones, "Now you may hear me talk during the Prema Sai Avatar. Let that be made public in the newspapers." Did His words imply that He found it impossible to accede to my request to talk to me during His lifetime as Sathya Sai? I complained plaintively, "O Baba, if you go away from me now and I wait for you till your Prema Sai Avatar, it will be so long a period that I shall grow old by then." I was not able to tolerate the idea that all my life He would not talk to me. The dream ended.

Baba Blesses My Book on Bhajans during Public Darshan

The next day, not merely in a dream, but actually during darshan, Baba blessed my bhajan book, but did it very discreetly in a way that it went unnoticed by the others sitting by my side. As I stretched out my hand, He continued to ignore me as before and stood talking to the lady on my left, giving her vibhuti that He had created. Just when my heart was crying out at not being fortunate enough to be acknowledged for my written composition, He gave a knock at my book on which His hand had been resting (palm upturned). He then sprinkled the left over vibhuti from His hand on to it, and at the same time continued to talk to the lady, without looking at me even for a moment.

Dear readers, I state with regret that while shifting residence I lost the original bhajan book that Baba had blessed. It contained bhajans in Hindi with English translations. However, fortunately, I had retained the Xerox copies of the Hindi bhajans (prior to editing) which are still with me.

Baba's Explanation on Why I Shouldn't Insist on Uncle Living a Long Life

It was a happy trip back home. Jyoti's ticket had been reserved in another bogie as she had to alight at Sholapur. But I didn't mind in the least bit travelling alone, as by now I was used to it. Sometime in the morning I had the most excruciating pain in my back. The slightest movement brought unbearable agony and tears to my eyes. I had to lie down. And then the breathing got choked. No amount of prayers to Baba proved effective. And after an hour or so, I knew for sure that I had to be shifted to a hospital if I wished to live. I was desperately in need of oxygen. When finally I was about to let the co-passengers shift me out of the train at the next station and see to my hospitalization, I fell fast asleep only to be questioned by the Lord in a dream. "If you were in the hospital in place of your uncle, bed-ridden and having to put up with this intolerable pain for the rest of your life, would you still wish that I grant you a long life?" (Here, He was referring to Kainaz Aunty's husband who lay in the hospital in utmost pain, with no hope of recovery.) "No, Baba, I am very sorry," I replied. The next moment the scene in the dream changed and I saw myself having a look at the calendar and told myself that it was 8th June '94 and all of us at home were dressed to attend the funeral rites of that uncle.

With that the dream came to an end and as I woke up in the train, miraculously I found myself relieved of all pain. (Actually uncle passed away on the 6th. As revealed in the above dream, my family attended the special prayers – Uthamna on the third day after his death i.e. 8th June '94. I knew it was as it should have been instead of having prolonged his suffering.)

"I'll Always Keep Coming to You," Baba Promised Me

There was a gnawing uneasiness that grew stronger and stronger as each day progressed. What had my Lord meant by saying that I would now hear Him only during His Prema Sai Avatar? Had He implied that He would stop appearing in my dreams and visions? If so, how would I bear that blow of separation for so long a period? But that was not to be my fate. My Lord knew my need for His constant presence in my life and appeared to me on 12th June '94. From the window of the car in which He was seated, He kept on peeping out at me every now and then with a mischievous smile playing on His lips, and He brought down the screen and looked at me one moment and elsewhere the next. This game He continued with me for a long while, enjoying Himself thoroughly. In a voice full of compassion, He finally addressed me, "I come to you. Yes, I'll always keep coming to you." A long pause and then in serious tones, He added, "What is the purpose of service? What is the meaning of life?" And the next moment His eyes were searching for Nargish Aunty or so I assumed. In sad tones, He said, "I miss her."

My Guru's Training to Me on Understanding the Higher and Nobler Purpose of Human Life

Though I have always heard devotees talk of Baba performing miracles such as materialising things from air, for me He never performed such feats / miracles which would have overawed me. Rather, as you must have noticed in these Volumes, He always interacted with me as a parent and tried to awaken the good in me and make me responsive to moral and spiritual obligations. He wanted me to understand that human life has a higher and nobler purpose and that the destiny of a human being is to move higher up in the cosmic order to reach perfection and to realise supreme bliss.

Baba again and again brought my consciousness back to the fact that it was indeed possible to become His image. And I found life taking on a totally new meaning and giving inspiration to me every day.

On 15th June '94 at 6.15 a.m., I had the following dream: "They deride Me, they laugh at Me, they are petulant, so what? I am here to make the cripple walk." Our dear Lord thus addressed the devotees gathered in thousands. Thereafter, fixing His gaze upon the lady sitting next to me, He said, "Come, get up, have faith and you shall walk again." "But Baba," she cried out, "I don't think I shall be able to walk again unless someone from this crowd moves and makes way for me. How do you expect me to rise without the help and co-operation from one of these people here?" Without a moment's hesitation I made an effort to give her the extra space she needed by shifting myself to an even more cramped position than before since I didn't wish to inconvenience anyone else on my account. This provided the lady with an opportunity to get to her feet. Not that she was strong as before but could at least once again manage on her own – and that was some consolation. Now I turned to Baba, whose eyes were fixed on me with a note of appreciation in them! As I held out my hands to Him, He caught them firmly and in very gentle, loving tones said, "There is an improvement in this eye." While saying these words He had pressed His finger upon the centre of my forehead. Once again He held my outstretched hands and said, "You have to rise. You have to rise some more. Like this, like this, like this." While saying so, He pulled my hands upward by an inch or so each time and His own fingers loosened the grip on my hands. Gradually, by gestures of His own hands, i.e. by raising His upturned divine hands a little at a time, He conveyed that slowly and steadily I had to continue to rise, that it was to be a gradual process.

To rise little by little would be possible. One of the ways by which I'd really know if I was progressing spiritually would be to analyse myself honestly. My consciousness was still not completely engrossed in communion with God and in love and concern for my fellowmen. Therefore, I had to admit that I still had a long way to go on the spiritual path.

My dear guru encouraged me to strive to lift up my consciousness to divinity little by little. He wanted me to keep striving to improve myself.

Baba Expects Me to Abstain from Food Once a Week

On 24th July '94 in a dream I told my Lord, "Baba, don't ever stop coming to me in my dreams." Hearing my heartfelt appeal, He placed His hands into mine and held them in a firm grip and in order to let me fulfil my wish of touching His feet, He left my hands. As I bent low to touch His feet, He lightly touched my head in a gesture of blessing and assured me of His never-failing love by softly saying, "No, I shall not stop coming to you in your dreams." My next prayer to Him was a silent one in which I questioned Him as to why there was any need for me to go hungry once a week (since fruits and curds I could not afford on the days that He expected me to fast) to which He answered, "You have also to think of those poverty stricken people all around. Try to see life from their point of view too." Perhaps He wanted me to spare a thought for those who couldn't even afford two square meals a day.

My guru had built on my faith in Him. In spite of what I'd have liked to believe, He had time and again confirmed that I never need worry on losing His love. He had unconditionally accepted me. Of course, He'd always keep His promise and continue to hold my hand.

Baba Advised Me to bring My Temper Under Control and be More Humble

When on 7th August '94 Jasmine (my sister) opened a book at random seeking an answer to her query which was, "Isn't Khurshid bossy?" the words my sister's eyes fell on were, "I shall sweeten her tongue." And right enough to put me in my place, He passed on the message to me, though in a humorous way, so that I shouldn't take it too badly.

The dream of 5.15 a.m. on 8th August '94 was as follows: Among the crowd I had taken my place and awaited the Lord's darshan. To my surprise I found myself sitting far away from the rest. Moreover, it was not on the floor but on a high pedestal more than eight feet in height! To my embarrassment, my Lord in His human form at five feet stood at the foot of the pedestal, His one hand stretching out in my direction in order to bless me. But the height I had placed myself on was such that it was beyond His reach! My predicament could well be understood. If I did not want to miss this beautiful opportunity of being blessed by the Lord, I had to do away with the barrier of my own creation. The Lord was aware of my repentance, and came to my aid by immediately materialising a ladder for me to climb down. A few hurried steps on my part brought me to the lowest rung of the ladder from which I jumped to the floor and stood before my Lord with folded palms. Our guru regarded me with silent compassion. He said, or rather it came as a statement more than a question, "You are happy." "Yes Baba, I am happy. May I touch your feet?" Before He could give me His approval, I bent low and was about to touch His feet when He took a few steps backwards and gently said, "You should always be happy." After hesitating for a long time, finally when I gathered enough courage, I asked Him, "Baba, are you angry with me?" And He softly enquired,

"What makes you think that way? No, I'm not angry." Now He went on to give me some sound advice of which all I could remember on waking up the next morning was, "Khurshid, you should control your temper. Controlling one's temper makes a lot of difference in one's family life, career..." (On waking up, I couldn't recall the rest of His counsel).

My guru then vanished from sight and the dream came to an end, leaving me to my tears and reflections. I was full of remorse at the thought of the trouble our Lord had to take to bring my flaws to my notice.

Only humility could help me get rid of my ego. To be a disciple was to surrender. Every experience would then become my guru. But no amount of experience could help me realise my mistakes unless I cultivated and adopted the humility required to be able to surrender myself. If I had claimed that I had completely surrendered to God and was full of humility, the dream had proved it otherwise. There was still a lot of ego in me. My belief in my own humility was only exaggerated, a cover.

Ego issues, if not handled with care, could create problems in my personal, social and professional life. Hence for better relationships, it was very important for me to understand and handle the ego – both of my self and of others. Humility had to be surrender of my self, of heart, mind and soul. I needed to completely surrender at the feet of the Divine. Humility was necessary if I wanted the Divine grace to pour on me.

When I injured others with words the bond of friendship broke. Even if the relationship could be mended there was a possibility of knots remaining there. Of course, I did not have to be afraid to speak the truth but I had to be sensitive in my words. If I caused pain to any human heart, I could not aspire for a place in His heart. So I resolved to keep my temper under control at all costs.

Just when I was wondering whether Baba was aware of my conscious effort to be humble and calm, on 15th August '94 He appeared to me with a strange message. In all humility He said softly, "Thank you very much, Khurshid." It was so unexpected and strange that no words would form in response. Moreover, it humbled me to hear Him talk in that manner.

Baba's Intimation of Remorse on the Part of a Child of His

A week after the Parsi New Year, in a dream, Baba wished me a Happy New Year. And He puzzled me even more by later on assuming the form of an acquaintance who addressed me in a tone full of remorse, "I admit it was my anger that had come in my way." Once again Baba was His own self.

And within hours of the above mentioned dream, the postman delivered greetings from the lady in the dream who had earlier on not been on talking terms with us!

Sainath's Assurance of Coming to Receive Me unto Him when the Time Came

Coming back to where I had left off, I now pen down the dream I had on 13th September '94, in response to my prayer of the previous night that He should let me know if He would ever come to my house in His physical form and sit and talk to me at least once during this life of mine. The dream at 6.30 a.m. was as follows: I found myself lying on the floor, with dad and mum sitting at either side of mine. My body seemed lifeless. Just then my Lord entered our room, stood watching over me and raised His hands in a gesture of blessing me. From His divine hands flowed rose petals in abundance until my full body was covered with them. And with that the dream came to an end. On waking up, I prayed to Him to make it more clear for me to be able to understand what He was trying to say by that message of His.

Within half an hour (7 a.m.), I was fast asleep and He appeared in my dream once again. The dream was exactly the same to the minutest detail with the exception of one addition to it at the end. Once again the rose petals were flowing from His divine hands and as before it covered my body completely. Then my Lord started rising into the air and from above (He was floating in the air close to the ceiling) now it was ash (instead of rose petals) that flowed from His hands right on to my body until my full body was covered with those ashes. By these two above-mentioned dreams, He had conveyed to me that I would have to wait for Him till the final moments of my life.

To Visualise Him in all Humanity is what He Wished of Me

On 17th September '94 in a dream, Baba was moving among the devotees and as He walked towards me, I made a silent prayer, "Baba, do come to me too as you move among the rest. Have I not waited long enough? Don't I deserve to get padnamaskar?" The next moment He stood right before me and to my utter confusion and bafflement I saw His usual orange robe vanish into thin air and all that His body was covered with was a nappy that little children are made to wear! It was with great difficulty that I was able to contain my tears. I was just not willing to accept Him in any other than His usual robes. Just when I was about to cry out in anguish He stopped me by saying, "It doesn't matter if my old dress has flown away, does it?" My eyes brimming with tears, I bowed down and touched His feet, telling myself, "Yes, as He says, it shouldn't matter what dress He wears, I have to see the God within, however difficult it may seem."

My dear guru wished me never to become attached to or dependent on His limited human form. He wanted me to love and seek Him in all humanity. He might have been hinting at my future with Sunbeam which was to be an NGO (my brain child) catering to the needs of underprivileged children. He wished me to visualise Him in the child beneficiaries.

Visions of the Lord in His Krishna and Shiva Avatars

On 19th September '94, before I could go to sleep, I was blessed with a lovely vision of a searchlight frantically moving from one place to the other looking out for something in the darkness all around. It suddenly stopped at one point, to reveal the most angelic face of little baby Krishna!

In a dream on 22nd September '94 upon telling Baba that my vision was not good, He simply replied in mock worry, "What a big problem!"

The lovely visions continued and on 1st October '94 I found myself going into ecstasy upon having before my eyes the divine form of Lord Shiva with His consort, Parvati. And the same vision repeated itself the next day when I sat to pray for a minute or so.

"I've Held Your Hand throughout Your Life," Baba Reassured Me

The dream on 3rd October '94 revealing something about my life was as follows: Barefooted, I trekked the streets in the hot sun. After a while, I took up speed, and began to run as fast as my feet could carry me. I had taken the same direction as those of others, only the mode of travel differed. They were having a comfortable ride in their cars, autos, scooters or cycles. In the scorching heat, I continued with my journey without a moment's rest until I reached a point of exhaustion where I had to walk on all fours as the road had an upward slope and my feet didn't have enough stamina left in them. During the journey, I soiled my palms as I passed through big muddy water puddles. Eventually, when I found myself at the gate of my Lord's ashram, it occurred to me that I'd have to wash my hands clean before making my entrance. After washing them, I entered the grounds and took the only place available, far at the end awaiting my Lord's darshan. Something strange came to my notice. On the lifeline on my palm, there were cuts and bruises and at the end of it, was a tiny miniature form of a sealed envelope stuck on it! The wound at the end of the lifeline just above the envelope bled profusely and I pressed my thumb of the other hand on it to check the flow until I could have my Lord's darshan. The minute my eyes fell on the form of my Lord who had come to give darshan, I managed to pull away the sealed envelope from my palm, and handed it over to someone sitting to my left. Now I felt free and no more tried to cover the wound but let the blood gush forth as I looked at my Lord moving among the devotees. My Lord's robe had changed colour from orange to grey.

Now the scene changed and I saw the Lord coming out for darshan from the temple grounds. The way He clutched at the shawl around His body and yet shivered gave me the impression that He was unwell. As the devotees grabbed at His feet, He gently addressed one by pointing out to me, "My dear child, there is this girl who is waiting patiently for me and it would be so nice if all awaited their turn like she does." Then He walked up to me. Though unsure of being granted the request, I made it all the same, "Baba, may I hold your hand for a while?" From the pained expression on His face, it was clear that my question seemed to have hurt Him as He replied, "But my dear, I have been holding your hand throughout your life. Not for a moment have I left your hand. Yet, if you actually want to place your hand into mine physically, here you are." So saying, He stretched out His hand to me. I clasped it firmly. Love poured from His eyes and I experienced bliss at the assurance I had just received from Him. Now I asked Him, "May I kiss your hand?" His spontaneous response in a tender voice was, "Of course, you may." After kissing the divine hands of my Lord, I removed my glasses and pressed them on to my eyes. With that the dream came to an end.

Yes, my Lord had always held my hand. He had always given me company. It was I who was away from Him, because my mind was too busy fighting for the little self, 'I am misunderstood, I am unloved.' If my life was unhappy it was because I was giving insufficient attention to Him and did not do enough meditation.

How could I ever accuse Him of inattentiveness towards me? He had always held my hand, never once left it. I was fortunate to have been blessed with such an intimate relationship with the Divine and had to strive to be mentally and spiritually in tune with my dear guru.

Our Guru's Guidance on Personal Matters Relating to My Dad and Brother

Suddenly we found ourselves in a situation that demanded wise, rational yet sensitive decisions. Peshotan requested that he and Nandini be allowed to shift to our Charni Road home and that mum and dad move to his premises at Virar, in the suburbs of Mumbai where he and Nandini currently stayed. Though he was justified in the first part of his request since staying at Virar meant daily travel of 2½ hours in overcrowded trains which left him with little time for personal life, the second part of the decision (to me) seemed unfair on dad. As for the worst consequence if this request were to be considered – that of dad having to leave his job, Peshotan's patient explanation to me was as follows: "Nandini would be able to work and supplement my income, leaving dad free to have a peaceful retired life that he fully deserves instead of having to work at this age."

My own perspective on the matter slightly differed from his. I was of the opinion that dad ought not to be made to quit his job because of his age, especially when he had immense job satisfaction where he currently worked for the Banajee Trust; just at 61 it would have made him feel aged overnight. Besides, putting in his resignation would have meant giving up his economic independence. He and mum would have had to completely rely on us for financial support since he had no savings of his own. Sudden withdrawal from his full time job could have resulted in accelerating the process of an unhappy ageing. Dad was still physically fit, so it would have been unfair on our part to expect him to quit his job, I reiterate, especially when he enjoyed his work.

In order not to put Peshotan to the inconvenience of having to travel long distance in overcrowded trains and understanding that his daughter-in-law who hailed from Delhi was not used to commuting in overcrowded Mumbai trains, dad took a tough decision. He resolved to resign from his job and shift to Virar with mum. Luckily, Mr. Alpaiwala, the Chairman of the Charitable Trust where dad worked, did not accept his resignation. Moreover, Baba too intervened.

On 3rd December '94, for the first time in his life, yes, for the first time in his entire life, dad had a dream of Sathya Sai Baba. (This was just before he could put in his resignation for the second time and perhaps, out of exasperation, the Chairman might have even accepted it this time.) These are the exact words of my dad as he related his dream to me, "Khurshid, Baba appeared to me in a dream. At first I saw Him sitting in our room hearing out Peshotan and answering his queries, though I don't remember any of the conversation they had had. But I vividly remember what took place next. As I entered the room and was about to say something to Baba, He turned to me, and said along with gestures of His forefinger, 'You go on working. You go on working.' So Khurshid, don't stop me from carrying on with my job even if it means that I have to travel from Virar daily i.e. from the suburbs of Mumbai. Having given my word to my son that we shall move to Virar and that he and Nandini can come and stay at Charni Road, I have no option but to travel from Virar instead of my son doing so. This new development is in view of Baba's command that I can't quit my job." It tore my heart apart to hear him say so; not that Peshotan would have ever let our father travel that distance but I felt that now the situation had become even more complex than before with dad not willing to disclose Baba's dream to Peshotan.

My brother had full faith in my faith in Baba so he requested me to check it out with Him as to what was His will in the matter. The most natural and effective form of prayer for me has always been informal conversation with God. In my silent prayer to Him before going to bed, I told Him that it was an emergency call. In a dream the same night, Baba appeared to me and let me know that my dear brother was soon to be transferred out of Mumbai.

The dream came true very soon and Peshotan got a transfer order from his company. In less than a month's time he and Nandini, his wife, moved out of Mumbai.

Friends, to me spiritual practice did not merely mean sitting in a lotus posture and meditating. It meant much more. It meant service to mankind, beginning with my own ageing parents – being a moral support to them and of course to continue to share the financial burden to whatever extent possible from my salary at CRY. My dear brother was there to supplement my income when I couldn't manage on my own, thus leaving dad free to save his own salary.

Before I move on to the next incident of my life, I take pride in sharing that dad dutifully served the Banajee Trust for almost another decade where he found fulfilment of his dream of being useful to the society.

He Desired that I be at the Driving Wheel with My Vision Fixed on Him Alone

On 25th November '94, I prayed to the Lord thus before going to sleep, "Baba, what makes you so strict with me as to punish me even for errors that seem to be insignificant to me? Why can't I enjoy life a bit by watching the television serials once in a while? At times I admit that my vision does shift to the world." The next morning in a dream I saw my Lord's car pass by me. Not receiving a glance from Him, made me sulk. And I was puzzled as to why He had been at the steering wheel with others at the back seat and wondered at the strangeness of it. The few of us upon whom His eyes had not rested stood feeling let down and I was surprised at my own voice ringing out loud and clear, "O you people, there is no reason for us to feel sad. By this action of His, He has passed on an important message to us. The one who is at the steering wheel is expected to keep his vision fixed ahead at the traffic on the road and not fail those seated in the vehicle, ones who rely on him/her for a safe journey to their destination. The driver can achieve that only by not getting distracted by anything on the way while performing his/her duty." What better answer could my Lord have given me than the one in this dream? I resolved not to let my mind waver anymore.

Sai Grants Me Permission to Allow Aban to Edit all My Books

On 11th December '94 the Lord appeared to me with some more messages. In the dream, among the devotees I found myself seated on one of the chairs arranged on both sides of the hall with our Lord on the stage. Because of the many obstacles in the way, I could not have the Lord's darshan. Putting in great effort, little by little I began to learn to sit straight instead of with the hunch. Finally, when I sat completely erect, did I gain the Lord's darshan. The lady sitting next to me said, "All of a sudden you seem to have become taller than the rest. Isn't that strange?" To my surprise, I found that to be a fact and replied somewhat puzzled, "To be very frank, I was myself totally unaware of my height increasing. All that I can remember doing is putting in an effort to sit straight even at the cost of severe exhaustion because my sole aim was to be rewarded by the Lord's darshan." As my Lord came and stood before me, my lips moved though no sound came, "Thank you, Baba." And He replied almost in a whisper, "Happy, very happy." He really seemed pleased with me. As He now walked away, I noticed the small tumbler of water that He held in His hand from which He sprinkled the water on His devotees. The moment He left the hall, the crowd dispersed. Now as He re-entered, I counted myself very fortunate to be the only one in His presence. (The full conversation that took place between the two of us now was in Gujarati.) "Baba, will my vision become all right?" I asked Him doubtfully. Very gently, in His usual loving tones the reply was, "Yes, your vision will become all right, it will still improve further." (Actually, my eyesight was becoming poorer by the day and it was much later I understood that He was referring to my spiritual sight.) "Baba, may I hand over my book for editing to Aban?" The Lord appeared a trifle unsure as to whether she would be able to cope up with the assignment and said, "But does she know to write?" "Yes, I think so, since I have seen her drafting letters in the office," I replied rather baffled at His question. My Lord was smiling away mischievously as He said very softly, "In that case, you may let her edit the books for you." In order to clarify further I asked Him, "Baba, do you wish me to give her the complete matter for editing? The entire set of volumes? What I mean to know is if it's OK to hand over to her every page of what I have typed which includes all your messages to me till date i.e. all that I have mentioned in my book till date?" He assured me in the same soft, loving tones, "Yes, you may give her the entire text, every single thing that I have told you till date." For long He stood before me, looking me straight in the eye and with a smile, He departed.

Persistent Effort in Order to be Blessed by His Close and Frequent Darshan

Baba continued to bless me with darshans and messages in dreams and the next time He appeared to me was on 22nd December '94 at 6.30 in the morning. A large crowd sat facing a huge wall that ran for miles at length. Upon inquiring with one of them, the response I received was, "We are sitting for the Lord's darshan. If He wants to grant us darshan, let Him walk up to us since we are not going to budge from our places or take the trouble to walk the long distance that those few people over there have covered." I looked to where she pointed and decided to move there in the hope of finding an entry to the temple and thereby the Lord's darshan. For the time being I let my friends be with the crowd, thinking that it would not be right to take them along since I was myself unsure of my success. As I walked the long distance and finally reached the small group seated there, I was glad to notice that one of the windows of the Lord's temple was open. Someone remarked, "We are blessed with His darshan whenever He passes by this window."

Not one to be satisfied with mere glimpses of His, craving to have His darshan every moment of my life, I continued with what appeared to be a never-ending journey until I finally reached the temple gate that was wide open. Only a few people had managed to reach here and there was adequate space for me to sit in the front. Now I thought it was time to call out to my friends who still sat with the large gathering facing the bare wall. My voice failed to reach them. And I tried to draw their attention by gestures. The results were instant. They came running at top speed without stopping on their way till they reached the gate and took a step more than me by getting closer to the Lord who now stood at the gate with a smile on His face.

My Guru's Gentle Reminder to Keep My Commitment to Jasmine

On 26th December '94 at 3 o'clock in the morning, He once again appeared in my dream. "What are you doing? Why are you asking for some of this? At the moment I am distributing it to those whom it is meant for. Why should I give you kumkum just yet?" He said it not so much out of anger but it was clear that my actions had irritated Him. I had already collected a bit of kumkum that had spilled from His palms, so I begged of His forgiveness and stood aside, making way for Him to go and give it to the others. Full of remorse, I stood quietly until my Lord came back to me and gently asked me, "What would you like to have from me?" In a barely audible voice, I replied with a view to give an explanation of my action that seemed to have displeased Him, "Baba, it's not as though I wanted kumkum. Kumkum as such has no value for me. If I did take it, it was only because it was lying in your palm and anything touched by you becomes invaluable for me. It is a thing very sacred which I would treasure utmost." After hearing me out, He gently placed His arm around my waist and took me to a cloth shop where He went and asked for the material that belonged to Him. The man at the counter produced a beautiful cloth material. I did not have any desire for material things from the Lord, hence, I addressed Him thus, "No, no, Baba, I have no need of such things. If you wish to give me something then give me any little thing blessed by your divine touch." Now He left me to move up to Jasmine whom He held by the waist and escorted her to the same shop. He purchased the material and presented it to her. With that the dream ended.

The above dream was just a simple reminder from the Lord to keep my commitment to Jasmine to begin purchasing / saving for all the household items that she would require to set up her own home after her marriage.

The Book on Divine Knowledge – Mother Saraswati's Blessings

The dream on 27th December '94 was as follows: An aunt of mine questioned me, "Of what use is all your writing? Will it serve any purpose?" "Well, Mother Saraswati opened Her eyes and cast upon me Her loving glance. This is the message I am trying to convey through this book," I replied. Her next question was, "How are we to believe you unless She looks in our direction as well?" In response to that query, I led the crowd to Mother Saraswati's temple where She stood awaiting us. As I ran to Her, to my great joy She pulled me even closer to Her and assisted me in climbing the few steps in order that I be able to stand facing Her. She helped me move to Her left to make way for the next person who approached Her. Upon each individual She cast Her loving glance, helped him/her rise and then requested them to make way for the others. Perhaps through this dream my Lord had tried to say that each individual would in some way benefit by reading the books in which Aban and I had put so much of time and energy.

For Once I Fail to Notice the Love He Showers on Me

That night in a dream, I found myself standing at the door of the train in which I travelled. Another train from the opposite direction crossed mine. I waved out to all the passengers in that train. They happened to be my family members, friends, colleagues, relatives and acquaintances. To my disappointment, not one of them waved back at me. Not a single person acknowledged my presence or gave a smile of recognition in return. I called out in despair, "Is there no one who can give me a smile?"

My Lord's answer came in the form of a dream that Aban had had the same morning. Let me quote her words, "Khurshid, the two of us were travelling by bus. At one of the signals our bus had halted. You were busy saying something to me when my sight fell on Baba who stood on the road, smiling at us and waving out to us. Upon asking you if you recognised Him, you gave Him a mere glance and without taking much notice of Him, carried on with your talk."

Via the above dream of Aban's, my love for the Lord had been proved so fragile that by mistakenly thinking that He had forsaken me, I in turn had actually forsaken Him. If I wished to receive unconditional love from Him, I also ought to be willing to return that kind of love.

Baba gives Me a Glimpse of the Effect My Books will have on the Readers

On 28th February '95 I was blessed with a vision of Shirdi Sai and He once again appeared the next morning, this time in a dream and in the Sathya Sai form. Our Lord stood at a distance, handing over to one and all a copy of the book from the hundreds that lay displayed on a table. The minute the crowd dispersed I walked up to Him. My prayer to Him was "My Lord, I'd like to have a glimpse of the effect my Volumes of 'A Glimpse of Joy' would have on those who will read it." The scene before my eyes changed.

I elbowed my way through a thick crowd of people gathered at the gate of a sports ground eagerly watching the happenings within. Curiosity got the better of me and I proceeded inside to gain a better view. Each contestant took a long jump and the distance covered indicated their progress. The person in charge of measuring the distance gave out the results. Nearby, a cameraman stood clicking shots and I moved away hastily, only to his amusement as he chuckled, "In spite of your best efforts of trying not to come into the focus of my lens, in the background of each successful contestant will be your reflection."

As regards the effect my book would bring about on those who read it – I feel there would always be a few seekers who would profit by it; it would give them the necessary inspiration to take the leap in the direction of the Lord.

Sai Hinted that He Dwelled in My Maid as well

My aim in life is to reach my goal – my Lord; the surest way to it is to endeavour to see Him in one and all I come across. The time allotted for one's life passes off quite soon. So I have decided to be ever vigilant, ever alert not to hurt or displease my Lord dwelling in each individual, transforming every moment into a sacred interaction with God in his multiple human forms.

Sitting in the Prashanti grounds on the 5th of March '95 at 4 p.m., I made this silent prayer. "Baba, though I have promised to do so and am trying to acknowledge your presence in one and all, it does not stop me from demanding an occasional sign of love from you to assure me that I have not strayed and that you are always there by my side."

The incident that I am now about to quote is to underline how easy it is for Him to give us proof of the divinity in all. Moreover, it is also to stress His inexhaustible patience in dealing with me. It is because He allowed me such liberties (of demanding proofs and assurances) that I could continue treating Him as my dearest friend, besides accepting Him as my Guru and God. Always that which floated before my mind's eye was His compassion, His guidance at every step of my life. Nothing less could possibly have made me stake my all for one who, to all outward seeming, lived completely ignoring me so far as any contact between the two of us (on a physical plane) was concerned – and yet could inspire me with a deep sense of fulfilment.

My mind stopped wandering, worries fled, peace descended and an everlasting joy seemed to have taken possession of me. Nargish Aunty and I had put up at a lodge in Parthi. On 6th March '95 at 9.30 p.m., prior to going to bed, I had a strange vision of my Lord Sathya Sai approaching me in hurried steps. His hands were full of utensils which He was about to hand over to me when the shrill sound of the doorbell abruptly ended the vision. Very hesitantly I opened the door only to find our household help, Bhaubi, who stood gasping for breath at the doorstep with her hands full of utensils that she handed over to me and apologised for disturbing me at this late hour! It was all so very clear as I understood that my Lord had wished me to recognise the divinity in that dear lady who served us so dutifully.

Leading a Life of Service to Others was far More Important than Craving for Divine Visions

I had neither attained nor come anywhere close to a state of pure consciousness. Yet, during meditation I had so often been blessed with divine visions. This was simply His grace. More often than not when I closed my eyes to meditate on God, I was blessed with beautiful visions of His in His multiple forms. Thus meditation for whatever little time that I did at any time of the day helped me establish a relationship with God that in turn gave meaning to everything else in life.

Yet, there were times when I tried to bring before my mind's eye 'the flame' but in vain; nor would He bless me with His vision. These then turned out to be times full of frustration. I would endeavour to concentrate on Him as never before. At one point in time, I thought I saw a flicker of light, but I concluded it was just my mind playing tricks on me. I tried several more times to bring back that vision – then gave up. The more I persevered and met with failure, the deeper grew the gloom and the mental agony till, on 8th March '95, when I felt like one completely stranded, I prayed thus: "You talk of self-realisation and reaching the state of consciousness where I am at all times aware of my oneness with Divinity," my heart protested, "but it is something impossible without your help." After uttering this prayer I felt even worse – more depressed than ever which, in its turn, made me fear that this time He might be forced to give up on me. But it was not to be so.

My dear Lord – my parent and friend, continued in His effort to help me reach perfection. He blessed me with a vision of Himself the next morning. His smiling face stood clear before me as I sat in token lines with closed eyes. This was followed by a vision of the light, a steady flame that grew brighter and began to rise till it placed itself at the centre of my forehead. I lost all body consciousness and was enveloped in a state of bliss – of oneness with God, oneness with every living being on earth. The vision faded away after a minute or two.

Chanting the sacred gayatri mantra lifted me to a higher state of awareness. One morning while chanting the mantra, the Jyoti (flame) was clearly visible. But this was not all. The light slowly took the form of the symbol OM, bright in its splendour, as if the sun had changed its form to OM. All my gloom of not having had His vision since the past two days, vanished as though by magic.

As time marched on, I became progressively conscious of the fact that I need not give undue importance to these visions which were but signs of the grace of the Lord; what I was supposed to do was to simply live a life of good thoughts, good words and good deeds.

Baba never encouraged interest in visions or the desire for them. He made me realise that psychic power was not to be condemned in itself. It was the desire for it and preoccupation with it that would distract me from the true goal. When I was hoping for miracles, it was not God that I desired; I only wanted Him to prove Himself to me. Miraculous experiences were not necessarily evidence of spiritual progress. I had to also forego my desire for Him to prove Himself repeatedly.

Baba Blesses Me with a Vision of the Direct Link Between Him and the Divinity in Each of Us

Baba's greatest interest in me was to help me to realise consciously the link between my soul and God; between my soul and the God dwelling in all. The link was already there. My guru had taken it upon Himself to make me consciously aware of my oneness with Him and all of humanity. I suppose, that is why He blessed me with the most sacred vision on 16th March '95 at 7 a.m., the first of its kind, not only in a wakeful state but with wide open eyes as I sat in the darshan grounds.

My Lord entered the grounds for morning darshan. To my amazement and joy I saw the sun in all its splendour shining right on to His chest! The light emanating from there was blinding and I blinked time and again to make sure that I was not imagining things. Throughout the darshan wherever He moved – the vision continued. Later, as He moved towards where the gents were seated and His back was turned to us, I could still see the same blinding light – now on His back. Every time I shifted my gaze from Him to the devotees gathered around, I was stunned to see a beautiful flame right before each person. Never had I expected to actually see others as the spark of the Divine, the way I had just then. As I passed through this wonderful experience I could behold myself as well as everyone around me as Divine.

That morning long after my guru's darshan, my consciousness remained merged with Him. I had perceived Him as light and also the devotees in the form of light. Suddenly all delusions seemed to have got destroyed. My consciousness at that point in time was effortlessly identified not with the body but with God and all humanity. At that moment I knew my guru, everybody seated in the darshan grounds and myself as the omnipresent spirit that each of us are. Such visions only confirmed that we were spiritual beings who had taken manifestations in physical form.

No doubt, I had often experienced the omnipresent, omniscient and omnipotent nature of my dear guru oftentimes during the past two decades. But it was only today in the human garb that I saw the Divine dwelling in Him and in each of His children seated in the darshan grounds. It was comprehensible because I had been blessed with His cosmic vision in a wakeful state.

A Glimpse of Him Dwelling in My Aged Jal Uncle

On 20th March '95 in a dream, my Lord stood in the balcony of my Jal Uncle's flat, purchasing some vegetables from a vendor. I promptly walked up to Him and took my share of vegetables from His divine hands. Two of the tomatoes spilled and went rolling on the floor for want of a proper carry bag.

I could not dismiss the above dream as a joke nor could I understand it until 12 hours later when Jal Uncle (dad's elder sister's husband) called me to his house on my return from the office. Today as he spoke to me, I felt ashamed as I realised that I had never made an attempt to see the goodness in him. I had avoided him for fear of having to listen to his comments on my faith in Baba as I daily passed by his house. In gentle tones he addressed me, "Khurshid, when you were away at Parthi, in order to reduce your dad's work we have been purchasing vegetables from the vendor who comes here with the handcart. Now even though you are back, we don't mind continuing with the same so as to save you the trouble of going to the market after a tiring day at the office." So saying, Freny Aunty (his wife) and he handed over some vegetables to me. The carry bag not being sturdy enough gave way and a few tomatoes rolled on to the floor, reminding me of that morning's dream – and I was literally in tears of gratitude.

This experience too had been an eye-opener like the rest. The Lord indeed dwelled in Jal Uncle. So what if he didn't believe in Sathya Sai? He did believe in his own religion and lived a life of good thoughts, good words and good deeds – the way Baba would want each of us to.

One Needs to be Aware of His Presence in Every One and at All Times

The dream on 23rd March '95 at 5.50 a.m. was as given below:

My friend and I were on our way to school dressed as students (with school bags in our hands) when we came upon a bunch of boys seated on the pavement, blocking our path. Taking a sharp curve, I walked past them. But deviating from the path once decided upon did not appeal to my friend whose request to the boys to give way proved futile. She marched up to their parents with her complaint, and, in the event, missed the opportunity to meet the Lord who in the meanwhile walked past us very casually, mingling in the crowd! I found myself blinking time and again only to make sure that He was indeed amongst us. Running up to Him, I asked Him the question that lay uppermost in my mind, "Baba, are you happy with me?" My Lord held my eyes for a few seconds in silence and then smiled. "Very happy. Yes, I am very happy," He said at last, in His loving way which I found so reassuring.

As for the message of the dream, I infer it to be as: The Lord exists all around you and one must be ever vigilant for Him, otherwise, like the breeze, He will visit and pass by, unperceived.

All the experiences I had had in the recent past were in themselves a beginning of a true understanding – something that shed light and brought up a spiritual truth that mere thinking would not have given, also a truth that brought with it so much joy in life. It was now easy to understand that the human form was a temple of bliss. But though this truth was not by any means yet unknown to me, I stumbled occasionally, I repeat, because of my reluctance to surrender my will to the Lord's Will.

Visions of Lord Ganesha and Lord Zoaraster

Visions of my Lord continued as before, mostly in His Sathya Sai form and occasionally in His other forms. For instance, in March '95 I had a vision of Lord Ganesha and, a few days later, on 5th April '95 to be precise, that of Lord Zoaraster. The vision that followed on the next day was of my Lord Sathya Sai spinning wool for 'Kusti' exactly in the manner my dad did. Perhaps He was hinting that I ought not to miss out on visualising Him in dad. (Kusti is the sacred thread worn over the waist by the Parsi community.)

Honesty Should be a Way of Life – My Guru Taught Me

The next morning (7th April '95) in a dream, my Lord appeared to be displeased with me and didn't let me get anywhere near Him. Yet, when I did go very close and my hand slightly brushed the sleeve of His robe as He passed by, He recoiled at the touch, muttering something inaudible and leaving me in tears. But I knew that the Lord would not discard me for my shortcomings: He appraised me by my aspiration for spiritual knowledge and my all out efforts to improve myself. Always patient but never compromising, He helped me overcome my ego with His simple counsel when He next appeared in my dream on 18th April '95. Refusing to grant me permission to touch His feet, He stood silently awhile, with a faraway look in His brooding eyes. There was an undertone of subdued pain in His voice when He finally spoke, by lightly touching my chest for a moment, "You still have a wee little bit of Satan in you that needs to be removed if you desire to be at my feet." He did not seem cross with me though. (And in the days to come He proved that He had forgiven me even before I could forgive myself.)

Fear gripped me as I fervently prayed for an explanation. Within minutes I was fast asleep. This time in a dream He showed me a lady (one of my superiors at CRY) to whom I had not dared to speak the truth that I was going to Bangalore in answer to my Lord's call. Instead, I had made an excuse of going to Bangalore for an eye check-up. On coming to know the truth from other sources, she had questioned Him at not being able to teach the basic lesson of honesty to His child!

I was contrite. How could I have let down my Lord? This was not the first time I had been confronted with my own self in such a vivid manner; it had happened on earlier occasions as well. Now that He had brought to surface the flaw in my nature, I had to do my best to eradicate it. The determination to rise to His expected level grew stronger and I knew I had to make an all out endeavour to outgrow my lower self.

I commenced my next short trip to Whitefield on 9th April '95. I had put up at Nagmani's house and every day I was blessed with beautiful close darshans of the Lord. What had made me utter a lie to the office staff upon being asked for the reason for availing of my leave? Fear. It was His call I had answered. What did it matter if others found it difficult to believe that He had appeared in my dream and called me for His darshan? He understood – and that was all that was necessary. Though praise did not affect me in the least, sarcastic remarks from others about my Lord's call cut me to the quick and the fear of being scorned made me resort to falsehood. But my Lord withheld from me even that right to self-pity.

It was better to be honest than to appear honest. Perhaps I suffered on account of my ego, because I believed that I was a better person than what others might make me out to be if I were to speak the truth! I would have succeeded in justifying my lie and even persuaded myself that the Lord was helping me all along since it was only 'white lies' that I uttered. It was because my Lord cut at the root of such self-deception that I got a chance to rectify my behaviour. He taught me to be ruthless with myself and it helped enormously. By saying that I still had 'a wee little bit of the Satan in me' He did not infer that I was doing anything criminal, but the small harmless looking enemy – of bothering about the world's opinion – was dangerous, that it hampered my progress which made it all the more necessary that I fight it out of my life. According to Him, nothing was too small to prove an obstruction for me and nothing too big to be overcome by sincerity. I had to change instead of deceiving myself and justifying my mistakes till the end of time though it proved difficult to see myself as I really was and not as I had believed myself to be.

From then on my personality began to undergo a change, I saw myself emerging as a totally new being who only felt the pinch of what she was not yet able to give to the Lord and to the world. I learnt to accept all that came as a gift from my Lord and all that was denied as withheld by Him. So when I was called upon for my appraisal at the place of work (CRY) and rated as 'very good' and not 'excellent' it didn't affect my mental peace. Nor was I elated a few days later when I was informed that the management had decided to revise their earlier rating and had now rated me as an 'excellent' performer. Where I stood in the world's eye held no charm for me – my only desire was to be rated by Him as an excellent student of His.

My Everlasting Longing for His Darshan

On 23rd April '95 as I sat up in bed at 3.45 a.m. and the scenes of the dream I had just had flashed before my eyes, I felt a thrill of vivid joy and blessedness. In a horse-driven chariot, my Lord had passed by Aban and I who were seated amongst the devotees, giving both of us a grain of rice. When I silently complained that what He had given was just enough for Mum and Jasmine, He turned back His chariot and gave me a half grain of rice for myself and one each for the rest of my family. My gaze followed Him until the chariot was out of sight.

In another dream on 27th April '95 my Lord and I sat on chairs facing each other. He patiently answered all my queries and counselled me on various topics. (Unfortunately, I cannot remember any part of that conversation.) In a timid voice I asked half expectantly, "Baba, I know I have been fortunate enough to see you at such close proximity and for so long a period. Yet, my thirst for your darshan has not been quenched. Now in the afternoon when you go to sleep and nobody else will be around you, is it all right if I sit by your side and keep my vision fixed on your Divine form till it is time for you to once again wake up and be among the people?" My Lord seemed pensive for a while. Then, with a beatific but sad smile flickering on His lips, in soft tones He addressed me (in Gujarati), "I don't know." The dream ended.

I had never done any penance. Neither had I practised deep austerities nor studied the scriptures. And I had never felt the need for any 'channels' or 'rituals' to approach my Lord, my dear parent. My only claim on His grace was that I loved, adored and needed Him. When He stayed away from me everything went dark before my eyes and I suppose my soul sought His presence all throughout to plead with Him not to have His physical form move out of my sight even when out of sight from the rest of the world i.e. beyond daily darshan time meant for devotees.

His Guidance to Me to have a Balanced Diet

I had another wonderful vision on 30th April '95 at 8.30 a.m. Let me write about it with an explanatory introduction. An earlier vision I had had in Bangalore a few weeks ago, that of the Lord giving me an apple to eat, was His way of reminding me that the body is a temple of God which was why I had to keep it as perfect as possible. (At the same time, I understand, He does not want this preoccupation with the body to grow into an obsession. Though the body has to be kept in good health to help the spirit to evolve, it should never be at the cost of the spirit by wasting too many precious hours of our daily life keeping it fit!)

When in end '93 He had expressed His wish that I give up my evening meals, had He not also told me to have apples and pomegranates? Hadn't it then been utter foolishness on my part to have taken His advice only in part and starve myself? My dear Lord took pains to remind me even of such a simple thing. It was brought home to me, through this simple gesture of His, how spontaneously humble He was.

Efforts to Raise the Series of 'A Glimpse of Joy' to His Ideal of Perfection

On 2nd May '95 at 6.30 a.m. in the dream I was reluctant to step into a smaller hall in which a lesser crowd had gathered. When He saw me take my seat in the large hall in one corner far away from where He stood at the gate of the small hall, He, out of compassion, sent a blanket flying in my direction and it fell straight on to my lap. (Shall I call it a protection of love and a blanket of His acceptance of me?) A volunteer walked up to me, took the blanket which changed into a beautiful carpet the moment it reached her hands and she spread it out from where I sat right up to the spot where my Lord stood looking at me!

I was not exactly what I seemed to others who saw me only busy with my daily chores at home or at work in the office and attending to trivial and mundane matters. They could not visualise my heart that longed for Him. The blanket of love taking the form of the series of 'A Glimpse of Joy' being woven steadily as days pass and, His lessons to me, continue. I sincerely hope that in the future it turns out to be the carpet to lead people to the Divine.

Dear readers, as these books are being written in compliance with His wish, I thought you would be interested in the history of its development as regards the emergence of its edited version. Aban had corrected my first typescript as far as grammatical errors were concerned. Upon going through the text once again, I got a brief survey of the work accomplished and what still remained to be done. Thus began a series of alterations in the transcript in order to raise the series of 'A Glimpse of Joy' to His ideal of perfection – a project that was as time consuming as was the original scribing of the material. Every evening after office hours and over the weekends, dad and I slowly read through the text, striking off unnecessary or repetitive stuff, rearranging the passages to get the link, incorporating points that had been missed out earlier, etc.

A Precious Gift from Sai – His Autograph

It will not be out of place to mention here that busy as I was with my work at the office (and His writing work at home), I sat dispiritedly at the desk wondering where I had slipped; what was it that had kept my beloved Lord away from me for 17 days since His last darshan that I had had during His visit to Mumbai in May '95. But from the dream that followed on 1st June '95 at 5 a.m. it was apparent that there was no reason for despair on my part.

Bestowing special grace on me, Maiji (my parents' guru) led me by the hand right up to the Lord's inner chambers. Baba, in turn, came running to the doorstep and greeted me with a smile. I was about to touch His feet but stopped short when by gestures He told me not to do so. Bending low, He gently lifted me, His child, by the shoulders and enfolded me in a loving embrace. As I clung to Him, entreating Him not to ever leave me in mid-stream, He whispered with an almost apologetic smile, "Wait a while till I go and get a special gift for you for all your hard labour." So saying, He left – only to return in a trice in hurried steps with a card in His hand. Opening it, on a beautiful photo of His within, He wrote: 'With love, Baba.' He surprised me even further by handing it over to me (the card had now changed into a book), saying, "Now on the same page down below, write your own name. Give me your autograph as well." The next moment He seemed to have remembered something that required His attention and rushed to His inner chamber, leaving me disconsolate. To seek solace, I turned to Maiji and put forth the question that had persistently bothered me. "Maiji, at times I keep calling out to the Lord but to no avail. And if at all He does come, He refuses to grant me permission to touch His lotus feet. Am I to surmise that I have committed a serious error and displeased Him? Or do I attribute it to something altogether different?" With abated breath, I waited for her response. Placing her arm around my shoulders, she said, "No, no, you shouldn't think that way. Just a little while ago, didn't He reward you with this beautiful gift as an expression of His appreciation for all your hard labour, instead of merely letting you be at His feet? Besides, in the future, if He does not come to you as often as before, it is because there is so much unfinished work to be attended to on a priority basis by Him. Many important assignments may take up His time. There are so many loose ends to be tied up." (This time Maiji spoke in English instead of Gujarati.)

Mysterious indeed were His ways to put my troubled mind to rest. I was taken aback by Maiji's explanation and had no heart to make any more demands on my Lord's time. The unexpected touch of His grace left me overwhelmed and I am sure that each of us, dear friends, must have had such occurrences / Divine experiences to treasure in our memory.

As for the gift of His photo with His autograph, the dream materialised many years later when Vivek, a Board member of Sunbeam and a friend of mine, got Baba's photo autographed by Him once when our guru had called him and his wife Rashmi for an interview. Vivek then passed on the photo to me.

The Sweet Manner in which Baba Reminds Me to Update His Books

It seemed that my Lord's visits to me would stop to all intents and purposes as a consequence of His busy schedule and I saw no chance of their resumption. But it was not meant to be so. In the recent past, I had been indifferent towards my health, especially the pain in my chest. Now it had increased considerably and it made me resolve to consult a doctor. Knowing that the pain was beyond my limit of physical endurance, He and Maiji once again appeared to me in a dream on 4th June '95. Both of them individually granted me my heart's desire by allowing me to rest my head on their lap. My Lord placed His hand on my head and blessed me. When I rested on Maiji's lap, she placed her hand on my chest and said, "Ah, there is so much pain in here. I know, I know." 'Maiji is aware of my pain and it has got to subside,' I reflected on waking up. My resolution (of consulting a doctor) melted into thin air.

From March '95 onwards I had discontinued writing about my experiences other than those that involved my life with God, my own progress on the path to reach Him. This decision I had taken because, instead of wasting time complaining that others were being unfair to me, I chose to focus on what I wanted from life and how to devise strategies to attain it. I had learnt to pay attention to my weaknesses (which I shall not fail to mention) and improve upon them. No longer did I assess my happiness on the basis of others' behaviour or opinion. Moreover, I resolved never to resort to self-pity to prop myself up but to use my Lord's assessment of me as a measure of my progress on my journey towards Him.

On 16th June '95 at 3.10 a.m. this is what I saw in the dream. At a short distance from where I stood, I saw a little boy of about 10 (who every now and then kept changing His form to Sathya Sai) with a wounded leg trying to get a foothold on a wheelchair that kept shifting backwards, not allowing Him to sit. In a trice I ran to Him and helped Him on to the chair. He let me caress His face and gently reassure Him of my presence in His life. Then, to my surprise, it was my Lord in the little boy's place. I crossed over and sat at His feet, asking Him a few questions. Though I vaguely remember having spoken on many more topics, all that I could recollect of our conversation (on waking up) was the latter part of it in which I kept trying to convince Him of my genuine efforts to improve myself, "Baba, but I am trying my level best to become perfect." "How perfect? Perfect in what way?" He demanded incredulously. And I went on to explain, "Perfect in the sense that I don't ever harm others, do service to mankind." There He cut me short by saying, "Ah! There you are! Service to mankind. That is good, but not only so that when you reach old age you can look back with satisfaction that you did not waste your life." His tone expressed that I was still lacking somewhere. With that the dream came to an end.

Baba's words had left me feeling guilty for having tried to delude myself into believing that I had reached near perfection. But at the same time I believed that if I ever went wrong (in spite of my best efforts to improve) He was sure to guide me. Every night my prayer before going to bed was, "O Lord, indicate to me the areas in which I need to improve." An answer came to me in a dream on 24.6.95 wherein I saw Him (dressed in clothes of a household help) float from the sky and place Himself on a shelf of books (handwritten manuscripts and typescripts) just above our heads as Aban and I sat enjoying our lunch. He diligently began to clean the books and all the dust which fell into our plates He said He expected us to eat with relish instead of the delicious food at the table. Once again He proclaimed aloud as though for us to take the hint, "I shall certainly not allow dust to collect on these books of mine."

My Lord, in His own sweet way, had brought my fault to light – a fault that lay in my thinking which made me give more importance to other services than devoting all my spare time in editing my books (work that I had been lethargic about in the past few months)! Each one of us has a task to accomplish in His plan of things – and mine was to complete the books in the best manner possible. Once again I began to work on it with renewed zeal only to think of taking a short nap. The minute I was about to doze off He blessed me with a vision of a snake charmer making the snake dance to the tune of His flute! He knew that my mind was not without a latent spark of a longing to serve others, and refused to be discouraged in His attempts to fan that spark to a flame by letting me know that in devoting some of my spare time towards the completion of the books, I was actually serving all those in whose hands a copy of it was to reach one day.

Ultimately, I had Begun to Grasp the Divine's Language

Within 24 hours of a dream in which Jasmine (my sister) had assured me of taking care of my accommodation in Parthi if I had agreed to join on her trip, I received a call from an acquaintance of mine, Roshan Bhathena, whom I had met at Pushpa Kunj where I attended bhajans. She inquired if I'd like to accompany her to Parthi for Guru Pournima and added that accommodation would not pose a problem since she owned two flats in Parthi – outside the ashram premises. Taking it to be an invitation from my Lord I longed to give a positive reply but decided against doing so unless the Lord Himself confirmed it. (Perhaps Jasmine was shown in the dream because Roshan was to be considered as a sister.)

The next morning the dream was full of scenes of my forthcoming trip: being in no position to enter the darshan grounds, I had to console myself with a mere glimpse of my Lord from outside though, of course, I saw myself being blessed by a close darshan when He passed by in His car. The latter part of the dream in which Yasmin Aunty commanded me to put aside my bottle of nail polish and run for darshan had me baffled. But instead of deterring me from making the trip, if anything, the dream made my resolution even stronger and our tickets were confirmed for the 8th of July.

What followed on 29th June '95 was a dream that shed light on more than one important aspect of my life. In order to escape from a room engulfed in total darkness, I ran up to the top floor into another house where I witnessed a beautiful phenomenon. A whole new world opened up for me. It was a house lit up with sunlight that came in from all sides and in a corner stood my dear Lord. As I silently stood before Him, He held out His own photograph to me but the minute I reached out for it, He teased me by withdrawing it. A playful smile was on His lips as He continued with the game until He finally presented it to me. As He spoke in Marathi, a language I found difficult to converse in, I found myself complaining, "Baba, please talk in Hindi instead, a language I can understand better and am fluent in." To His amusement, I had all the while been talking in Marathi! Without being aware of it, I had already grasped His language and begun to speak it as well! What I lacked was self-confidence and He laughed away merrily.

The above dream gave me immense satisfaction. Instead of living in darkness I had to learn to open the windows of my heart. My aim in life had to be to open my consciousness to the Divine, to learn to express His will in all my actions so that I might grow out of ignorance into the light.

Baba Kicked Me when I Insisted that He should Wipe Away Madhu's Karma and Heal Her

One day I paid a visit to Madhu (name changed) as she was very ill and undergoing radiation treatment for lung cancer. Seeing her condition generated a feeling of intense sorrow in my heart. When she called me to her bed and wrote on a piece of paper asking me how to do away with her pain and that I should talk to Baba about her (for she had lost faith in ever getting better), I found it hard to believe that the same lady who had time and again mocked at my faith in Baba now had made this request of me. (She had lost her speech completely, hence she wrote in order to communicate.) Attempting to assure her of our Lord's mercy, I told her I would pray for her and was sure that she'd be relieved of her pain. For the next 2 days I spent fruitless hours in prayer. Finally, in desperation I called out to Him even more fervently, insisting that He either stop her pain or at least give her His darshan. What didn't strike me was that I had begun to dictate terms to Him, little realizing that indirectly I was hampering Madhu's progress towards God for she (like all of us) was merely working out her karma – hence she underwent all that pain. My prayers continued until He lost His patience and appeared to me on 7th July '95 in a dream at 5 a.m. What He demanded of me meant an inner discipline (and an understanding of His way of functioning according to the theory of karma) that was far more exacting and difficult than mere prayers. On waking up and recollecting the events of the dream, my mind froze. Words rose to my lips, but I could not utter a syllable. I couldn't express the dread I had of facing Him again after the dream, which I shall now give details of.

In a hall packed with devotees I found myself seated on a chair in the corner. It was apparent that each of us was awaiting the Lord's judgement on the roles we had played on stage before taking up our seats for the inspection that was to begin. Baba entered and I watched as He moved amongst the people, giving an approving smile, a look of reproach, a mere shrug of His shoulders with a sad look in His eyes, and many other expressions as He scrutinised each individual. With a sweet smile He approached me and in order to stop Him from moving on to the next person before hearing me out, I stretched out my hands in His way saying aloud, "Baba, what answer should I give to Madhu?" His mood changed swiftly to annoyance because He had to take a step out of His way as my outstretched hands proved to be an obstruction. Assuming a huge form, His eyes bore into me angrily as He spoke in stern tones, "How dare you stretch out your hands in this manner! Do not come in my way, you bad girl." I stirred uneasily and felt a moment of alarm as He came closer. Before I knew what was happening, He kicked me in my face and the impact of it sent me reeling to the floor. Then I turned over and crouched on all fours. Inch by inch, quivering with uncertainty and hoping against hope, I reached out for His feet and clasped them, begging for forgiveness, "Baba, I'm sorry." Once again He grimaced and repeated His words, "Do not come in my way, you bad girl." Another equally forceful kick from Him, straight on my face, made me once again lose my balance, leaving me too bewildered to make an effort to rise again.

I sat up in bed, wondering at being labelled as 'a bad girl'. I told myself, my imagination had got the better of me to think that my Lord could call me a bad girl and actually kick me. And yet, I knew that those were the very things I had just dreamt about. All my enthusiasm to go to Parthi vanished and was replaced by fear. The next morning after waking up and before leaving home to board the train to Dharmavaram, I had a vision of my Lord in His Shirdi Sai form and He raised His hand to bless me.

In the past month I had been exerting myself a lot at the office and felt overtaxed and driven. A strong bout of flu had left me weak and on my way to Parthi too I was still running a slight temperature. The scene of my Lord kicking me kept flashing before my mind's eye and I became blank. Self-pity would not help, but I could have a moment's private rebellion. Had my error been so grave as to have received such harsh treatment? For the first 2 days in Parthi I found myself stuck to bed, swathed in blankets and yet shivering with cold. My body temperature fluctuated, leaving me perspiring one moment and then suddenly it would shoot up, especially in the evenings.

On the 10th evening when I lay all alone in the room unable to go for darshan, just like the day before, I wept, "Of what use is this body if it stops me from coming for your darshan? I look forward to the time to come where all physical limitations will drop; where I shall be with you all the time (in spirit) and I shall be engaged in greater service than what I can do with this weak body of mine." For several hours I alternated between unconsciousness and a mild delirium. I'd wake up asking Him if it was humane on His part to let me suffer so all alone when His attention was fixed on the devotees performing before Him (a music festival was on and devotees from countries all over the world performed before the Lord). "Baba, it seems my cry is falling on deaf ears. Today you appear not to notice my tears of repentance either. Can you not understand my pain?"

I had two photographs of His in a plastic cover – one side had the photograph of my Shirdi Sai and the other of Sathya Sai. As I lamented with His photo in my hand, something made me turn the cover to the other side. What met my eyes left me awestruck and speechless. From my Lord Shirdi Sai's left ear blood oozed out and a drop of blood trickled down His cheek from the left eye (inside the plastic cover). And this was not a dream! The nightmare of feeling abandoned by Him had come to an end and the fury within subsided. I gazed at this sad but divine spectacle for a long time, shedding tears of joy. (A fool that I was, I took out the photo from the plastic cover, wiped off the blood but it got smudged and I washed it with water as a result of which I spoilt the photo completely.) The sight of Him bleeding made me feel that He had gathered me up and held me very close, while I wept out how sorry I was to have doubted His love for me. Feeling warm and relaxed for the first time in 4 days, I slept peacefully.

The next morning I had very close darshan of His as I walked out of the Sathya Sai General Hospital where Roshan had taken me, but the crowds there had compelled me to leave without consulting a doctor. As I felt weak, I walked with faltering steps when Roshan drew my attention to a car that had to slow down for me to pass by; it happened to be the Lord's car with Him gently looking at the two of us and smiling! That full day I was again stuck to bed due to weakness but felt happy beyond words. Next morning, after Roshan and Beroze had left for darshan, Yasmin Aunty's words uttered in a recent dream rang into my ears, "Khurshid, leave behind your nail polish bottle and run for darshan." Now I understood the meaning of her words. Instead of giving too much importance to my health (self-importance by pampering myself) I decided to go for darshan. With the crowd becoming unruly (where nobody bothered about token number queues which otherwise was the normal procedure), I found myself being pushed into the darshan grounds, thus securing a front row and feeling blessed with the close darshan I had on Guru Pournima day.

This particular trip had left me drained of all energy, but the next morning I was back to office, never missing a beat. A week later I picked up enough courage to visit Madhu at the hospital. She was on life-support systems in the Intensive Care Unit and I didn't see her lasting very long. As she pushed the notepad lying next to her expecting me to give an answer from Baba, I ignored her action because the thought of speaking His exact words was unsettling. But the next morning Madhu appeared to me in a dream at 7 a.m. and she was her old picture of health as she said, "O Khurshid, I am no longer in pain and just want you to know that I am happier this way." Later that day I got the news that she had expired a little before 7 a.m.

Break the Seal of Your Heart to Allow the Lord to Enter therein

I had also been blessed with another symbolic dream a few days ago, i.e. on 23rd July '95. Baba moved among the devotees with a bagful of toffees in His hand to be distributed among all those who looked up to Him expectantly. He approached each one individually and offered that plastic bag of toffees to break open the seal. Each in turn tried his/her luck without success. Though our Lord appeared amused, there were times when He looked sad as He moved on from one person to the other, giving me a fleeting glance now and then. As I was confident of breaking open the seal if I made an attempt, the moment He passed by me, I promptly suggested, "Baba, shall I open that parcel of toffees for you?" He smiled kindly at me and said, "No, you may not." So saying, He moved on to the next person, leaving me in a daze as to why all the people found such a simple task so formidable and that if they didn't succeed at the first go, did it mean they had to give up?

Perhaps the above dream implied that it depends on the individual to break open the seal of his heart and mind and reach out for the Lord's grace in order to let the sweet nectar of Divinity find a place in his life.

"I shall Certainly Come to You as Promised," He Reconfirmed

31st July '95 – 6.30 a.m. dream: I ran up to Him and held His hand tight. "Baba, my sister has come of marriageable age. Why not look out for a good husband for her?" Knowing that my fears were unfounded, He replied softly, "Don't worry." It was a heart-to-heart talk that followed. "Baba, do you at times feel very angry towards me?" "No, no," came the hurried response. "Baba, do you too hate me at times? Or else how could you (who had all along loved me and hugged me to your heart) have kicked me so mercilessly?" He winced at my words and looked so sad and hurt that I'd have done anything to take back my words when I heard Him say in a trembling voice, "But I never kicked you!" To freshen up His memory I reminded Him of the Madhu incident. "But that does not mean I hate you. You were very obstinate, in not trying to understand what was good for her and for you too. Hence I had to behave in the harsh manner I did. But I have always loved you." After these soft, comforting words of His, He seemed very tired and expressed a desire to rest by laying down His head on the table. Quite unexpectedly I found myself close to tears and nothing could stop me from shaking Him up and imploring, "Baba, Baba, don't go to sleep. Not yet. Please may I ask you one more question?" He shook His head in the negative, but I had decided not to take 'no' for an answer and insisted, "Give me at least a few minutes of your time before going to sleep. And I promise it will be my last question to you." The silence that followed was granite-like until He finally sat up and said, "OK" To my shock I noticed a man sitting close by, listening to our conversation and I immediately lowered my voice almost to a whisper, "Baba, you have promised me that you are going to take rebirth and that I shall be the chosen mother then." His puzzled look frightened me all the more. "Baba, hadn't you yourself promised me so?" I wailed. Appearing to be taken up by my cries and as though much against His wish, He replied, "Well, OK." He had bent forward and whispered those words into my ears, giving a side glance to the man sitting nearby. "Baba, is it because the man over there should not overhear us that you were feigning ignorance? Perhaps you don't wish anyone to know of your coming to me as my child," I whispered back. Bringing His face still closer to mine, He said, "Yes, I don't want him to hear of it. That is precisely why I took so long in answering that question of yours. I shall certainly come to you as promised." With that He got up and walked out of the room.

Friends, you might wonder as to what made me question my Lord the way I did, but at times when I thought of His anger and gave way to panic, I felt the world around me shatter and needed a reassurance from Him that He had still decided to be with me, accepting me with all my faults.

A Devotee's Heartfelt Prayer being Answered by Baba

On 1st August '95, I had one more dream of Baba. It was as follows:

My one hand held Rustom from falling and the other stretched out towards Baba who stood before us, His face expressionless. My prayer was, "Baba, please do not get angry for I shall not insist that you give what I ask for; I merely beg of you to consider my petition. Give some relief to Rustom for he can't see his loved one suffer thus. Don't punish him so. Please let me know how he can come out of the pain." Baba put His hand in the side pocket of His robe that overflowed with what seemed like bits of paper. Then He poured out a little vibhuti into my palm which I put in Rustom's mouth. Rustom was surprised and almost in tears when He admitted unashamedly, "Khurshid, I never believed in your stories about Baba's visits to you but today, though I haven't been fortunate enough to have His darshan, He has proved His presence in the room." Farida came running to me, weeping that she could not dream of living with an important part of herself snatched away from her and asked if I could help her. With that the dream came to an end.

(A week later, I received news from Farida that she had actually felt our guru's presence all the time in the hospital. A part of her body being snatched away referred to the miscarriage that she had suffered. But with God's grace, in the months to follow, she once again conceived.)

It is up to the Devotee to Scale the Ladder of Spiritual Success

As usual, my Lord was always there to express His appreciation at every single effort on the part of a devotee to become a better human being and to bring to the notice of wrongdoers even their minute flaws. I was erring and He came to let me know of the same. It had never occurred to me that I had lacked somewhere when I didn't clean dad's puja table on a regular basis. It was Jasmine who always took up that task and that of cleaning up of our house as well. Hence, in a dream on 8th August '95, Baba showed that He was all the while standing next to her, watching her fruitful efforts at bringing about cleanliness, even Himself being completely drenched as water was poured over Him (perhaps signifying the action of His photo-frame being washed by Jasmine).

It came as a pleasant surprise when Aban, and then Jasmine, decided to make a short trip to Parthi provided I joined them. The tickets were booked but I awaited the Lord's message which came on 9th August '95. In the dream He declared, "The tree that can provide you with all you seek in life, that tree is your father and mother. Come, all of you come to this tree." He stood in all majesty with outstretched hands, calling out to us – His children. By the time I reached Him, He had vanished from sight and in His place stood a huge tree and an equally long ladder resting against its trunk – a ladder placed there for any of us who wished to climb it. But no one seemed to be enthusiastic to do so and felt satisfied by merely bowing down to the tree. And I found myself asking if it were right to follow suit and be content at merely being at this place when the Lord had provided us with a ladder to help us in scaling the otherwise unattainable heights. Yes, as seen in the dream, He leaves it to us to decide to climb the ladder to success on the path that leads to the fruits that He wishes to offer us.

I Learnt to give due Respect to Another's Perspective

On 15th August '95 on our way back home from the short memorable trip to Parthi, I tried to recollect everything that had been taught to me by my loving parent to whom my prayer had been, "Baba, this time instead of asking for any worldly gift, I beg of you to show me my shortcomings so that I may overcome them and come closer to my destination." The images that rose to my mind were of the moments of my life in which the innumerable weaknesses in me such as anger, annoyance, insensitivity to another's pain and the like propped up. I felt as if a timely message had reached me: "Khurshid, learn to look at things from another's point of view. If you wish to scale the heights, learn to be the loving reflection of God."

The rail journey back home left behind beautiful memories of the visions that followed as I chanted the 'Gayatri Mantra' and dived into the depths of silence for almost half an hour. The moment I asked the Lord if I still stood a chance of improving myself or if it were already too late, the vision I had was that of an old lady walking on the railway tracks, ignoring the train coming from the opposite direction until it had come too close – and in panic she put in her best effort to climb back safely to the platform. That's when she noticed Baba standing on the platform. Our Lord's hand from the above pulled her out of danger in the nick of time.

Now, happy to know that my Lord was there to pull me out of the pit of selfishness to selfless love towards all, I asked Him if my prayers had reached Him and the instant vision was that of a garland of flowers placing itself around His lotus feet! The vision implied that silence did not mean absence of experiences. But the inner silence (with cessation of thoughts) and peace have first to be established in order to open up to the Divine consciousness.

"The Books are Going on Well, as Per My Expectations," My Guru Reassured Me

Baba was there to hold me in a close embrace in a dream on 17th August '95 early in the morning. On waking up, all that I could remember of the dream is as follows: Dad and I found ourselves seated in the back seat of a car that drove by itself without anyone at the wheel! The minute it came to a halt (which happened very often) I'd call out to Baba (this time He had appeared in His Shirdi Sai form) who was walking right ahead of the car all the while. He, my dear parent, came running up to me each time I called and I in turn flung open the door to let Him in. Dad and I made enough space to accommodate Him with us. Holding His hands tight, looking straight into His eyes, I asked Him, "Baba, may I ask you any question?" "Of course you may," came the usual gentle response. "Baba, now that your book is progressing and I have it typed out, even started with the second editing, should I do away with all the old manuscripts?" I went on to provide Him with my justification, "Baba, it is because I have made innumerable changes since the first handwritten manuscript until now in the second computerised manuscript. For instance, I have deleted some incidents in my life or have added a few happenings in my life which I had earlier on felt hesitant to put on paper. And I've made some changes in other ways too i.e. correcting the spelling errors, grammar, etc." Sensing my uneasiness at retaining any of the old manuscripts, He said in soft tones, "But whatever changes you have made are fine. You don't have to worry on that score." (I took that as a go ahead of doing away with the old manuscripts.) After a pause, He suddenly objected vehemently to one of my errors in the book by saying, "But in that book of ours don't use words like: I can't interpret this particular dream." The next moment I hugged Him tight and to my joy He reciprocated with His feeble hands going around me, His head resting on my shoulder. And I kept patting His back as though He were a little child whom I helped rest awhile. As He gently pulled Himself back after some time, I said, "Baba, I have always been asking for some selfish wish or another. Today I won't do that. Just tell me if the book is going on fine and whatever editing has taken place is as per what it should be." "Yes, it is going on well, as per my expectations," He responded. "Baba, are you happy with the book's progress and Aban helping me with it?" "Yes, I am happy about that." With these words He ventured out of the car and the dream came to an end.

My Resolution to be Severe with My Own Shortcomings and Charitable to those of Others

Here are a few more important messages that came through as I dwelled on my relations with my family and friends:

I had to learn to take criticism in the right spirit. Through family and friends it was the Lord helping me to progress spiritually. In order to have everlasting relationships I had to try to look calmly on others with an open mind, not overstressing either their virtues or defects. It was best for me to be severe with my own shortcomings and charitable to those of others.

Forgetting all the hurts and disappointments of the past, I apologized to my dear ones for the misunderstandings between us. I visualized my Lord in all and held friendship as a sacred thing, not wanting to see it broken due to my ego, destroyed by a moment's anger. Ingratitude did not become of me. Hence, friendship with my family and friends was indispensable to me. But attachment had to fall away and unless I remained in the true consciousness centred on the Divine, my friendship towards fellow human beings would be selfishness disguised as love.

I had scribbled the above mentioned thoughts (my resolution to become a better human being) in the middle of the night when no one was around.

Early next morning, i.e. on 19th August '95 in a dream He came up on the stage from behind the curtain, smiled at me and raised His hands in a gesture of blessing.

Serving at Sunbeam was Equal to Serving the Sai Organisation, According to Him

With what seemed like being forced by circumstances, dad had taken upon himself to earn more (by way of tuitions after office hours) in order to meet the sudden expenses. It was sheer torture for me to see him tire himself out thus and with the Lord's permission stopped him from carrying on with it any longer. Instead I decided to go in his place – but only on weekends, teaching for a longer period of time. But my conscience wouldn't permit me to do so at the cost of the Lord's writing work. On the one hand I needed money and on the other I had been assigned a job by the Lord. It was a very tough decision but my mind was made up – not only to make dad give up his weekend job of giving tuitions but at the same time if possible not to take any part of his monthly income. And to carry on running the household expenses from my salary alone so that I could save his salary for a rainy day. My Lord immediately responded in a dream the next morning i.e. on 25th August '95 at 4.30 a.m.

I found myself at the entrance of a small hall with Baba on the stage, giving a discourse (in Telegu) on what He expected from a Sathya Sai Organisation worker. The audience comprised of a group of permanent members of the organisation, sitting hushed, expectant and eager to hear what He had to say. Slowly I inched my way inside and took my seat among the members. My presence was not noticed. So far it was good. But the minute they spotted me, there were gasps of shock – and one of the ladies harshly commanded me to leave immediately. I tiptoed out of the hall. My Lord found it hard to address the crowd until I returned by obeying His instructions given to me through gestures; and He resumed His discourse – but only after addressing the public thus, "Let Khurshid come in. She belongs here." Every now and then there was a break in His speech when He turned to give me a loving glance and asked me, "Tired?" After another long pause, He repeated, "Tired? Very tired? Ah, I know!"

This dream was His way of indicating that I had taken a step in the right direction and that He considered me to be a member of His organisation while I actually continued with my tireless efforts at Sunbeam in bringing about a positive change in the lives of its child beneficiaries. Moreover, the dream also indicated that no matter how busy He was, He always kept a close watch on all my actions.

Looking at the World from Lord Ganesha's Viewpoint

The next morning, I had had a live vision of Lord Ganesha in a huge form with myself in a miniature form seated on His trunk, looking at the world from His viewpoint! Yes, I reiterate that it was a vision I had while wide awake, and it wasn't a dream.

Lord Ganesha, the Lord of Wisdom, had blessed me with His vision. As I began to grasp the significance of this unique and unusual vision, I felt humbled. He wished that I look upon life and the world at large not from my own limited viewpoint but from His Divine point of view.

Instead of Merely Seeking His Forgiveness, I Decided not to Repeat My Error

On 1st September '95, I heard one of my office colleagues talk to others once again in the most indecent language. Instead of either correcting her or trying to understand that the chief cause of her weakness was the growth of her ignorance in the knowledge of the

Divine, I committed the mistake of mentally comparing her with a vile character in one of the recent television serials that I had been watching! O dear, I thought to myself, there I had again displeased Him for sure.

The wait for His appearance was difficult. I feared that He would withdraw out of sheer disgust. How would He react, I couldn't predict. Within hours He took me by surprise when He appeared in my dream at 4.15 a.m. on 2.9.95. Giving me a quick glance and a beautiful smile He passed by, waving out to me before He went out of sight, only to return in a trice, running in my direction with outstretched hands. Just when I was about to touch His feet, He lifted me gently by the shoulders and I flung myself at Him, curling into His arms, resting my head on His shoulder. "Baba, have you forgiven me for that error of mine?" I begged of Him. "There is no reason for you to still remain so disturbed about it. Not only have I forgiven you for that error of yours, but for the other errors as well," He told me with warmth. The dream ended.

It was a day to rejoice; in my mind's eye, I saw myself so gently held in His loving embrace, the caring apparent not just in that gesture but in the obvious large-heartedness in forgiving me. What appeared very clear was how pointedly the dream showed the lack of any true ground for the apprehensions I had felt while approaching Him for asking forgiveness, especially now that I kept a check on my thoughts, words and deeds and was full of remorse the minute I came to know of my mistakes. I had expected Him to get angry, to perhaps even stop appearing to me. I had expected all kinds of punishment, undefined in my imagination, which had made it all the more frightening – but not the way He actually so lovingly responded – as though He was trying to say – 'Think no more about it except to retain the lesson.'

"Khurshid, for the Next Few Years I'll be Quite Busy Setting Your Vision Right," said Shirdi Sai

My dream of becoming a good human being was perhaps coming a little closer to fulfilment. But His dream of making me reach perfection could materialise only after a prolonged struggle on my part along the lines in which He wished me to move; rather more of a struggle on His part is what He seemed to express in a dream the next morning at 3.15 a.m. i.e. on 3rd September '95.

My Sai (in Shirdi Sai form) sat on His stone in Shirdi. As I placed my hands underneath those feet of His, bent low and pressed my eyes on them, He enquired gently, "Shall I stand up?" I nodded my assent and He stood on my palms, His weight next to nothing as I lifted Him up and next, when I put Him back on a seat, it was not in Shirdi but at my home in Mumbai! Now with folded hands I stood before Him, awaiting His instructions.

You can imagine my shock when He placed His thumb and forefinger right into my eye; with great concentration and patience He began to adjust the pupil of my eye, moving it in a circular motion so very slightly and stopping awhile to examine the effect His effort had on my vision! I wailed, "Will I ever be able to see clearly?" In a sad tone He responded by saying, "Khurshid, you are all the time talking of improvement of vision in your physical eyes whereas I am referring to that inner eye of yours. So let me make it clear once and for all that your physical vision is never going to improve." Then He softly added, "Whenever your inner eye shifts from its place blocking your vision, I set it right so that it may focus only on what it should." With that He was once again busy adjusting and readjusting the pupil in a manner He deemed fit. Not at all satisfied with the result, every now and then He stopped to query, "Has your vision cleared? Can you see better now?" But what moved me to tears was what He said next, "Khurshid, the change won't come about overnight. For the next few years I'll be quite busy setting your vision right. First you will have to undergo the surgery and only upon removal of the bandage will you be able to see clearly. Till then you may carry on with your work and let me do mine." With that He continued with His job of adjusting the pupil of my eye. The dream ended.

It was difficult for me to conceive of a correct view of the world from a human angle; hence all that effort on His part to set my vision right. By surgery, He could have meant His efforts in the direction of making me do away with all my weaknesses. And the bandage that was needed to be removed from my eyes, I suppose, was the bandage of 'illusion'. It certainly was a harsh reality which could not be done away with overnight; it required persistent effort on my part as well and not just His.

8

His Labour of Love to Mould Me into His Image

I Checked Myself in Time Before I Could Act Contrary to the Voice of My Conscience

Evidently, my Lord kept His word and set my vision right each time it got blurred. I recall an occasion when the solution I had thought of with regard to a particular problem faced by a friend of mine would have proved disastrous had it taken shape. But my Lord intervened in time and I postponed my suggestion to an indefinite future.

On another occasion He emphasised that though man pretends to act according to God's Will, his actions are moved by self-will. The devil (the restless, dissatisfied mind) makes suggestions influenced by this motive (self-will) and persuades him that it is the will of God. Here let me quote an incident in my life in support of the above statements.

On 15th September '95 at the inquiry counter of the tourist office, I was informed that if I wished to book our tickets for the 21st of October I could do so only after the 21st of September, i.e. a month prior to the date of the journey. This meant wasting a few more hours waiting in another long queue a week later. So it was natural that I felt overjoyed when a stranger walked up to me and said, "If you are willing to bribe the supervisor at the counter, he'd do the needful and you'll be saved the trouble of making yet another trip here." My mind grabbed at the opportunity and even dared to suggest to myself that it was God who had sent timely help! That I checked myself and didn't take the wrong step, didn't make me feel less contrite for having entertained such a thought.

Being Trained by the Dance Master Himself to be in Tune with His Steps

In truth, I lived from moment to moment, according to the supreme guidance and, consequently, was incapable of making plans on my own. The dream that followed on 16th September '95 at 3.15 a.m. would support the above statement depicted by Him in His own unique way.

A rare sight met my eyes – that of a group of devotees heading for the sea for the immersion of Lord Ganesha's idol with Lord Sathya Sai leading the procession! Along with thousands of others, I ran up to Him. We kept a respectable distance from Him and sat in neat rows before Him. In the red wet mud He drew a line, thereby indicating the limit up to where we were supposed to come. We ran to take our seats and in the process soiled our clothes in the mud that splashed on our bodies, making us all look horrible. What happened next came as a surprise. All of us, including the Lord, were dancing away in ecstasy. While the rest of the people danced to their own merry tunes, I couldn't take a single step of my own free will. But then, unlike some who stumbled and fell deeper into the mud and soiled themselves further, I was very fortunate to be saved from falling every time I stumbled. Why? For the simple reason that the Lord, busy dancing His own unique dance, different from the rest, never once let go of His firm grip on me. His divine hand held me by the hair and oftentimes I was taken unawares by the sudden unexpected steps He took and I got tossed about from one side to another. It began to rain heavily and I looked on in a dazed state as He now held me by the hair with both His hands and squeezed away whatever little mud was still stuck on me. The dance continued and it was scary as I couldn't master the steps He took and I suppose wished me to imitate, until I realised my good fortune of being upheld by the divine hand and letting go of all my fears, surrendered completely to His will. It was only a matter of trust that He'd never let me fall. My progress in mastering the dance was slow and painful but He was patience personified and never once gave up on me.

The moment He stopped dancing for a while, I took the opportunity to ask Him a question that had me bothered for quite some time now. "Baba, why don't you go to others just as you come to me?" "O but I do go to others as well," He said in a defiant tone. Now I queried, "What about my mum? Will you grant her your darshan?" "I shall certainly go to her," He replied. Then in a disturbed tone He said something that had no connection to any of my questions, "You know, there is a student of mine who repeatedly attempts at handing over an appeal letter to me in which he requests me to grant him permission to watch a movie. But I brush aside his request. How can I grant such a request at the cost of his reading work?" And the dream ended at that.

All messages of the Lord have a significance of one kind or another. But the growth of an inner knowledge was necessary to understand and interpret them properly. My Lord helped me in doing so. His grip on me was too firm to ever let me fall whenever my foot slipped. The rain water (His grace) was there to wash away the mud (worldly desires and attachments) that splashed on me; my Lord taking pains to squeeze it away from my very being. As for my weakness for television (wasting time watching a few of the TV serials), He very gently had expressed His disapproval of the same.

If He asked for surrender without reserve, on His side He was giving Himself entirely, without reserve. To attain perfection in the art of dancing to His tune, I needed to focus my consciousness on Him alone.

Merely His love for me and thereby His frequent visits to me were in no way a sign of a high spiritual progress on my part. To falsely imagine so would be a delusion of my mind and never in my wildest dreams has it been the intention to persuade you, dear readers, to think on those lines; hence my frank confessions of all my human weaknesses in the books. On the contrary, if I persisted with the type of life I led (caught up in worldly desires however few they might be), I was sure to lose altogether whatever closeness I had gained to Him till date.

Whether it was to give up watching movies or fasting once a week, He wished that my attitude towards such things need not be one of forceful suppression but of detachment with regard to the object of desire, and the sweet loving manner in which He had referred to that flaw in me had indeed put me to shame. I had to be prepared to renounce at the higher call the natural desires for worldly things in life or else it would clash with my progress towards Him.

His Consistent Efforts in the Direction of My Spiritual Awakening

25th September '95 – Dream – People flocked around Him in large numbers, eagerly awaiting the golden moment when His eyes would rest on them and the toffees He distributed would fall into their laps. Unlike them, I coolly remained in my bed far away. The Lord took pains to walk up to me every now and then to place a handful of toffees under my pillow!

The above dream message was yet another attempt on His part to indicate that He would not leave me until I was thoroughly awakened (spiritually). Till then He was there to give top priority to my spiritual progress. Once that awakening came about there would be no need for Him to occupy Himself further in that direction.

Yet another realisation that had dawned on me was that I needn't merely go on living the way I desired, awaiting Him to pull me out of the pit of errors. A question that my inner voice raised and the answer it provided left me in tears. Was it not expected of me to undergo a feeling of uneasiness when I did certain things, not because I had been told not to do them, nor because I feared His displeasure – but spontaneously? If I listened to my conscience, that feeling of uneasiness was sure to arise when I did that which was contrary to what my inner voice told me.

"Strive Consistently to Reach My Height," My Guru said

The dream on 5th October '95 was as follows: Baba's form before me was very blurred and it made me feel lost. I prayed to Him to help me see better. The very next moment my vision improved and I could see Him clearly. Our eyes met and I prayed, "O Lord, help me see clearly. Give me your Divine counsel." He smiled back and the scene changed. At the CRY office, I looked on with contentment at the height I had gained which made me a few inches taller than the rest of my colleagues. I ran to Baba. He said, "Khurshid, I feel it necessary to counsel you. How can you stop your efforts at becoming taller? Merely gaining a height that has made you taller than others at your office, does not mean you are the tallest. Stand before me." As I stood up, it surprised me to see Him grow in height. I, in turn, stretched myself and finally when I did manage to reach His height I was quite satisfied with myself. But my joy was short-lived because within seconds He had assumed a much larger form and I was once again busy stretching myself to reach His height. When I managed to do so He played the same trick and He was again much taller than me. The thought of Him having to look down upon me was crushing, but He put my mind to rest by holding my hands in His and giving them an upward jerk, helping me gain further height and said softly, "Khurshid, never give up. Don't ever feel satisfied at gaining any height lesser than mine. Keep me before your mind's eye at all times and carry on with your effort. And I, on my part, will never leave you."

The above dream taught me more than one lesson. If I always dwelled on the idea that I was going to be transformed, then I would help the process of my progress on the path that led to Him. If, on the contrary, I gave in to dejection and bewailed that I was not fit or that I was incapable of realisation, I hampered my own progress. My belief in my potential had to be moulded by my faith in the Lord. It was impermissible to have a lack of faith in my own capacity. To have constant self-distrust was as bad as the pride that made me feel that I had reached perfection and no more efforts were needed in that direction. Yet, to attain a likeness (to Him) seemed a distant reality. At best I could aim for getting closer to becoming His image.

Every Single Effort of Mine at Sunbeam was being Cemented by His Blessings

The next lesson came in a dream on 10th October '95. He, my beloved Lord, brought to my notice that I still thought and felt in terms of a separate existence from Him who was the in dweller of my heart.

In the dream, for what seemed like eternity, I prayed before the Lord's photo-frame hung on the wall. My prayers were not in vain. Finally He stood before me, in His present human form. But alas! it was too late. My thirst for His darshan had not yet quenched when I received a call and was told that I had better hurry as my ticket to Baba was confirmed and the train I was to board would be leaving shortly. I sat by His silent, sleeping Divine form, wiping the sweat off His brow, caressing His face and kissing Him lightly on both the cheeks, wishing Him a fond farewell as it was certain that I was to board the train that would bring me to Him via a different route! "O Baba, I wish these lovely moments could have lasted longer. But it is not to be so since I am supposed to leave and be on my way to you soon," I whispered into His ear in the hope that in His sleep He would not come to know of my agony at the separation from Him, now to be united with Him at a soul level. My dear Lord, who had pretended to be fast asleep till then, now took me by surprise by lifting His head so very slightly and kissing me on my right cheek!

Suddenly the scene changed and the dream continued. Perhaps in order to let me know that He was playing the role of the director of my life He, for a fraction of a second, assumed the form of Mr. Bhagwat (the then Director of the CRY – Child Relief and You where I worked). Within seconds He was back to His own form. "Come my child, let's carry on with our respective jobs," He said. As I walked up to Him I knew exactly what He expected of me. From the heap of bricks that lay on the ground, I picked up one at a time and placed them on top of each other and also sideways in order to build a wall. My Lord, in turn, plastered each brick with cement. In no time the structure grew in size as a result of our combined effort.

Dear friends, in a few years time, I was to be on a journey with Him via the karma marg, doing social work. Perhaps, that's what He had tried to convey via this dream. But just at that point in time, the dream hadn't made much sense.

Equally symbolic was the latter part of the dream. Now that I think of it, He must have given me a glimpse of what was to happen in the future. This had perhaps been His way of foretelling about the structure of Sunbeam that our combined, tireless effort was to bring about – a long, lasting structure of an organisation that was to cater to the psychological and educational needs of the underprivileged children of Mumbai. He would never let the structure of my efforts crumble. He was there all the time to cement them with His love. Recollection of the above dream always brings tears of gratitude.

"Never Doubt what God Tells You in Dreams. It's Bound to Come True One Day," Baba Declared

On 24th November '95 my Lord was there to assure me of keeping His word! In the dream I was one of the few assembled in the interview room where He offered to bless us with His divine counsel by saying, "All of you, feel free to ask whatever you wish."

When the rest had finished with their queries and He had answered them patiently, I enquired, "Baba, to those who don't get the chance to be physically close to you, you appear in their dreams. What if things you have promised in the dreams don't materialise for months together or even years at a stretch?" My Lord appeared hurt as He replied, "Never doubt what God tells you in dreams. So what if years pass by? One day it is bound to happen as per the word given."

Visions of Lord Christ and Baby Krishna

On 29th October '95 my Lord had appeared in my dream, this time in the form of Lord Christ. It was after a long, long time that He granted me darshan in that form. Glad to be blessed thus I took His permission to visit Him in Parthi where He was presently staying.

(In December '95 I did make a one week memorable trip to Parthi along with some Sai devotees from Mumbai.)

1st December '95 proved to be a glorious morning beginning with a clear vision of baby Krishna during my short period of meditation.

I Missed out on Him Dwelling in Nandini's Father

On 11th November '95 Peshotan's father-in-law was supposed to arrive at our place any time that morning and yet I had not woken up early enough to be ready to receive him. My Lord had to take the trouble to come and inform me of the error. In the dream I stood with joined palms patiently awaiting the Lord's darshan. Someone passed by me unnoticed until I cared to look at him again and to my shock I saw him turn towards me and it was my Lord who looked at me laughing away that I had failed to recognise Him and still awaited His arrival – arrival of one who had already come and gone. For a few moments He had changed His form and a close look revealed that He had appeared as Peshotan's father-in-law!

On waking up I was full of shame and remorse. That the train was delayed and he actually arrived at our place close to afternoon, was not the point.

Baba Agreed with Me that I Needed to Save for a Rainy Day

I was adamant that dad save his salary for his old age. But this insistence on my part was not looked upon with kindness. On the one hand dad claimed that it inferred a lack of faith on my part; a lack of faith in Him as the sole provider, and live in the present instead of worrying about the future. On the other hand, in my view it was imperative to fulfil my duties towards my parents while carrying on with my efforts to reach God. If I could assert my rights as a member of the family, I had no right to forget my duties either. Had my efforts been directed in making my own future secure, dad's statement would hold true.

My Lord was the sole witness to see that my work was without attachment to any fruit or reward, without any egoistic attitude or motive, simply an act of what I felt was my duty. How could I then by my simple act of love set a wrong example to others?

"Baba, had you been in my place, what would you have done? Should I spend whatever little I can spare or save, invest and multiply it for my parents' future though I know you are the one to see to everyone's needs?"

The next morning i.e. on 28th December '95 it made me feel happy to hear Jasmine relate to me her dream of that morning. She had seen Baba perform an unusual miracle before a gathering of devotees. Displaying a one rupee note to those around Him, He surprised them by changing it into two rupee note by a wave of his hand. And then by another wave of His hand it turned into a five rupee note.

There lay my answer. He had assured me that I hadn't gone wrong. Wrong I'd have been had I begun to shirk my duty.

Be Humble and the Lord will Open out His Heart to You

In the days to follow, Baba continued to grant darshan in dreams as before. On the 29th as well as on the 31st of December '95 He appeared to me. One particular scene that left a lasting impression on my mind was that of people sitting in two groups, one full of those who claimed themselves to be His devotees and the other comprising of people who considered themselves to be His students. As far as the first group was concerned, their vision of Sai was blocked by a huge wall between them and Him and I felt sad for them as against the group of students (young and old) who had a very clear vision of Sai. And I watched from behind a pillar the way He patiently dealt with each student.

Via the above dream, how sweetly He had brought home the point that only those who were humble, opened out their hearts and were willing to learn all that He had to teach were worthy of His darshan as against those who merely claimed themselves to be His devotees and let the veil of ignorance block their vision instead of making an effort to move in the direction which could enable them to see Him clearly. Yes, that is the drama I had seen myself watch from behind the pillar and prayed that I continue to be His student and He let me be in His Divine School to help me reach a higher standard of perfection with every passing day.

Baba Expressed His Joy at My Shopping Spree

One evening before I could decide on whether I had done the right thing or not in uttering a lie, He responded by once again appearing to Jasmine. First let me relate the lie I had spoken in order to avoid unpleasantness at home. When from my own hard earned money, I purchased 9 pairs of clothes for the children of construction labourers at the site opposite our office, I told my family that these were purchased from the money Nargish Aunty had given me. Not that my family would have found fault in this action of mine but it would have been one more cause of concern for them that I didn't buy anything for myself, thereby neglecting my own needs. Jasmine's clothes fitted me well and she had of late been buying more of Punjabi suits than jeans, skirts or dresses in order that I may have a decent range of clothes for myself! (This is because I wore Punjabi suits and no other dress to work.)

"O Lord, I know I cannot expect you to be telling me every moment all that is not perfectly spiritual in the details of my actions from morning till night. These are things to see for myself. Yet, I implore you to come to my aid and let me know if you too would have done Christmas shopping the way I did had you been in my place." Immediately in response to my silent prayer (which I had not shared with anyone at home), He appeared to Jasmine in a dream on 29th December '95, a dream in which He climbed up the stage, His hands filled with parcels – the day's shopping!

Sai Expects Me to be as Patient with Others as He has been with Me Throughout

An early signal that my relationship with family or relatives was in danger, I found, was harsh criticism. At times their expressions of disliking me or completely disagreeing with me, affected my peace.

I knew that if I took offence at that moment, I would no longer hear them out without distortion or respond with clear-headedness – hence I kept quiet. I had begun to put in an effort to understand others by editing what I heard, ignoring the hostility or the nasty tone by being non-defensive and concentrating on the principal message. It helped me understand things from their perspective.

Yet, I lacked somewhere and it showed at times when the tensions and pressures at home and office grew unbearable and it made me snarl and snap at somebody, usually those who were nearest and dearest to me.

One day, I was quite upset with Jasmine, my younger sister. To my surprise, the same night Baba appeared in her dream and hugged her. This was in response to my silent prayer as to how He wanted me to react to her insensitivity towards me. This made her feel all the more that she had been right and reiterated that she prayed to God to help me improve! That was the last straw – and I told Baba that hugging her, instead of reprimanding her, to me was a questionable act on His part and I needed an immediate answer from Him as to how He wanted me to carry on in such a situation. His answer in the dream astounded me. The dream was as follows:

I found myself in the compound of the Byramjee School (where I had myself studied as a child). The bus driver refused to take the responsibility of driving Jasmine to her home. Just then (in the dream) Jasmine had taken the form of a 1st standard child dressed in school uniform, her hair tied in 2 little pigtails, sitting stubbornly on the floor and not willing to budge unless I carried her in my arms. Upon confronting Baba who was at the driver's seat, this is what He had to say to me: "Listen Khurshid, you have been one of those who always had me at the steering-wheel of your car and I had taken full responsibility of your studies. So I patiently carried you in my arms right from the time you started attending primary classes. I saw to it that from primary class you reached high school and then college and finally other advanced courses. Considering that I never gave up on you, don't you think it's only fair that you too deal with utmost patience with this kid as well as the others whom I have left under your care?"

Once again my Lord's simple but clear explanation had left me full of remorse. True, I had been very fortunate to have the Lord Himself at the steering-wheel of my life's car. My error was that I had compared the spiritual understanding of a primary school child (as per the standards of the Lord's university) in need of constant unconditional acceptance and guidance to that of a person whom the Lord had personally taught innumerable lessons in life. This attitude of intolerance did not become of me. Embracing Jasmine would be my first step towards coming up to my guru's expectations. In that moment she was a six year old, waiting to be taken into my arms.

"Have a Broader Perspective and be Ever Alert if You Wish to be at My Feet," Baba Hinted

Once again I found myself questioning the Lord's behaviour of treating with utmost affection those who (in my sight) needed to be brought to their senses quickly. Smita (name changed) was one such person who I believed was getting away with treating me shabbily. How could I have committed the grave error of being ever on the alert to find fault, discover apparent defects even in the Divine?! In questioning His actions wasn't I merely trying to succeed in finding some superficial shortcoming in Him! It was not at all correct on my part to evaluate Him by such human standards of the obvious and apparent. And I begged Him to forgive me by guiding my steps.

The joy surging in me after the revelation in the dream to follow on 14th January '96 at 3.50 a.m. was the true sign that my soul had awakened and had sensed the truth. Now I found it easy to open to the influence of the descending truth and be shaped by it. But before I carry on any further, let me narrate to you the dream which was as follows: My Lord was giving a discourse to a large gathering and I found myself in the far corner at the other end of the hall. Slowly and steadily I inched my way to get closer to Him and with each new effort moved in His direction until I found myself at His feet, away from the crowd. He carried on with the discourse, His eyes resting on me every now and then with tender, motherly affection flashing in them. The minute He stopped addressing the public, I grabbed at the chance of asking Him if I could remain at His feet to which He gently responded with, "Do you know how you can be at my feet? Demonstrate to me as to how you can do so." Before bending low and pressing my eyes to His lotus feet, I promptly removed my spectacles and He retorted approvingly, "Yes, you have to remove your glasses. That's right." As I was about to press my eyes to His feet, I found Him stretching Himself and standing on His toes. I looked up to catch Him smiling merrily and He said, "This is how you should be if you wish to be at my feet." The next moment I got up and stood facing Him and He pressed His thumb over my eyes in order to improve my inner vision further. He gently rubbed my eyes, saying, "You know, she can appear directly for her final year of graduation, skipping all the in-between classes. It is possible for her to do so, don't worry." As He let my eyes open I found Smita next to Him, whom He had obviously been referring to! With that the dream came to an end and I sat recapitulating all that I had seen.

There were tears of gratitude and repentance streaming down my cheeks. Of course I had to be on my toes at all times – i.e. always alert to ever remain on the right track. I had to view the world without glasses – from another's point of view in order to understand their perspective. And His final message about Smita made me feel ashamed of myself at having underestimated her potential of the possibility of extremely rapid spiritual progress.

My Lord had implied that I was giving up on Smita too easily. The qualities of understanding and selflessness that I had hoped for in her were there all along. They would appear when they were ready and not before. I didn't have to expect too much too soon, but try to set a good example by being a patient and unselfish friend and parent to her. Expecting too much of her was unfair because (as shown in the dream) she was still a primary school kid – in His sight. It was silly of me to expect a child of her age to exhibit traits of selfless love and recognise the Divine in one and all – something that had taken me years to develop (with His constant guidance) and over which I still had only a slippery hold.

My Longing for His Darshan at the Cost of Duty Met with His Disapproval

On 20th January '96 at 6 a.m. He responded to my request of

permitting me to make a short trip to Parthi at the cost of missing out two lectures at NIIT where I was receiving computer training free of cost (part of NIIT's contribution to CRY). Besides, very often my mind wandered to the Lord while the classes were on and as a result, Kevin, our instructor, had to repeat to me the different commands which he always did with great patience.

In the dream, a child was seen performing his dance, trying his utmost to keep everyone's attention focussed on him. Baba sat at a distance watching the little boy as he painstakingly tried to teach the audience his dance, step by step. Every now and then my gaze shifted from the child to Baba and in the event I missed out on a few of the steps the child had taken. This made it impossible for me to understand the steps that followed. But the little boy performed those steps all over again. Though at first my Lord seemed amused at my behaviour, a time came when He reprimanded me by gestures that I keep my vision focussed on the child performing before me and not on Him. I did obey Him but wondered if this dance was worth mastering at the cost of giving up on my Lord's darshan. Soon the performance came to an end and the child looked downcast and sullen when he found me staring at him with a blank look on my face. The fault lay not in his teaching but in my mind that had wavered so often. In very gentle tones our Lord addressed the child by pointing out to me and with His eyes that shifted from the child to me and back to him, "You know, her sight is always fixed on me, hence she missed out on how well you performed." So saying He began to clap and the audience also applauded the kid's performance and I knew I had to follow suit to learn to appreciate others' efforts. With that the dream ended.

The purpose of the CRY management making me attend the computer classes was clear – they expected me to update my knowledge so as to serve the organisation better. Hence, I was betraying the trust they had placed in me. Besides, by not paying attention during the lectures, I was showing disrespect to Kevin, who was a good teacher, fully dedicated to his job. While I lived in this world I had to learn to respect my guru, be it a spiritual guru or the one who guided me to enhance my knowledge to help me advance in my worldly career.

It's Unwise to Spend too Much on Rituals, Especially when there is Paucity of Funds

One issue over which I argued with dad was his monthly expenditure of approximately Rs. 1,000 which he incurred merely on lighting lamps at home, at the fire temple, at the tomb of Maiji's guru or adorning the tomb or photo-frames of saints with flowers or burning incense or sandalwood. To me it was a sheer waste of money given the fact that dad's salary was barely around Rs.4,000. The idea of paying priests in the fire temple to pray for the departed souls of my grand parents or younger brother who had left the world years back also made me feel angry at what I mistook as dad's negligence towards me. I toiled day and night to make two ends meet and was compelled to take monetary assistance from friends when my salary didn't suffice for the family. My sister had been saving her salary for her marriage. My brother had stopped giving any financial support after his own marriage. (He did start contributing a few years later though and eventually he took care of the entire expenses for our parents.) Dad loved me utmost and had a serene conviction that the Lord would guide us on the issue, and the minute He would command so, he'd cut down on the expenditure he incurred otherwise on rituals.

I wanted dad to surmount his only weakness and ignorance; to create a place in his heart where the well-being of his living child (myself) would get precedence over the satisfaction of having spent money on rituals for the peace of the departed souls (granny or Jehangir) or burn oil on lighting lamps that Maiji had lit daily during her lifetime.

Now I demanded an answer from the Lord. In the dream to follow Maiji appeared to me and I found myself pleading that she tell me if I had done the right thing in telling dad to stop spending money on rituals. Maiji blessed me and then moved out of sight. The scene changed. Right before my eyes appeared a curtain covering a stage. Then the same curtain began to lift, making the stage gradually visible. Finally the full stage was in view. And who but Lord Ganesha – the Lord of wisdom – in all His majesty sat on a throne! After this dream never once did I feel guilty at having made dad give up his expenditure on rituals and lighting lamps and incense. (At a later date, Maiji again appeared in my dream and specifically told me to advise dad not to spend more than Rs.100 per month on lamps and the like.)

According to My Guru, I Still had a Long Distance to Cover to be an Exemplary Devotee

The year 1996 began with a beautiful lesson. "Pride and satisfaction with oneself are the worst obstacles in one's progress." The dream I had early in the morning on 1st January '96 left me in a state which cannot be expressed in words. In the dream I entered a shop where tiny statues of Lord Ganesha were kept for sale. To my surprise there were no customers for the same and as I looked about me in a baffled state, one of those statues fell into my hand and I tried to hold it in my fist. I had not yet succeeded in my effort, when the owner of the shop came in my way and snatched it away saying, "Before you can claim to be able to hold Lord Ganesha in your fist, you have to pay its price. What you have given till date is barely half its value. The day you pay me the balance you shall be able to hold Lord Ganesha in your fist." "What do you mean by that?" I queried, taken aback, and pat came the reply, "Have a look at this."

The scene in the dream changed and I found myself explaining to Nandini (my brother's wife) that she shouldn't partake of the food from the same plate as mine since there was a possibility that I still suffered from tuberculosis, a contagious disease, as I bled from the mouth occasionally. Once again the scene changed – this time I was at the office with Neerja (my colleague) who was eating with relish from my lunch box. Not having enough courage to let the whole office know of my illenss, I justified my sin of hiding the fact by consoling myself that there was every possibility that the bleeding from my mouth was either from the gums or caused by ulcers in my stomach and could not be tuberculosis. With that the dream came to an end.

To transform my ordinary human consciousness into the divine and live in that divine state every second of my life was expected of me – and here I was, a selfish human stumbling the way I was as shown in the above dream. To be able to hold Lord Ganesha in one's hand was symbolic of gaining mastery over oneself, equal to having gained spiritual wisdom. At this point it struck me how far from it I still was. It would be sheer arrogance on my part to believe I'd achieve it in this life of mine but the least I could do was to take steps to rectify the errors brought to my notice. From then onwards, though I let colleagues at the office partake of the food from the extra lunch box, I didn't hesitate to stop them from eating from the same tiffin or use the spoon with which I ate. Soon I got the necessary blood tests and tuberculosis tests done and fortunately the reports were negative.

My Guru Declared that I Had Passed out from His University, Hence Had Stood First

20th February '96 – 6.45 a.m. Dream. As our Lord walked in the midst of the public, I closely observed His movements, the way He poured out consolation to the suffering, advised those who sought His counsel, Himself walked up to others who needed Him yet were too obstinate to budge from their place to take any step in His direction. I watched Him at His work of bringing about a transformation of the hearts of one and all whom He came in contact with and decided to try and follow His footsteps.

The scene changed and I found it surprisingly easy to love even those who harmed me by reminding myself of the Lord's teaching to see the spiritual age and not the age of the physical body of the person concerned. Once again the scene changed and to my great joy my Lord was in sight. People gathered and took their seats. All eyes were glued to Him. Every single place was occupied and I squeezed myself between two chairs and sat on the floor. Though I was seated right in the front, strangely enough His voice never reached my ears. His lips moved, repeating a word that I couldn't catch. Then a faint sound could be heard and I couldn't believe my ears when I heard His voice so desperately calling out my name, "Khurshid, Khurshid, Khurshid, Kh..." When all eyes turned to where I was seated, I now felt for sure that He was calling me. The faint whispers were by now quite audible and I could clearly hear Him call my name.

I ran to Him and He gathered me in His arms. Not wanting those blissful moments to end, I clung on to Him like a little child. A few seconds later, I fell at His feet. It seemed I had met my Lord after an eternity and not just the two weeks that had passed without His darshan. The fear of losing Him once again gripped me and I pleaded with Him, "Baba, don't ever forget me. Don't you know I can't exist without you? Baba, when I die please grant me mukti or when I am reborn at least let me be close to you so that I don't miss you." Gently moving His one hand over my head and with the other hand holding me by the waist, my Lord replied in sweet loving tones, "But I've never once forgotten you, Khurshid. And I'll never forget you." Then gently pulling Himself away from me and placing His hand over my shoulder, both of us stood facing the crowd as He declared, "She has passed from the Sai University, hence first."

Perform Your Duties Without Expectations of the Fruits Thereof

Barely two months had passed after the above dream and without any reservations I asked the Lord if at all it was possible to gain His darshan and at the same time tread the road that the majority of the worldly people did.

In response to my above prayer, the dream next morning i.e. on 3rd March '96 was as follows: After waiting for a long time for His darshan and His non-appearance on the scene, I decided to take a stroll and tread the path that led me away from the place where Baba was supposed to give darshan. On and on, I walked; yet there was no end to the road. Gradually, darkness began to descend and I decided to turn back and run to the Lord before it was too late. But in doing so, I faced a major obstacle. Both my feet had disappeared and laboriously I dragged myself with the help of my hands. Though it was very difficult I finally managed to reach the destination and there stood my Lord right before my eyes, smiling.

I received my answer via this dream that one cannot have both – the world and the Lord – at the same time. Here let me clarify that by my above statement I do not claim that one should renounce the world, but be in the world, amidst the worldly work or duties assigned to oneself, and yet be above all attachment to the fruits of one's effort.

Don't Limit the Indweller of all Merely to His Physical Form

In response to my prayer that a friend of mine wanted to know why she didn't get His darshan in spite of trying her utmost to live up to His expectations by giving up all worldly desires, the dream that I had the next morning (on 4th March '96) provided me with an insight to the reason that kept Him away from her. In the dream my friend's vision was focussed on the chair placed on the stage for Baba to occupy. Hence she failed to have His darshan though He was right there on the (world) stage, not on the chair but moving amongst people from all walks of life busy with some job or the other. The minute I pointed it out to her, she shifted her focus and was blessed with a glimpse of Him every now and then as He moved amongst His children – of all age groups, from different countries, rich and poor.

Indeed, He is the indweller of all. Then how can we make the mistake of limiting Him to His human form? If each of us put in an effort to visualise the divinity in others, we are sure to have His darshan in people whom we come across in our daily lives.

Jasmine, My Sister, was Blessed to have the Lord Himself Choose Her Life Partner

Now I come to the topic of surrender – total submission to His will in every little matter of our lives. We at home had coaxed Jasmine into meeting eligible grooms. On 3rd March '96 she went with our parents to meet Yezdi for the first time. Though she liked him instantly, how could we have expected her to take such a major decision of her life merely on the basis of one meeting? Her fear and hesitation in taking any further steps were justifiable. To my great surprise she requested me to ask the Lord for His advice. The answer I received was a favourable one. Yet, I could understand her feelings when she stated that it would have made a world of difference to her were the Lord to appear directly to her instead of giving any answers through me. Here, I believe, she was completely justified in her expectation and I felt proud of her faith in God to the extent of wanting to go by whatever He willed for her in such a major decision in her life.

I had a dream on 6th March '96. Jasmine and I were travelling by road. The scene changed and now the journey was by rail. Jasmine and dad were also in the same bogie as mine. At a particular station I expected Jasmine to alight but being in a confused state of mind she didn't know what to do and didn't budge from her seat. I ran out and went up to Baba who was at the driver's seat, requesting Him to wait awhile and not start the train because though He expected Jasmine to alight at that particular station, she needed time to decide. He put my disturbed mind at rest by saying, "Of course I shall give her time. I shall personally help her take the decision. She has to be made to understand that she has reached her destination and cannot travel with you and parents any further." The train had halted a little longer than usual and finally it began to puff away, leaving me in tears that Jasmine had not been able to take a decision for she found it difficult to believe me when I conveyed to her His message. The train was now out of sight and to my great joy I saw Jasmine on the opposite platform. She had eventually alighted from the train at the station that Baba had wanted her to. She had after all taken the right decision before it was too late. With that the dream ended.

As I sat ruminating over the different messages I had received, my sister woke up with a smile because He had appeared in her dream as well. She seemed so relaxed, so much at peace with life because God had answered her sincere prayer. The previous night, she had asked Him to give her darshan in the dream if He approved of Yezdi. Though from her side she had liked the boy she had awaited the approval from the Lord who was the only guide she could rely on. That early morning for the first time in her life she had Lord Vishnu's darshan in a dream. Lord Vishnu had taken a very, very huge form and she saw Him in a reclining posture on a big serpent. The bus in which she travelled circled around Him. Later in the dream she had darshan of the various avatars but all she could remember of that part of the dream upon waking up was that she had also had the darshan of Sri Krishna, Shirdi Sai and Sathya Sai. How symbolic the dream was. Isn't it true that our lives revolve around our Lord? And He had blessed Jasmine with a dream of multiple forms of His. Once again He had proved that He is always there for us – we only need to call out and He will reply.

Today, when I'm at a re-edit of the book, I'm so full of gratitude to Baba for having guided Jasmine in choosing her life's partner. Yezdi is a gem of a person, caring and loving. My sister is blessed to have him as her husband. With their two lovely children, Pearl and Jehan, they are leading a happy life together.

Our Divine Professor Guiding My Steps Once Again

The same evening I was in a lazy mood and felt like resting at home instead of attending office the next day, availing of casual leave on the pretext of mother's illness. As I had leave to my credit that would have lapsed otherwise, I thought that was good enough a reason to lie!

Next morning i.e. on 7th March '96 the message of the Lord put me to shame and I soon dressed up and was on my way to the office. The dream was as follows: In a disturbed state of mind I found myself at the cross-roads of an unknown place and was puzzled as to which turn to take to find my way back home. As I looked about desperately in need of direction, I saw Baba in a tearing hurry rushing towards the marble building on the opposite road. On approaching Him I told Him about my predicament and He in turn replied, "Khurshid, I shall show you the way." He walked briskly and I kept pace with Him. He said, "I am on my way to the college to coach the batch of newcomers awaiting me." I looked on in awe as the Divine Professor took me up to the main gate of that marble building that looked more of a temple than a college building. The gate-keeper asked Him in surprise, "How come she is back here?" Giving me a kind look, He turned to the man and said, "Even though I have hardly any time on my hands, busy as I am training the batch of freshers, I always spare time to show the path to my ex-students as well. And she happens to be an ex-student of mine who has lost her way at the moment and needs guidance. Each time that she passes through my gate she finds her way." Now in a much kinder tone He addressed me, "Khurshid, walk straight and take the right turn." Not grasping the import of His words I mumbled a thank you, saying I'd make sure not to take the left turn. To that He replied a trifle annoyed, "There is no such thing as left turn. It is either the right turn or the wrong turn that one takes in life." The dream ended.

Tears slid down my cheeks as I thought of the patience with which my Lord (the Professor) treated me (His ex-student) though He was always busy with the newcomers (who were yet to be trained by Him personally just the way He had for years at a stretch trained me). I needed to be alert at all times and not justify my wrong actions. If I could realise that, then even the smallest thing to which I did not usually pay much attention to or cared for, ceased to be trivial and insignificant, and became full of meaning and opened up a vast horizon beyond.

The Lord's Disappointment at My Inability to Love all Equally

With Jasmine's marriage in the air, lists of items to be purchased were being prepared – jewellery, furniture; utensils, clothes and other household items besides the expenditure we'd have to incur on dinner for the guests, expenses for the rent of the wedding hall, lighting, music, flowers, wedding cards, etc., etc. We had shares that could be sold to meet the above expenditure in part and for the balance I was sure that Peshotan would come to our aid. So much of my time I spent in preparing for the wedding. Thus my life had become a round of various desires and attachments towards my family. As long as I was preoccupied with them, there could be no lasting progress in me, even if that desire was for the well-being of others – simply because it was limited to the well-being of my own blood relations.

What was duty after all? Was it really my attachment – attachment that had become established and I called it duty? Duty was good to a certain limit. But when attachment became chronic, I had made the mistake of elevating it with the high-sounding name of duty. Yes, this is precisely what I was doing – as pointed out to me in two different dreams to follow on 8th March '96 and 13th March '96.

8th March '96 – Dream: From where I stood on the balcony of a building next to the open grounds where crowds had gathered for darshan, I had to stretch myself and always stand on my toes to have a full view of Baba where He sat at that moment. My Lord turned to me but the look in His eyes as they met mine spoke that He was displeased with my behaviour. By gestures He let me know that merely standing on my toes was not good enough, whereupon I joined my hands in reverence and He imitated me once again, conveying by gestures and with a smile of satisfaction that this was how I was expected to be if I wished to have His darshan. It was easy to understand His message that simply feigning obedience to His command to be alert at all times, was wrong. I was expected to be full of humility. Where had I gone wrong? Had I failed Him in some way? "Baba my vision is going from bad to worse," I cried, and He in His usual manner referring to my spiritual sight replied, "Go to doctor." After a long pause He added the word "Shaila". Since I thought I hadn't heard Him right I requested Him to repeat His words and He complied to my request by saying, "Doctor, Shaila." Once again there had been a long pause between the two words He had just repeated. I had jotted down the name in a notebook, telling myself that I was supposed to contact her. Not wanting to miss the opportunity of His closeness, I queried, "Baba, I am writing the book as per your wish. Will you sign it?" "Of course," He said in soft tones. Before handing over to Him the 100 pages rough notebook which contained merely short notes of His messages to me, I told Him, "Baba, in the crowd I feel lost because you don't come to me as close as you are now." Not paying any attention to my complaint, He glanced at the book and then at me and with a pinch of sarcasm in His voice He exclaimed, "Now don't tell me that this is the book and that's the way you have made it!" "No, no Baba, this is merely a rough copy. My fair copy is elsewhere yet to be completed," I replied hurriedly to which He responded by saying, "OK so complete that and then bring it to me." With that the dream ended.

On waking up I wondered for a long time as to who was this doctor by the name of Shaila whom I was supposed to contact, something over which He seemed upset and had to remind me in order to improve my vision. Suddenly everything came back in a rush. The scenes that flashed before my mind's eye left me dumbstruck. Of course I had once again failed Him. Just opposite CRY's office, a building was under construction and the staff members had personally taken on the responsibility to run a small project for the children of the labourers at the site. Besides giving the monetary contribution (voluntarily) which was a mere Rs. 50 from my monthly salary, I had been requested to call up Shaila (an ex-employee of CRY) and arrange for her brother who happened to be a doctor to come and give a free medical check-up to the children. I had noted down Shaila's name and number in the notebook but busy as I was with the work at office and home, this matter never got priority. Would I have treated the matter with such negligence had it concerned the health of my own family members?

As for scolding me for His book being incomplete, here again He was right because I had not been updating the fair copy by adding the recent messages I had received, and I merely noted them down on loose sheets.

Let me come back to the dream message to follow – on 13th March '96. Baba was followed by a bunch of poorly clad, undernourished children and He approached me. He asked if I had food to spare for all these children. Though I was sorry for them, I felt helpless and said I didn't have enough to feed so many mouths. This angered Him and He thundered, "I am the protector of the destitute. If I wish I can provide them with the best of food-stuff but I was merely testing you as to how large-hearted you can be. Nothing ever goes unnoticed by me and you dare to lie to me! You claim you don't seem to have much to offer to these kids. You even dared to calculate the amount you'd have to spend on them if you were to daily give them biscuits whereas you never once give it a thought while planning about making the life of this one child very comfortable by going to any lengths, all the time carrying her in your arms and not letting her be on the streets."

After this dream how small I appeared in my own sight. My Lord had opened my eyes to the fact that it was maya, a veil of ignorance, that blocked my vision – or else how could I have been so senseless as to spend the maximum possible of what dad had kept aside for me (since Jasmine's share couldn't suffice for her marriage expenditure) to see her in comfort and at the same time be so small-minded as to calculate the measly sum that I spent on children's biscuits if I were to buy enough for 10 children daily?

The strings that bound me to my family were too strong and had to be loosened. Our Lord in His own unique way taught me the lesson of my life. He wanted me to be in a perpetual state of joy; at every minute of my life I had to make a choice between what dragged me down and what brought me closer to Him, between what made me progress and what hampered the same. It so happened that I myself didn't know what I needed from life, perhaps in some corner of my heart there was this longing to win over the love of my family members. He knew a little better than myself as to what I needed and He had already resolved to give that to me – an awakening to the truth that I was creating chains that bound me up tight and that I needed to let go of.

What right had I to talk about renunciation or to say that I must renounce attachments? He, my guru, felt it was high time I understood that so long as I had to renounce anything I was still not on the right path; for so long as I had to make an effort to reject attachments, I was not ready for realisation. To renounce meant giving up what I was attached to. By using my own family members as instruments, He opened my eyes to the fact that my attachment towards them hampered my progress and it had to be uprooted from my very being once and for all.

Every Soul on the Path to God Realisation but at his / her own Pace

A dream I had had on 28th March '96 made me look upon people more kindly, to accept human beings with their weaknesses and patiently await the time when they'd realise their mistakes and retrace their steps. The dream was in answer to my desperate plea to the Lord as to how could some individuals not think and act selflessly. Or for that matter why did their conscience not prick them when they hurt others.

The dream at 5 a.m. on 28th March '96 was as follows: Ambica Aunty (a family friend who had expired about a decade ago) alighted from a car and rushed in the same direction that the multitude around me had taken. Catching up with her, I enquired, "Aunty, how come you are back on earth and what for?" "Khurshid, all I have done is that I've changed my clothes. And I have returned in order that I may gain His darshan. If not this time, I shall once again change my clothes and keep coming back till I succeed." Her reply had stunned me.

The dream continued. The sea of humanity that rushed past me claimed that their sole intention was to gain His darshan but also claimed that they were in no hurry, that they didn't mind travelling hither thither nor did it matter to them if they had to change their clothes a number of times before they finally gained His darshan. What puzzled me was their shocked expressions at hearing what I had to say. I informed them of my resolve to have the Lord's darshan before changing my clothes even once. The public insisted that I had taken upon an impossible task and many of them blocked my way to Him. It was clear that I'd reach my goal only by not letting any of them come in my way. As I cleared my path by gently pushing them aside one by one, and took steps in His direction, gradually the distance between the Lord and myself became lesser. At the end of it I was exhausted but felt refreshed the moment my eyes fell on the Lord. He, my guru, my God smiled at me understandingly when I bowed to Him and thanked Him for giving me an opportunity to have His darshan even before changing my clothes i.e. during this lifetime itself; before I had to give up this mortal sheath. With that the dream ended.

The above dream clearly indicated that union with the Divine was not an easy matter and it could possibly take an almost indefinitely long time if one kept worldly affairs and achievements on the priority list. Of course the length of time (of union with the Lord) depended on each individual's effort, but it could be considerably shortened if one made a really firm resolve. Whether we reached God-realisation during this lifetime itself or took a number of lives to achieve that, solely depended on our own efforts and eagerness to do so.

His Multiple Teachings to Me

Once again my Lord stood before me in a dream on 8th April '96 at 5.15 a.m. Patient as He was, my dear guru had yet again taken upon Himself to lead me by the hand towards my destination. This time our Lord stood talking to Nargish Aunty and me and it was a long conversation. He patiently answered all our questions but the only part of the conversation I could recollect on waking up was my confession to Him, "Baba, there are these rare moments when I long for the world though more often than not it's you alone that I have an intense longing for." In a very stern tone He admonished me, "It is not right to want God and the world at the same time. You should seek the Lord alone." I requested Nargish Aunty to leave us alone for a while since I wished to talk to Him in private. She gladly obliged – only to rush back with a book in her hand – a book on Baba. As she still struggled to read the name of the author, a glance was enough for me to know it was one of my volumes. Still straining her eyes she said, "Baba, this book..." and her voice trailed away. Our Lord completed her sentence by saying, "is that of a soul." With that the dream ended.

What was it that I had confessed to the Lord? I confided that I still craved for human love, at least the love of my family members. Firstly, wasn't it very silly and ridiculous to boast about my sacrifices and expecting my family members to sing praises, and yet that is exactly what I had done.

Secondly, I had to remember to express gratitude but didn't have to expect it from others. If I help someone I should let virtue be its own reward. Henceforth I'd do it merely for the satisfaction of lending a helping hand, but never expect anyone to be grateful to me and stand by me in my time of need. On the other hand, if someone else lent me a helping hand at a difficult time in my life – I would remember to thank that person. If I were to give myself, I would do it for the sheer joy of being helpful and try not to recall whether the recipients bother to express their thanks.

Thirdly, in the days to come, increasingly I found myself mirrored in almost everyone I met. The people I saw had problems and obvious human weaknesses. Upon introspection, my innumerable failures and mistakes tended to appear before me like ghosts from the past. I had not always acted with total integrity; I had not always been completely honest. Perhaps some of my failures of the recent past had not been as gross or as obvious as those committed by a few others, but then I had always had greater advantages. I had known the truth longer, had been corrected by the Lord a million times, and was therefore in the wrong even though my failures may have seemed less blatant.

Every time my Lord's loving, comforting, encouraging and appreciative words had always given me way, they had worked magic on me. They had been able to remove all my tiredness and revived in me a sense of meaningfulness in life. Just like I wanted to be loved, wanted to be complimented (by the Lord), so did the others. So, if I had to learn to become an image of His, then – like Him – didn't I too have to be free with well-deserved compliments? (I mean genuine compliments and not flattery.)

Be Humble Enough to Seek Forgiveness of those Whom You Hurt

Having attained a mental state where I could easily forgive others who caused me pain was not enough. Was it not equally important to seek forgiveness of those whom I hurt? When a friend pointed out to me how one of my thoughtless remarks could have possibly hurt her sister and demanded that I apologise to her, in all humility, I did so. The poor lady seemed really embarrassed because she said that she had taken my suggestions in the right spirit, the way they were meant to be.

My genuine apology had not gone unnoticed by my Lord. The next morning at 5 a.m. (i.e. on 6.5.96) He appeared in my dream to let me know how even such a small step on my part had given Him immense joy. There was a huge staircase and people were free to choose their seats on any of the steps. Baba sat on His chair at the bottom of the staircase, but to the right. I ran up the steps and took my seat with a few others on the topmost step. But a huge wall blocked my vision so

I climbed down a few steps, the wall here was a bit low and the top part of the crown of His hair was visible; climbing down a few more steps enabled me to see His complete face. With the intention of having darshan of His complete form from where His feet could be visible, I continued climbing down until I was seated on the bare ground whereas the rest of the crowd sat on their respective, carefully chosen seats on the staircase. My Lord was all smiles as our eyes met and I mentally touched His lotus feet. He walked up to me in long strides. Within minutes He was seated opposite me on the bare ground. In a pleased tone, He addressed the lady next to me by pointing out to me, "Ah! Her heart has expanded and I am very happy for that change in her." With that the dream came to an end.

Experiencing Baba's Closeness as Before

In a dream on 15th June '96 at 5.45 a.m., I had a glimpse of the Lord as He sat in a glass cabin. From afar I bowed to Him and He got up and walked up to me. I took steps in His direction and as we got closer, He held my hand. We walked together hand in hand. Later, we sat on the floor next to each other with my arm around His shoulders and the other hand caressing His face. Just then, I visualised Him only as my child and not my guru. He let me be close to Him as we sat talking to each other. All the time people thought I was the one holding on to Him but the truth was that He too didn't want to let go of me though it didn't appear so to the public. Now and then a student of His passed by us after bowing down to Him in reverence and I wondered how in spite of His ever busy schedule He had the time to spare for an insignificant person like me.

Baba was playing the role of a parent in my life. How could He then let go of me? Just as with any of His millions of devotees all over the world, in my case as well, He was concerned about my spiritual progress and hence was not one to give up on me till the very end.

Our Guru's Prediction on Aban's Invaluable Support to Sunbeam

On 20th July '96 at 8.45 a.m. the dream was as follows: Our dear guru sat opposite me patiently listening to my requests. "Baba, Jasmine is getting married. Please bless her and Yezdi." My Lord smiled and nodded in approval. "Baba, is there any special message for Aban?" My Lord had changed His form to that of a little boy who was up to some prank. He said, "She will be spending her time playing with you." "Her future will be spent playing with me!" I echoed incredulously.

"Ah," He said patiently, "that means she will be spending her time playing with me and not you, Khurshid. I am referring to the time when I shall be coming back." So saying, my Lord, still in the form of the little boy, pushed me to the floor and stood on my stomach! The dream ended.

Today, on 30th May 2007 while I'm editing this Volume once again, I am dazed at the manner in which His prophecy has come true. Aban is indeed taking care of Him, my brainchild in the form of 'Sunbeam', a Public Charitable Trust reaching out to over a thousand underprivileged children in Mumbai. My dear friend now devotes her full-time to Sunbeam that takes care of the education and psychological needs of our child beneficiaries.

Baba Blessing Me with Vibhuti

It gave me immense joy to think of the innumerable incidents in the past when He had showered me with love. On 23rd May '96 at 2 a.m. (during my trip to Whitefield) in a dream He had blessed me by applying vibhuti on my forehead and also with a loving smile granted permission to touch His feet. The dream was symbolic and just when I was wondering if in reality I would be blessed with His vibhuti, Vimla (daughter of Khurshid and Indravadan D. Thakur, lovely friends whom I visited during my trips to Bangalore) came and applied Baba's vibhuti on my forehead, vibhuti that had formed itself in large quantities on His photoframes in their house.

Baba Expresses His Love for Dad in a Very Endearing Manner

Now let me quote an instance depicting Sai's sense of humour. In a dream on 25th June '96 at 4.30 a.m. our dear Lord surprised me by the strangeness of His request as He said, "Khurshid, will you make me a cup of tea? You know, actually I have given up tea since years but if you were to offer it to me yourself, it would make me only too happy." Not knowing how to respond since I couldn't fathom if He were serious or merely joking, I stood silent. And the next moment it was all crystal clear and I asked, "O Baba, are you talking about dad who has stopped drinking tea since so many years?" "Yes, I am talking about him. He may start drinking tea if he so desires. But too much tea is not good for health. So he should consume very little quantity of tea, say, like having it Sunday to Sunday," He answered with a mischievous smile.

The above dream had me puzzled that He should take the trouble to throw light on what seemed to me such a trivial matter while I still awaited answers on more urgent issues in life. But that is what our Sai is – a caring mother to one and all. Later in the day, when I shared the dream with dad, he confided in me that though he had given up tea, he had prayed to Baba that he would be glad to have it sometime but only if He Himself offered it to him. And that is why the above dream! Not a single prayer of a devotee goes unheard by Him. Perhaps it was because dad had been earlier addicted to tea that He had advised that he consume it in small quantities.

Now coming back to my own journey with my guru, I felt that He was the toughest taskmaster in the whole world. No matter how hard I tried, rather I didn't try as hard as I should have, and judging by His standards I at times fell short of His expectations. The purpose, I believe, was to break me down (the 'I' in me) and rebuild me into a person who, someday, would walk tall.

He had set so many rules for my behaviour in life out of which perhaps there were a few I couldn't adhere to. The messages contained in the book are those in which He has tried to convey the whole essence of the necessary teachings in the simplest and briefest form. Mine is a very exceptional case for the Lord to spend so much of His time in the direct teaching of one individual, but through these Volumes, His messages shall, as per His will, reach out to tens of thousands of others, and may help them to an extent. I am sure that the good that will come about by these books shall far outweigh the trouble it might bring to my family who might feel hurt and embarrassed to face the world in the event of my personal life full of faults becoming public.

By being Harsh on a Child Beneficiary, I had Ended up Hurting the Sai Dwelling in Her

Let me quote an instance in my life via which He reminded me of one of His rules to which He expected strict adherence – Never hurt others by your speech or action.

Our Lord in the form of Shirdi Sai appeared in Jasmine's dream on 15.7.96 and permitted her to touch His feet. But there was something more to the dream then just that. On waking up she also remembered to have noticed that our Lord's nails had grown, that they were not neatly trimmed as expected. It was something that made no sense to her but long after she had spoken, her words kept ringing in my ears, reminding me of my error of the day before of hurting a little kid of our CRY neighbourhood project by scolding her for not trimming her nails which were so full of dirt. (I was unaware that the nail-cutter we had provided the crèche teacher with was never put to use and had made the mistake of assuming that this child didn't pay attention to her personal hygiene.) Little 5 year old Parvati had piteously cried out, "Had I the privilege of owning a nail-cutter or even a scissor, I'd not have given you the opportunity to rebuke me so." It was the Lord dwelling in her whom I had wounded with my thoughtless speech and Jasmine's dream put me to shame. I was contrite.

Jasmine's dream had set me thinking on other issues as well besides hygiene. Whenever the kids had asked for biscuits I had obliged. But wasn't that a cruel deed instead of a kind one? If I really cared for them, I had to teach them never to receive anything for nothing. The character of the children had to be made strong and self-reliant. Hence, in the days to come, with the help of the contribution from CRY staff members, I saw to their education (schooling and tuitions), and a daily supplementary nourishing meal, took them out to excursions, taught them hygiene, etc. Thus I learnt that children are charming saplings, full of promise, who can be made, by wise care and well-directed love, to blossom into ideal citizens. It was a learning for me that it is not wrong to love children but one must know how to channelize that love. Obligations towards these kids do not end by giving them a rupee coin or a packet of biscuits. They should also be provided with a nourishing diet, education and also be made aware of the right values in life. I needed to work more closely with their parents to ensure a steady decline of their dependency on us for their children's education and healthcare.

Puja Marwaha, HRD Head at CRY Extends Support and Cooperation at all Levels

On 27th August '96 in a dream I was a silent spectator watching the scene from afar. The Lord it seemed was playing my role as He turned to individuals who were the managerial level staff at CRY. Surprisingly, His voice could easily reach them though they stood at quite a distance from where He was. They were even sympathetic upon hearing of His problems.

Let me explain the message in the dream in which my Lord's voice reached out to the CRY management. My failing vision proved a hindrance at my work, especially when I was expected to be at the computers for long periods of time. With vision in one eye gone and the vision in the other eye getting affected, I was worried and shaken. Over the years I had developed a strong sense of self-reliance. Yet today, I realised I would need to request Puja (HR Head, my boss and a very dear friend) to give me assignments that wouldn't involve much work on computers. Till date I had a compulsion to prove that I could succeed at anything a person with normal vision could do. Hence, when Puja had sent me for computer training on 'Windows', I had attended it regularly; and when I was expected to work on 'Windows', I plunged into the new challenge with determination by magnifying the letters to almost 3 times their normal size but that was not possible at all times since I worked in Human Resources Division and was supposed to keep matters confidential. Most of the time my eyes watered and there was a lot of burning in the only eye that still had vision in it. A shadow of dread came over me. Yet I had to stay on the job because I needed the money. The dream had indicated that frank disclosure of serious personal problems was the best policy. How true that advice proved to be. Puja was very understanding and reduced my computer work considerably, even allowed me to send hand-written letters.

The day after my talk to Puja, I had another reason to be grateful that I had raised the issue. It also gave me a chance to voice my concern and my feeling of inability to take up the new position she offered me – that of an HR executive instead of continuing to work as a secretary. I had no writing skills nor possessed any HR skills or qualifications but she was very confident I'd be able to manage things well and encouraged me to give it a try instead of asking for a transfer to Admin. where she felt my aptitude would be wasted. I could see that Puja appreciated me for giving my best, even if I couldn't be functioning at my usual level with my physical handicap coming in the way. After obtaining permission from the Management Committee, she appointed an assistant in the HR department who proved to be of great help to me for he was hard working and took on much of my computer related workload.

On 28th August '96 my Lord appeared in my dream twice within a span of just a few hours. The first time He let me touch His feet but the second time, by gestures, told me to remain seated where I was.

The Sai Dwelling in Jyoti, the Caretaker

One evening, just before I left for my own home leaving Nargish Aunty in the caring hands of Jyoti, I had made the mistake of feeling sad that I had not had the Lord's darshan since the past few days. He responded immediately by appearing to me in the Shirdi Sai form in a dream early next morning where I saw Him seated on a mattress spread out in Nargish Aunty's puja room and, being unaware of His presence,

I saw myself enter the room and bow before His photo frames in different forms until my eyes fell on Him seated so humbly on the floor – and I regretted my foolish behaviour.

In the above dream, my Lord had been representing Jyoti who had, at one word from Aunty, left her job and home in Sholapur to be at her bedside in Mumbai within 24 hours of my call to her. The first night of her stay there, I was still around, sleeping in Aunty's room and due to lack of space, Jyoti had slept in the puja room by spreading out a mattress on the floor, precisely where I had had Lord Shirdi Sai's darshan.

Our Guru Addressing My Dad as Shankar and Searching for Him in the Front Rows

On 8th September '96, in my dream Baba granted dad the permission to travel to Parthi with Yasmin Aunty who had offered to pay his airfare both ways. She felt that dad would be doing her a favour by accompanying her on this particular trip when she desperately needed someone to be with her to deal with the builders with whom she had booked a flat at Parthi. She needed to make the final settlement and get possession of the house. Papa too had been planning to make a short trip to Parthi in order to hand over Jasmine's wedding invitation card to the Lord before he could distribute it to others.

The dream of 8th September '96 was as follows: Dad sat amongst Seva Dal members (which was a sign that dad was to make the trip to relieve Yasmin Aunty of the tension of having to handle the builders on her own) but I was shooed away from there to a place where CRY staff members had seated themselves. (This I took as an indication of not being permitted to travel to Parthi myself.) Now to my surprise I saw Baba walk straight up to me. He was dressed in a white pant and shirt and limped just like dad, who had in the recent past developed severe pain in his knees. Coming up to me and giving me a searching look, He enquired of me, "Where's Shankar? Where's Shankar?" Being positive that He was referring to dad I guided Him to where he was seated. Somehow the Lord found it impossible to reach him.

The latter part of the dream indicated that this time dad would not be able to get physically close to the Lord, but the dream was also symbolic in yet another important fact that could not be disregarded. By calling out to my dad as Shankar, the Lord had implied that He and dad were not separate.

A fortnight later dad did make a week's trip with Yasmin Aunty and as per the dream, due to his knee problem, only once could he sit on the floor. At all other times he was compelled to take a seat far behind amongst the sick. On one of the days, Baba had come quite close to dad but not close enough for him to hand over Jasmine's wedding invitation card to Him.

Perhaps He wanted dad to know that whether He showed any outward signs of acceptance or not, He had already acknowledged Yezdi as Jasmine's life partner in March '96 when He had given His approval by appearing in Jasmine's dream. Our guru wanted dad also to understand and accept that he himself was no different than Him whom he worshipped so selflessly and he therefore need not look for any outward sign of acknowledgement.

We are the Makers of Our Own Fate – by Our Own Karma

On 15th October '96 in a dream early in the morning, Lord Shirdi Sai's face radiated love as each person in the room walked up to Him and handed over to Him whatever he / she wished to offer Him and expectantly stretched out the other hand in the palm of which He gave them a glimpse of what He wished to give them in return. Soon it was my turn. (Unfortunately, on waking up, I couldn't recollect if I gave Him anything at all.) Very nervously I stretched out my hand to receive whatever He had to offer and the love glowing in His eyes encouraged me, or rather, gave me the required courage to dare look at my palm where He was to give me a glimpse of my future. Therein I saw Lord Rama in His full splendour and then the form changed to that of baby Krishna – and my joy knew no bounds.

Via the above dream, I suppose, the Lord wants us all to learn the value of long term investments. For instance, in a devotee's life that long term investment could take the form of total surrender to His will. There are times when a human being resents being treated in a particular manner by the world and feels God has forsaken him but in truth he is simply paying for his own karma. In my life He was patiently training me up in building my faith that it was not an impossible task to become His image. Though it would take me some time, probably more than one life, there was no way I would lose hope – in each life He would surely be there to hold my hand and guide my steps towards the destination. Thus, even if my investment in going as per His Will was to take a lifetime to mature and blossom, it was still worth the wait. Before I'd close my eyes in this very life itself He was sure to be by my side as per His repeated promises.

Humility Alone can Grant us the Lord's Darshan

The fact that anger still existed in me made me feel ashamed. I resolved to unfold within myself sympathy, affection and tolerance. I had to realise that there were points of view other than my own, and that they could be just as worthy of attention. When I saw the drawback of intolerance in myself, I resolved to take it in hand effectively. On 11th November '96 before going to bed, I begged His forgiveness and promised Him that I'd apologize to Shreya (name changed) for having lost my temper with her.

At 3.45 a.m. on 12th November '96 I woke up and noted down the dream I had just had: To my dismay I found myself seated amongst thousands of people who had placed themselves on a high platform, far away from where the Lord sat below on the floor with just a handful of people around Him, the only ones who had His clear vision from where they sat. Realizing the futility of remaining seated where I was if I wished to have a better view of my Lord, I decided to join the few people from my group on their way down though thousands remained stuck where they were. As I reached the last step, I found Baba coming towards me. After a while both of us stopped short in our tracks. Not knowing whether I was fit to be at His feet, I kept a respectful distance from Him. My Lord once again resumed His walk in my direction and by gestures let me know that I could be at His feet. After touching those lotus feet, I placed my head on them. He bent low and gently raised me up by the shoulders, then took my hands and held them in a firm clasp. With motherly affection He asked if I had anything to say to Him. I simply shrugged my shoulders and with a gesture of my hands conveyed my helplessness, thereby indicating that He was already aware of all the happenings in my life. He let me kiss His hands. Then loosening His grip over my hands, He turned and walked away. Suddenly He seemed to have remembered something important enough to make Him retrace His steps. To my surprise, He gently inquired of me, "Have you bought curds?" The dream ended.

The elimination of the 'I' in me (even if for a little while) had enabled Him to draw me closer to Him far earlier than otherwise would have been the case. It was not easy for me to forget myself entirely, to yield myself without reservation to the service of mankind, yet that is what He expected of me – that I should live only to be a blessing to others, and to do the work which I was meant to do. I had just made a beginning in the process of self-development, but much remained to be done. Sometimes I felt that my Lord had set before me an ideal which was too high, a goal or a condition impossible to reach perfectly as yet, but still one which I constantly strove at.

In case you are wondering about His last question to me regarding the purchase of curds, let me explain. Since the past two days I had severe diarrhoea and felt weak. Hence, His suggestion of a simple remedy. This little query of concern for my well-being acted as a morale booster. It was an indication that the same Lord who spent His life in working for all of humanity sometimes turned aside and paid personal attention to little details concerning me – one amongst His millions of pupils!

I was Full of Remorse at My Misplaced Anger

Dear friends, it often happens that we take out our anger on a person who isn't the one we wish to punish. I made the same mistake. There were times when with my sister and brother I couldn't retaliate – so I turned my anger on to my defenceless father. Since he was the kind who could take it without protesting, I got relieved. Soon I realised the gravity of my error – that it was displaced anger being directed on the wrong person and it solved nothing. On 18th November '96 guilt gripped me. My conscience wouldn't let me sleep. That particular evening I had been hurt by what appeared to be my dad's total silence in a matter where he needed to intervene and counsel my siblings, so I grew indignant. Such conduct on my part had nothing righteous about it. I had sought to establish dominance over dad by impressing on him that my anger came from my righteousness and therefore it was just and correct. How could I have accused dad of loving his other children more than me? How could I make him feel guilty? I chided myself each time I thought of that moment when he had come and apologized to me. Had he not been my pillar of strength during my period of trial? (So what if dad expected financial support from me alone now that my brother didn't support us anymore and my sister saved her salary for her own marriage.) Today I felt I had fallen in the Lord's sight and wouldn't be surprised if He too would forsake me for no longer did I feel worthy of His love. This time I was certain that He would punish me and decide to stay away from me.

Once again He proved me wrong. He came to teach me that my tears of remorse combined with my resolution of never again making the same mistake had wiped off my sin and made me worthy of pardon. On 19th November '96 in a dream my Lord was giving a discourse and I was one among the masses attending it. Unable to concentrate on what He had to say, my heart longed for His forgiveness. Finally mustering enough courage to interrupt Him, I said in an almost inaudible voice, "Baba, do you love me?" (What I meant was could He still love me in spite of my failings?) "Mother, I love you." This was something I had not expected to hear and it took me a while to imbibe His words so full of love – words that kept ringing in my ears long after they had been spoken. He had resumed with His discourse as before without showing any signs of displeasure at the interruption. The simple, matter-of-fact way in which He had responded left me in tears. He had addressed me as His mother!

Friends, His heart is a vast ocean of love. Hence, we need not despair if there are unintentional lapses from the right path, especially out of ignorance, because if we are repentant on coming to know of the same, and are willing to atone for it, He is sure to forgive us.

Experiencing Lord Krishna's Omniscience

Lord Krishna appeared in my dream on 25th November '96 at 5.30 a.m. His action of rushing into a temple with a garland in His hand, placing it around the neck of the Divine Mother, then turning back and walking away in long strides stupefied me. It seemed He was in a great hurry to attend to other matters and had come to the temple specially for the purpose of garlanding the mother! Calling out to Him in desperation, I followed Him, "Krishna, Krishna." Upon hearing my voice, He stopped and turned to look in my direction. "Krishna," I asked, "have you forgiven me?" And I anxiously awaited His reply. This time I had no particular error in mind but was referring to all my mistakes in life till date for which I wanted to be pardoned. Very gently He replied in one word 'Haaji' which meant 'yes' and added to it was a term of respect used while addressing people who are elder to us! Not convinced of my good fortune, I repeated the question and His answer was the same as before. He also let me touch His lotus feet after which He inquired, "What is your meet line?" And my immediate response was, "40." To that He responded with, "Well, as per the doctor's opinion it should be brought down to the 19th."

As I thought of the former part of the dream, from the recesses of the memory floated similar scenes that had actually taken place just 2 days ago, i.e. on 23rd November '96 – Lord Sathya Sai's birthday. Dilshad, a colleague of mine, had given me Rs. 5 and had requested me to buy a garland to adorn Shirdi Sai's neck in any of His temples. The money belonged to someone else and the garland had to be given to the Lord. That evening after the picnic with the CRY Neighbourhood Project children I was exhausted. Yet, before the gates of the temple could close I managed to rush in. Being very late, people selling flowers had already left for the day and I placed the money in the donation box kept next to His statue, mentally asking Him whether the garland had reached Him or not. The next second I took to my heels – to rush back home where the day's household duties were yet to be completed.

As for Him granting me forgiveness of all my sins till date, I do not know how to express my gratitude to Him. Of course, His forgiveness did not mean that I'd ever dare to knowingly err again. His grace can wipe away all the effects of one's karma. On the other hand, it could also have meant that He'd give me enough strength to suffer the effects of my karma. It was important that I keep in mind and understand that once a wrong act is done, I could not escape the consequences of such an act. It was of no use, however, merely giving myself up to repentance and remorse over past faults. The better attitude or real repentance would mean resolving never to go in for the same error again. I would minimise the future chances of wrong thoughts and deeds, and thus pave the way to a better life. Just as He continues to forgive me time and again, I too resolved to consciously cultivate a short memory for all wrongs, injustices, insults and injuries done to me and forgive freely those who hurt my feelings. In the absence of such an attitude on my part, it would seem impudent to approach God for forgiveness of my own wrongdoings.

And you might wonder what He meant by bringing down the meet-line from 40 to the 19th. Let me explain. As per what Nandini's doctor had predicted, her delivery date was to be 5th January '97. Accordingly I had decided to book my ticket for 4th January '97 which would have been 40 days hence. But dad had told me to book one for the 14th of December and I had obeyed him, though grudgingly. The night before I had prayed to Baba asking if He wanted me to cancel the ticket. Now Lord Krishna's statement made sense when within hours of the dream we received a call from Peshotan saying that as per the doctor's opinion the delivery would take place any time after the 20th of December '96 so I didn't cancel my ticket for the 19th! (Krishna could have disclosed the real date instead of letting me know of the date the doctor would be giving. But what I now feel – months later – must have kept Him from doing so was that He wished me to be in Satna where I'd have enough time to update my writing at leisure, which I was unable to do with my hectic schedule while in Mumbai.

Visit to Parthi Put Aside to Fulfil Family Obligations

2nd December '96 – A day that brought with it another message of love from Him. In the dream it seemed as though my Lord and I had been staying in the same guest-house but now it was time for us to part. My Lord was lying on the floor and I kissed His hand, kissed Him good-bye with tears in my eyes. "Baba, it's time for me to leave and I shall miss you terribly. I shall not be able to come to Parthi and will thirst for your darshan. But will you appear to me in dreams? You will, won't you?" In most loving tones He assured me that He'd certainly visit me in dreams. As I turned to have a final glimpse of Him, I saw Him stretch His neck, His eyes following me as I walked up to the door, shedding tears for me!

Upon her request, I had decided to be with Nandini as she was expecting her first child and needed someone to be with her. The dream spoke of the tough decision I had made of spending my one month's annual privilege leave in Satna in order to fulfil my duty towards my sister in law, the leave which I'd have otherwise spent in Parthi or Whitefield in His presence. And He on His part understood the pangs of separation I underwent and reciprocated my love on an ongoing basis via dreams and visions. Mum was busy with Jasmine's wedding preparation and Nandini needed someone to give her the emotional support during her difficult though wonderful and blessed months of becoming a mother.

Meera's Unwillingness to Go by Lord Krishna's Will

On 18th November '96, the Lord came to tell me to warn Meera (name changed), not to accept the flat her community Trust was about to allocate her. This house was being offered to her in response to her appeal to them for residential premises on a rental basis for herself and her husband.

The Lord in His mercy showed me scenes which foretold the impending danger (in the event of the old building collapsing) if she were to accept their offer. In the dream He told me to wake up Meera who lay in a semiconscious state. Thanking Baba for His timely message for Meera, I moved on. Lord Ganesha met me on the way and expressed His appreciation at my performance of a dance and bhajan before Him! Now Lord Krishna (in the form of a lad of 10 years) fell in step beside me! Then He ran and entered a flat, closing the door behind Him, though not bolting it from within. To me He was clearly visible from even behind the wooden door – but not so to others. Now He kept changing His form from Krishna to Sathya Sai and back to Krishna. Meera who couldn't have His darshan, called out to me in anger, "Where is your black Krishna? If you can see Him, why can't I?" Then turning to the door behind which He stood, she frantically called out to Him, "O you black Krishna, why do you keep yourself hidden from my view? How am I to believe that at the same time you are clearly visible to Khurshid?" The Lord from within responded with, "Meera, why complain that I keep away from you? Don't blame me if you are unable to have my darshan. All you need to do in order to see me is to open the door and to learn to bend. Bend, my child, bend." Meera began to bend gradually until her head almost touched the ground when she discovered a crack in the door through which the Lord was visible. "O Krishna, I can see you! Yes, you do exist. Now I also believe you must be visible to Khurshid," she exclaimed, full of joy.

Dear readers, after disclosing to her the earlier message of the Lord given a week ago, that she should not accept the house being offered to her, you can imagine her state of mind. Her anger towards me was justifiable because I had suddenly put an end to her dreams of a permanent roof over her head. Hence, the above mentioned dream in which she had accused Krishna of not giving her darshan. Moreover, just a week earlier, she had made it very clear to me that henceforth I should not interfere in her life, not even to pass on any of the Lord's messages to her. She claimed she believed in allowing nature to take its course and didn't want Baba's advice. And she added that she'd rather occupy the house being allotted to her, even if it meant facing severe consequences. If suffering came as shown in my dream, then she said she would attribute it to the Lord's will! Fortunately, she did heed the Lord's warning because after the initial worries, faith in God took over that He'd provide her with a decent roof over her head. Yet, angry she was with Him, hence, in the dream she must have called Him harsh and cruel, even 'black'! Soon Baba solved her problem of accommodation and she was glad that she hadn't accepted the earlier offer from her community Trust.

Oftentimes it so happens that when fate seems to be unkind to us, we take a gloomy view of things, get embittered and lose faith in the designs of the Almighty. Our mind being absorbed with worries, we refuse to see our own hand in the framing of our destiny.

Dear friends, we should not defile or belittle this most priceless gift from the all loving Lord – His timely messages in dreams. It should be our sacred duty to consistently maintain an attitude of peace, thanksgiving, reverence and gratitude to our Lord, the Creator, for coming to our aid. With His grace it's possible for people to transcend the traumas of life and themselves become loving individuals. I believe that grace is available to everyone. All of us are called by and to grace, and it's up to us to listen to the call or not, willing to open the door of our hearts to let the Lord in or not. By expecting us to bend further each time, the Lord wants us to totally surrender to His will.

There might be many people with absolutely no awareness or understanding of the immense value that the dreams of Baba (if interpreted correctly) can bring to them. Consequently, they discard from their consciousness all dream material as worthless and unimportant. They need to appreciate and perceive the treasure within them. To utilize dreams effectively, I have worked at being aware of their value and to take advantage of them when they come. However, I have never sought these dreams. They have been my guru's true gifts to me. Dreams are one form in which the gift of grace has been given to me. With these dreams of spiritual messages I have found that my journey of spiritual growth has been guided by the invisible hand and unimaginable wisdom of God. So guided, the journey has become a lot easier.

Baba's Unique Sense of Humour

A dream that I had had on the 29th of November '96 was as follows: It all began (I mean the dream) with my innumerable questions to Baba on topics worldly and spiritual and He, love and patience personified, responded to every single question. (Unfortunately, on waking up I couldn't recollect any of those questions or answers. Perhaps it was meant to be so as these question answer sessions merely signified the innumerable lessons He had taught me in life.) Finding Him a bit serious just when I myself happened to be in a mischievous and jolly mood, I queried, "Baba, of late you seem to have lost your sense of humour. There used to be a touch of humour even in the most serious lessons that you taught. Now why don't you joke as before?" He certainly didn't seem to mind my question nor my act of kissing His hand. Now I noticed a twinkle in His eye and a mischievous smile playing on His lips as He said, "Now just wait and watch." The next moment He had vanished out of sight.

The dream continued. As I looked about from where I sat amongst thousands of devotees, I could make out that they were waiting for what I assumed to be the Lord's darshan. I quietly resumed my work – writing down all His teachings. Suddenly the murmurs around me stopped. There was a hushed silence and I looked up to see what had brought about that change. People were craning their necks, their hands folded in reverence, some shedding tears of joy with ecstasy clearly visible on their faces, and others pleading that they have darshan more often. Turning my eyes away from the devotees, I looked hard, trying to search for the Lord's figure in the car passing by at a very slow pace in order that all those gathered could get a chance to have a glimpse of the Divinity within. From where I stood amongst the crowd, to my shock I saw my own self seated in the car where I expected my Lord to be! What stunned me even more was the way the eyes of those thousands of people, young and old, were glued to my form, yes, myself in that car! People kept calling out to me seated in that car as 'The Divine Mother!' I had never before found myself in a more embarrassing situation. I called out to them, "Will someone please listen to me? You have got it all wrong. That's me in the car you are bowing down to. Yes, it's me who has always been living a simple life as one amongst you. What has given you the impression that I am the Divine Mother? I do not possess a single quality that should invoke such reverence." Nobody seemed to pay heed to my pleas and I helplessly watched them continue worshipping my form in that car! With that the dream had come to an end.

9

Treading the Path He Wanted Me To

My Guru's Reminder that I Perceive the World from His Viewpoint

The last dream I had during my stay at my brother's place in Satna was at 1 a.m. on 5th January '97. In this dream I found myself shift my position a number of times, each time in an attempt to place myself where I could have clear darshan of the Lord. All of a sudden the Lord appeared from the direction where I least expected Him. "Now here you are. You may touch my feet," so saying He removed His slippers, worn out slippers that belonged to me, which I had removed and left at the entrance of the darshan ground! I bent low and placed my head on His lotus feet. In very gentle tones He said, "Khurshid, now you should throw away your spectacles forever and see everything in the world with what I have to offer you." It was clear now that He had meant spiritual and not normal human sight.

The dream continued. "Now go and buy 50 books which will cost you..," He commanded. (I can't remember the amount.) "Baba, I have only Rs. 150 in the purse. Then how am I supposed to purchase so many books?" He nodded understandingly and smiled. After a silence of a minute or so, instead of asking Him any more questions, I told Him not to come in my dreams till such time that I could complete to pen down and type out (from the shorthand notes that I wrote in) His earlier messages. He seemed to understand my problem and immediately vanished from my sight. It left me feeling empty within and I resolved to update my writing work.

By telling me to discard my glasses, Baba wished that I see the world from His viewpoint. The 50 books that He requested me to purchase probably referred to the stationery items that I needed for the children from the CRY neighbourhood project where, by this time, I was spending much more quality time then what I had done earlier. Now I handled all the activities relating to the children, with support from some of the CRY staff members (on a voluntary basis).

Acute Need of an Extremely Sensitive Staff for our Child Beneficiaries

Friends, my experiences at the CRY Neighbourhood Project (later registered as a Public Charitable Trust under the name of 'Sunbeam') transformed my life completely. It began as a project for the construction workers children. Earlier, when I would pass by a newly constructed building filled with smiling young mothers and healthy children, I never wondered about the people who built it; the labourers, the quality of their lives, lives of their children and families. Now with first hand experience of running the project I know their lives better.

I found myself being drawn into the personal lives of the children and their families. Many of the mothers, I was happy to note, had embraced me as a friend and confidante. The budget for the project was never a problem because my CRY colleagues contributed on a regular basis. Besides, we had a generous donor and friend in Ashish Sheth who contributed both in cash and in kind. My colleagues, Sangeeta Kapila and Leela Alvares helped me with maintaining the accounts, taking care of the medical aspect and also the non formal education classes. Yet, if asked to identify my biggest concern, I would say that a good teacher for the education classes was most crucial. The present candidate was not fit – not only because she had never before worked with underprivileged children, but also because she was mentally in no state to take up any responsible assignment as she had become a widow recently. Besides, she was not sensitive enough to understand the problems that these children faced in their daily lives. Her tactless attitude towards the parents and insensitiveness towards the children resulted in my relationship with the labourers (that I had painstakingly built over a period of one year) collapsing. Though I did sympathise with the teacher for her personal problems I would not have recommended that her services be continued.

I knew that the time the children spent with us or at school was beneficial, but regretfully short. In most cases, they would be withdrawn from school when construction work dried up near our area and it would be time for them to migrate once again with their families.

But I also knew that not all effort was lost on them. The parents by now had begun to take interest in the lives of their children, encouraged the little ones to continue with their studies and also began to contribute towards their education and healthcare expenses.

Baba's Message of Dad Meeting with an Accident Coming True

On 19th February '97 at 11.50 p.m. my Lord appeared in a dream. Sitting in a row far at the back, I could not get a chance to be at His feet though I'd have loved to do so. My Lord solved the problem by simply bidding the crowd to make way for Him to reach out to me. Every step He took brought Him closer to me and within minutes, He was standing right before me, looking upon me with motherly affection and just when I was about to touch His feet, He bent low and held my hand in a firm clasp.

On 30th March '97 once again in a dream at 4 a.m., the Lord was there to shower me with His love. Dad and I were happy to have a glimpse of the Lord who was passing by our way. "Baba," I called out and He immediately responded by turning to me and stretching out His hand. I held His hand and full of remorse said, "Baba, please accept my apologies for telling you not to come to me with any more messages till I found time to record in book form your earlier messages." "That's OK," He said tenderly. When He was about to leave, dad called out and once again He stopped and stretched out His hand to dad who held it in a firm grasp. Then He held dad and me together by the waist and the next moment the three of us were going in a merry go round as the Lord began to sing, "Ringa, ringa, roses,......" He stopped short at the last sentence of the poem. He didn't utter the words, 'and all fall down.' Instead, by gestures He told us to imitate His action of crossing His toes!

Friends, our guru was telling us to keep our fingers crossed and I sincerely prayed that this part of His message – 'all fall down' perhaps indicating an accident, would never come true for any of us. But it was not to be so. Our Lord was gradually preparing me for the worst. Soon, my dad was to have a fall and multiple fractures in his hip and thigh of which I was not aware.

On 31st March '97 at 3 a.m. my dear Lord appeared with His next message. Not in His usual jovial and loveable mood, this time He appeared quite serious as He sat cross-legged on the floor with me opposite Him. He had come to warn me of the impending danger to my father's life. "Khurshid, your vision is still very faulty." "Yes Baba, I can't see properly. Do you mind throwing light on how you can improve the same." In a serious tone He said, "An operation needs to be done. Will be required to take leave of absence from office for a period of two months and get admitted in my hospital for the operation." (What I did not realise at that point in time was that Baba was hinting that dad would be hospitalised for an operation very soon.)

The dream ended – leaving me in a confused state of mind. Two weeks later, on 13th April '97 to be precise, my dad met with an accident and had to be hospitalised.

That fateful morning one of the neighbours rushed in to say that dad had fallen in the passage and was lying there unable to rise. He who had been my support all my life was now lying immobile on the floor and in terrible pain. For a moment I thought he had had a massive heart attack. I was trying to figure out what could have happened but for a while he didn't give any clue. Pain was writ large on his face. He closed his eyes for a long moment and said, "Bring a chair; I have fractured my left leg." Though he was in pain, he could read the fear in my eyes and was at once in control of the situation. He himself called up the trustees of Banajee Trust and informed them of his fall, requesting leave of absence from office as he was to get hospitalised. The neighbours were a very helpful lot. After carrying him to his bed, they arranged for an ambulance as instructed by the doctor whom the neighbours had summoned. Dad was promptly shifted to the Parsee General Hospital.

X-rays revealed 2 major fractures in his left hip. The operation was fixed for the 5th day after his fall and I cannot adequately describe the agony I felt as I saw him lie on the bed so very helpless, not able to shift at all because of the excruciating pain that any movement on his part brought about. But no amount of pain could deter him from continuing with his daily prayers or his office work. With pride I watched him as he sat (his surgical bed upraised) giving instructions to his subordinates so that the office work may carry on without interruption.

Even though mum insisted that she stay next to dad day and night, I made sure to send her home every evening. She herself was not keeping too well with her slip disc problem and to add to that, now she could barely walk. The soles of her feet had peeled off because of a wrong application of medicine for corns that was prescribed by the doctor. Every single moment of those pain-filled days was torture for me and I had imagined that all would be well after the operation. But the night after his operation dad's condition became critical. I was grateful to the Lord for having sent help in the form of Dolly Mistry (a distant relative) who stayed with me at dad's bedside for the first 2 nights after the operation. Dad's hands and feet went cold. His urine stopped and the stomach bloated. Beads of perspiration appeared on his forehead. When I asked him if the oxygen being given to him was of any help, he quietly said, "Now oxygen or no oxygen, nothing seems to make any difference. But I'd like to have it removed immediately." And then I lost all hope when he started vomiting blood.

These were the worst moments of my life. My father, my friend, my guru and guide it seemed was about to breathe his last right before my eyes and I watched on helplessly, unable to do anything. But with immediate medical treatment, by midnight the vomiting had stopped, though now his temperature shot to 105°. Dolly Aunty lay awake the whole night attending to his needs and coaxed me to sleep for a few hours. The next night she was again there to give me moral support and with genuine concern in her voice asked me if I'd like her to continue to stay longer. By then dad's condition had improved and the worst was over – so I felt I had no right to take advantage of her goodness. Today, I take this opportunity to thank her for all the support she provided then and for standing by me during that difficult period.

Dad never saw himself as a 'helpless cripple' overwhelmed by depression or powerlessness. A rod was placed in his hip / thigh for one fracture. The doctor claimed that the other fracture was in a place where surgery was impossible and hence left untouched. That meant dad would have to put up with the pain till it healed on its own. Within 10 days he was back to his feet – first with the walker and then a stick. Had his heart condition permitted, he'd have left the hospital sooner. His spine too was damaged which, besides causing pain in his back, had also been responsible for the numbness in two fingers of his left hand. But nothing seemed to discourage him. Over time, he had come to accept his disability. Within 3 months he was back to his office as before. The medical bills were taken care of by well wishers – Dossan Masi (mum's sister), Mr. Ratnagar (a friend of my father), Nargish Aunty and Aban. My heartfelt thanks to all of them for helping me in time of need and not once reminding me to repay before I could get the reimbursement from The New India Assurance Co. where my dad had his mediclaim insurance.

Baba's Prophecies about My Impending Health Problems as well as our House being Taken Away

Hardly a week had gone by since dad had been discharged from the hospital when Baba once again appeared to me on 29th May '97 at 4.45 a.m. The scene was of my Charni Road house and Baba seemed to be searching for us. So I ran to Him and held His hand. To my dismay He loosened His grip. Then before I knew what was happening, He bent low and touched my feet! I was startled but regained my composure soon. "Baba, were you looking for us? Well, you know we have shifted to Forjett Street." No sooner had the words escaped my mouth I'd have given anything to take them back. How could I have imagined Him being unaware about anything in our life! But He didn't take offence. In very soft tones, He replied, "Yes dear, I know that." "Baba, I wish to ask you a few things, may I?" "You may ask as many questions as you like." So saying He led me into our room and sat on the floor beside me. "Baba, dad underwent a lot of pain after his fall. Now there won't be any more hospitalisation. Am I right?" I hoped against hope for a positive reply but He said with finality, "There will be hospitalisation. Yes, yes you will be hospitalised. You will have a fall and will have to be operated upon. And a big rod will have to be placed." My voice was barely a whisper when I queried, "Baba, can you not forgive me and wipe away my karma? Or can you not at least turn it into a minor operation with no rod being placed or better still altogether do away with this suffering from my life?" "That depends on you," He replied matter-of-factly. "Baba, will you intimate me about the fall in advance so that I can be prepared for the same?" "Yes, I'll let you know beforehand." "Baba," I continued with my next question, "I want my dad and mum to live a long life." "Yes, they will live long." Hearing His answer I was relieved. "Baba, what do You have to say about our Forjett Street house? Will my parents always reside there or will someone else snatch it away from them?" "It will be taken away," He said in a serious tone. With that the dream came to an end.

More than a decade later, as Baba had predicted I was hospitalised for multiple rib fractures and a hairline fracture in the hip that were a result of a road accident. This was the beginning of a slow and painful journey that had pushed me into near immobility – a process that continued steadily over the next few years even as I am at the final edit of these volumes in 2010. A brittle bone structure that resulted in severe osteoporosis took its hold and my health began to deteriorate gradually. Even then I had little time to rest because by now, Sunbeam was reaching out to over 1,000 children and as the Managing Trustee cum CEO of the organisation, my presence was critical for the well-being of our beneficiaries.

Almost 8 years after the above dream, i.e. in May '05, the house at Forjett Street as well had to be returned to the Banajee Trust authorities as Baba had aptly pointed out – "It will be taken away." And that is exactly what came to take place. Dad had worked with the Trust till the age of 73. That is when my brother Peshotan and I decided that he should retire in view of his advanced age. Given that dad had worked for14 years at the Trust with total commitment and dedication, Peshotan requested the Trust authorities to allow our parents to continue to stay in the same flat. Besides, moving back to our own home in a chawl building at Charni Road (with no proper facilities of a toilet or running water) was not at all a viable option. Peshotan also offered an amount of rupees three lakhs as donation to the Trust as we did not have any more than that to offer. The Trust authorities declined our offer (as this flat was meant for someone who actually worked for the Trust) and informed dad to vacate the premises as early as possible. We had no option but to move out – but where was the place to go? I approached a few of my friends at CRY and some other acquaintances with whose timely support I was in a position to purchase a flat in a Parsi Colony in Andheri (East). And with that we had to leave the Forjett Street house with a heavy heart.

Accepting His Will as the Final Word

On 25th June '97 He announced the 4 operations He wished me to undergo. I saw myself sitting in a row along with others awaiting the Lord's arrival. When He stood before me, I opened my palms ready to accept whatever He wished to bless me with. He terrified me by placing His foot on my hand, increasing the pressure gradually. As the pressure mounted, I had to put a considerable effort not to let out a cry of pain. For a while He lifted the weight and looked at me intently. My palms remained open as before, ready to accept all that He had to give. Once again He placed His foot on my hand and exerted the maximum amount of pressure on it. This time when He lifted off the pressure, I expected relief for a while but He crushed my hands, now by placing both His feet on them. As before, I did not complain. The next moment He was off my hands and I asked Him, "Baba, on an earlier occasion you had mentioned that I'd be undergoing 4 operations. Can you please throw some light on that? What sort of operations will they be?" "Uterus operation, eye operation, ear/throat operation and brain tumour operation," He replied instantly – and the next moment He began to move towards the other devotees. Someone from the crowd remarked, "How lucky Khurshid is to have Baba talk to her." Another retorted with, "But didn't you notice her open palms? How many of us have the courage to accept what He has to offer and never complain if it doesn't meet with our expectations?" The dream ended.

In the coming years, especially during the period 2006 to 2011, I actually did face tremendous pressure – at work with underprivileged children at Sunbeam or in matters relating to my health. There was an element of uncertainty in both – the moment I got respite and hoped to relax a bit, other problems cropped up unexpectedly that once again pushed me to the wall, leaving me feeling depressed and frustrated – as no ready solutions were at hand.

The above dream was in connection with my earlier message in a dream dated 21st June '97 in which people awaiting the Lord's darshan asked each other why they weren't blessed with such frequent visits from the Lord as I was. One questioned me, "Do you daily pray a lot as I do?" My answer was in the negative, whereupon another queried in a raised voice, "Then you must be meditating a lot the way I do." I thought it best to be sincere so once again the answer was a negative one. This brought upon me the wrath of yet another devotee who demanded in an angry tone, "You must be at least singing bhajans daily. But then I too do that. How come I haven't been blessed by His darshan?" In a calm voice I said, "No, I don't sing bhajans either." Now, all of them pounced upon me with the same question, "What is it then that makes the Lord appear to you? As compared to you aren't we far better devotees who sing His praises, pray and meditate daily? What keeps Him away from us?" My spontaneous response was, "Well, to my knowledge the only action on my part that seems to be enough to draw Him to me is that I act as per His Will. I have surrendered myself to His Will." Just then our guru, Sri Sathya Sai appeared and they approached Him with their query to which He lovingly responded with, "I am willing to come to each and every individual but to enable me to do that, doesn't each of you need to open the door of your heart?" The dream left me in tears of gratitude.

Striking a Healthy Balance between Caring for Others and for Myself, Meeting with Baba's Approval

With all the household chores, office 9.15 to 5.00 p.m., plus the additional responsibility of the Neighbourhood Project doubled with unexpected events needing my presence, events such as Nandini's delivery, a friend's illness, sister's wedding, daddy's hospitalisation, etc., etc., I had my hands full.

People tend to make you see things their way in an attempt to make you feel guilty. For instance, I didn't see any point in feeling guilty as relatives expected of me when I no longer stayed at dad's bedside at the hospital at nights after about a fortnight and left him instead to the care of ward-boys. No one seemed to have taken any notice when I had been with him most part of the day and every night for the first 12 days. Now that he had gained back his self-confidence and could manage on his own, I no longer needed to feel indispensable. Of course I had been loyal to him – but at the same time didn't I have to be loyal to myself as well?

Likewise, when friends complained that I was placing voluntary work and office work ahead of my relationship with them, it didn't make me feel guilty. In polite but firm tones I explained to each of them that I had to set priorities in life but that didn't mean I had cut off relations with them. They should still have enough trust in me to stand by them whenever they needed me.

Yet, to be doubly sure I prayed to Baba to let me know if the attitude I had adopted of setting priorities in life at the cost of not being able to spare as much time as before for old friends was the right one. The dream on 10th August '97, just a day prior to my journey to Parthi with Nargish Aunty, Aban and her mother, was as follows: Hand in hand a friend and I were travelling by foot. I took great pains to point out to every stone, thorn or anything lying on the ground that was likely to hurt her or make her stumble. Then along the way my eyes fell on another traveller in need of guidance and I left the hand of the earlier friend but not before handing over a torch to her to light her way. The same thing happened over and over again i.e. I moved on from one person to the next, never feeling guilty when each time upon leaving someone's hand, she/he reproached me with, "You can't do this to me. How will I find my path?" Each time I infused faith and courage in them with the same soothing words, "This torch that I have handed over to you will be as good as having me by your side." The sun was about to set when by chance I happened to see the outstretched hand of a man who claimed to know his path well but just needed a fellow traveller to hold his hand. The thought that crossed my mind was that it wouldn't be such a bad idea to place my hand in his and befriend the lonely soul even if it meant walking only a few steps together, because somewhere deep down in my heart I was aware of the sun about to setthereby bringing an end to my journey – though I continued to encourage my fellow friends to carry on travelling with the torch I had gifted them with.

The Lord had taught me to strike a healthy balance between caring for others and for myself by learning to set priorities and organising my time. I had to guard against the self-deception that I could give without being refilled. Yet the problem was that I seemed to consider myself dedicated and committed to caring for others, but the needs to be met seemed endless and I pushed myself to provide more and more care. Because I had feared doing anything that could be considered selfish, I had all these years failed to be good to myself. Very often what I had labelled as fear of being selfish was my fear of disapproval or my fear of being criticized or condemned for normal, legitimate forms of self-assertion. I learnt to avoid taking more than what I could physically or mentally handle. Or I would have to blame no one but myself for my victim status.

Let Each One Follow His / Her Own Path to Attain Liberation from Bondage

One of my paternal aunts, who was an ardent devotee of a well-known saint, lovingly told me, "I am aware of your struggle for enlightenment. All that you stand for meets with my approval. But there is one thing still lacking in you for full enlightenment, and precisely because I appreciate your efforts to reach God, I propose it to you. I have received a guru mantra from my guru. It must be more than a decade since I have watched you go to Sathya Sai Baba with no results on that score. Till date, He hasn't granted you a single personal interview. From that I infer that either He has not accepted you as His disciple or else He is not a Sadguru like my guru – in which case you better look out for one who is a Sadguru if you want mukti (liberation). Take my advice and get a guru mantra, mind you, the mantra should be only from a Sadguru and that you may keep chanting. That's all you need to do in life in order to get mukti."

I respected the lady's conviction and spoke gently in my answer. She meant well and was convinced she was doing the right thing in asking me to follow her guru, for she believed there was no way to salvation besides repeating the guru mantra. It is also true that I am by no means perfect and many things are lacking in me. But I certainly didn't feel that daily repeating a mantra at fixed times was the only way to salvation. Had she told me she wanted me to learn more about her guru's teachings, and had given me books to read, I would have gratefully accepted her offer and would have opened my mind to the new experience.

I totally agreed with my aunt that as a result of meditation or japa, the mind would withdraw from sense objects and the sensory world. But I felt that though this was one way of getting closer to God, it was certainly not the only way. Personally speaking, I strongly believe in the theory of karma (action). And it saddens me when religious people give up karma and take to inaction. Their argument is that if karma is engaged in, it leads the doer to either heaven or hell or back on earth, that is to say, to bondage of some sort. My counter argument to that is that karma will bring about bondage, only when it is engaged with a view to the fruit thereof. When done without any thought of the fruit, it leads one closer to God. Why, even a liberated soul like my guru, engages in karma, though He does not derive any benefit therefrom. Besides, with my heavy schedule of work at home, office, the Neighbourhood Project (later on registered as a Public Charitable Trust under the name of Sunbeam) and my writings in order to complete my books, I had no time to follow a well-established discipline. I believed that if my mind could be conquered and brought under control, I could immerse myself in meditation wherever I found myself.

However, I was careful not to discuss any of the above views with my aunt. This is because, to each one, his path will appear as the best. One who believes japa of the mantra as the only means of achieving liberation, was likely to treat my faith in karma with scant respect.

The Lord Taught Me to Listen to Others with Empathy

In response to my prayer to the Lord on how He would have helped a friend who seemed to be in so much of emotional turmoil, the dream on 17th August '97 was as follows: Baba was intently listening to a cassette, a tale of woes. After it came to an end, it rewound itself and Baba had to hear it all over again. And once again the cassette rewound itself and started playing all over again, leaving the Lord with no option but to patiently hear the same message over and over again, Himself not perturbed in the least bit.

The above message was clear. Of late there seemed to have cropped up a communication gap between that friend and myself. The Lord wanted me to know that just giving advice doesn't work. I had to be a good listener as well. I therefore understood that in order to interact effectively with others I really needed to listen to them. Yet, I did not possess the skill to really listen deeply to another human being. Now that I understood and accepted that, I created a habit of listening to others. I realised that most people who wanted to talk things through had the answer themselves and just wanted someone to hear them out. Hence, I didn't have to interrupt but just listen. The above dream especially taught me how important it was to make a person feel respected, heard.

He Wished that I Continue Treading the Divine Path without a Break

On 4th July '97 the Lord appeared in His Shirdi Sai form, giving orders to a troop of military men (amongst whom He ordered me to stand) to march forward. Then He ordered us all to run. People running ahead of me had been awarded badges by the Lord. My uniform had none. Somewhere I got too exhausted and stopped dead in my tracks and He immediately thundered, "How dare you stop running and block the way of those behind you? How and where will they proceed unless you lead them? Come on, run. Don't stand still!" I obeyed Him.

The Lord was right. His message in the above dream was so appropriate. He wished me to follow the example of those who had received badges of appreciation and approval from Him for running along the Divine path guided by Him. And whenever I felt too exhausted, instead of stopping half-way and not covering the remaining distance, my priority should be to help all those people behind me who trust me to lead them not only through these Volumes but by making my own life one of service to mankind.

Our Lord's Helplessness at having to give Me Fruits as per My Karma

On 13th July '97 at 6.30 a.m., when the Lord had appeared in a dream I found myself at the gate of the ashram, hesitant to enter because I was late – but the Lord by gestures bid me in. He placed something invisible into my outstretched palms and said, "Bad, bad." I couldn't figure out what He had said and asked, "Baba, please clarify what you meant by that." And He merely translated the word in Gujarati by saying, "Kharab, kharab." Then He sort of murmured to Himself (in Gujarati), "My daughter is as it is unhappy and I don't like to do this to her. But what can I do? I am totally helpless."

The dream indicated that what He had to offer me in life (according to my own past karma of this life and the previous ones) was not what

He wished to give but that He was helpless. Even He couldn't interfere with my fate which was the fruit of my own past karma.

To Check Myself Each Time I Knew I was Going Wrong

On 1st September '97, in a dream I asked the Lord, "Baba, what do you wish me to do to further improve myself spiritually?" His answer was inaudible. So I repeated my question but the second time as well I could not follow what He said. For a third time I asked the same question and this time I could catch His voice as He spoke, "You yourself know whenever you go wrong. Hence if you start making an effort to rectify your errors, you grow spiritually." With that He moved away and it appeared as if it was time for Him to give private interviews to other devotees of His. Someone from the public asked me, "Don't you desire to have a private interview?" From the depth of my heart I spoke of my conviction about Baba always answering all my questions via dreams and visions, leaving me with no desire or need for a private interview.

Reflecting on the way He had responded to my prayer that He guide me to help me grow spiritually, I was full of remorse. How right He was in saying that in order to grow spiritually I need not wait for Him to come and point out to me my errors every time I went wrong because my conscience already did that job for me and I had to learn to go by what it said.

On Living Out My Values in Life

Most of my evenings and even weekends were spent on efforts in bringing about a positive change in the lives of the Neighbourhood Project children and their families. With the success of the project (for the time being) I felt I had achieved my goal. But it had been at the cost of my writing work. As a result I was always left with a feeling of emptiness, of guilt. Yes, though it was good to do project work I should have set a limit to the amount of time to be devoted to its accomplishment. I was getting one thing (the satisfaction that I contributed to the Neighbourhood Project) but vaguely wanted something else (to update my pending writing work as well), hence didn't feel happy or fulfilled. In order to feel truly fulfilled and at peace with life, I needed to allocate quality time beyond office hours equally to both – to the Neighbourhood Project work as well as drafting out and keying in this Volume. Otherwise I would continue to have everything and yet feel like nothing. This was the power of values; values which were simply my own personal and individual beliefs about what was most important to me. It was apparent that the feeling of personal wholeness would come only if I fulfilled my values by my present behaviour. Though each of my responsibilities had its own place in the hierarchy of my values, I did not have to place any one of them above my writing assignment. When this was clear to me, my mind was at peace.

Friends, each individual thinks that some responsibilities in life are more important than others. Almost all of us have a bottom line – things that are most important to us above anything else. To deal with people, we need to know what is most important to them, specifically what their hierarchy of duties and responsibilities is. It will make it easier to understand other people's basic behaviour.

I felt fulfilled only when my life was led in accordance with my values. Let me quote an instance at my office which clearly indicates how different the hierarchy of values is for each individual. I was in charge of the Neighbourhood Project and did the fund raising. Trishika (name changed to protect identity), a colleague and a very good friend of mine, had offered to maintain the accounts of the project. I valued accountability to the donors above the consequence of confronting Trishika on the issue of not updating the accounts. In her hierarchy of values, doing that job of hers was nowhere in her priority list or else she wouldn't have (despite my repeated reminders) not updated the accounts and kept it pending for 5 months. (Of course, each and every entry of the income and expenditure made by her or by me was maintained. But how was I to know that the balance I was left with was the correct one and that we had been making all the right entries?) Finally in September '97 I felt compelled to personally sit with her in order to help her do the same when I realised that the balance amount did not tally with what she was actually left with. She simply told me that she would herself pay up that amount of Rs.1,500. Knowing her to be weak in accounting principles, I didn't think it fair that she suffer a loss where there actually must have been none. I scanned through the accounts from the month she had begun handling it and found an error of a wrong entry of Rs.1,000 in February itself and then some minor errors in entries made in the months to follow. It took the two of us not more than 2½ hours to update the accounts of the past many months. Nor did I see any reason for her to have been so upset with me when I demanded an explanation for not updating the accounts. If it was impossible for her to spare an hour per month to make entries, she could have simply said so. I would have gladly taken it on rather than face the donors (i.e. our CRY colleagues) who had every right to get upset with me for not being aware of the opening balance at the beginning of the month. If only she would have approached any of us from the office and sought our help rather than delay the job or make incorrect accounting entries, I'd not have felt as upset with her as I did just then.

This in no way made her less beautiful a friend than she was and still is. It was an enriching experience for both and she embarrassed me by begging my forgiveness time and again for having been rude to me and promised to henceforth maintain the accounts on a monthly basis. Our bond grew stronger now that we understood each other better. Besides, I was grateful that at least she had the time to spare for the project whether it was to maintain accounts or to accompany me to the construction sites whenever she could. (Dear friend, even though we rarely meet nowadays given our individual busy schedules, if you happen to read this book, I wish to thank you. I have always appreciated all that you've done for me at a personal level and also your consistent support to Sunbeam over the years – from behind the scenes.)

The Lord's Assurance that I was Singing in Tune with Him

There were happenings in life that hurt me. It wasn't fair that after the kind of labour I put in for the Neighbourhood Project, the Program Support Head of an NGO told me to my face that he doubted not only my capabilities but even my intentions in running the project.

My heart cried out to the Lord. "Whether it's the way I run the project or any of my other actions in life, if I am not going as per your expectations, do guide me."

The next morning i.e. on 14th September '97 in answer to my prayer, the Lord appeared to me at 3.30 a.m. The dream was as follows: At a very slow pace, I took one step at a time to reach the spot where Baba stood, giving darshan to the masses. My Lord in turn took long strides in my direction and came and sat at my feet! As I sat opposite Him, my face at such close distance from Him, I could notice that His eyes had sunk so deep, eyes that were pools of sorrow, eyes brimming with unshed tears. Thousands of people watched as I continued to have the privilege of His close darshan. He held my hands and in a melodious voice sang one bhajan after another, patiently teaching me one line at a time and giving me an opportunity to repeat what He taught. He appreciated my efforts and every now and then nodded in approval, His face glowing as though He was proud to have me as His student – someone who sang in tune with Him. One of the songs He taught me was, "Bada chitchor brindavan sanchala, Gopala, Gopala....." Next He materialised a plate full of vegetables, rice, chapati, and the like. With His own Divine hands, He fed me. As He placed one morsel after the other into my mouth, I felt transported into heaven, never wanting these moments to come to an end. Never once did He shift His loving gaze away from me to the others.

This dream acted as a healing balm. It was as though an awesome burden was off my chest. No longer did it matter if someone doubted my capabilities in managing the Neighbourhood Project and even my intentions in handling the project. The Lord had assured me that I was singing in tune with Him. What more could I ask for?

My Guru Wished that I Re-edit both the Volumes Once Again

For a long, long time I had kept aside my writing work and gave priority to other jobs until finally on 13th October '97 the Lord found it imperative to bring this to my notice. No doubt, I had been noting down the dreams on bits and pieces of paper but had not written it all down in a book form since almost a year. So His disappointment in me was justifiable.

In the dream I requested Him to sign my book. With a look of disappointment in His eyes, without even glancing at my book, He scolded me, "But it is incomplete. How do you expect me to sign it?" "Baba I shall update it immediately. All of last year's matter that is still on bits of paper, I'll put down in a book form. Will that make it complete for you to sign it?" I asked ruefully. He seemed to be in deep thought as He nodded in the negative and said as if speaking to Himself, "No, my updating it will not complete it. There is still a mammoth task left to be done. From page 1 of my book, I'll have to read the lines page by page till the end and do the necessary corrections, additions and deletions in the work done till date. To be able to do that, I'll need to put aside all my present duties and come and stay in Parthi in order to concentrate only on this work and no other." The very fact that He had used the first tense confirmed that it would be Him guiding my hand in the necessary corrections in my book – each volume – from page 1 till the end.

From the dream, I got the message and immediately applied for 38 days leave that I had to my credit, including the current year's leave. It was granted. Upon my request and with due permission of the Lord, Nargish Aunty agreed to accompany me and we booked the earliest available confirmed tickets to Dharmavaram (Parthi) i.e. for 8th November '97.

Urgency in Baba's Request to Finish Updating His Books

On 9th November '97, along with Nargish Aunty, I reached Parthi. Since I could avail of Privilege Leave from office only up to 16th of December I knew it wouldn't be correct on my part to extend my stay in Parthi beyond that. In so short a period I had set myself a goal of completing a second edit of the series of books written till date. Was I being unrealistic about what had to be accomplished? Had He set up for me an impossible goal? Not at all. All that was required was careful management of one of my most precious and most mistreated resources: time. Therefore I took time off to plan my work. This kind of planning of my daily work had positive psychological effects.

In the days to come, it made me feel comfortable when the work progressed in predictable cycles, but only till such time that my failing health and the excruciating pain in the abdomen began to prove a major obstruction. And I took the liberty to rest. This I could do without feeling guilty because I foolishly justified my wrong action by telling myself no matter how worthy the cause, no matter how necessary the service, there was no need for any further self-exploitation either. Hadn't I been working from 6.30 a.m. till 9 p.m. from the day I had reached Parthi, missing out on the opportunity of sitting in token number queues which could have given me a chance to sit in the front rows and have close darshans as against the distant ones that I ended up having? Besides, I couldn't possibly sit amongst the other devotees with my books and still keep the matter confidential. Of course I deserved a break – or so I believed, since I was way ahead in my work that would reach completion if I continued at the same pace for the next 10 days or so. The Lord conveyed His disapproval when He next appeared to me on 24th November at 4 a.m. The dream was as follows:

Baba was at the wheel with Aban and I seated in the back of the car. Suddenly, He took me by surprise. He turned to me with a gun in His hand and actually at gunpoint, He demanded for the books resting on my lap! Initially, I was too shocked to utter a word. Soon realisation dawned that I was His child, and He had a claim on me, a claim He rarely hesitated to express and this was one such occasion. Yet, I felt I had an equal right to ask Him why He was demanding my books at gunpoint. He responded to my query with gestures, telling me to look at Aban. Upon doing as told, I found her looking out of the window with tears streaming down her cheeks.

All I understood of the dream was that the Lord was trying to convey that time was finite and time lost could not be replaced. So I set about my work with renewed vigour and was able to complete the editing by 4th December, almost 12 days prior to the deadline that I had otherwise set for myself. It left me feeling jubilant, looking forward to a vacation ahead. Now I'd have all the time in the world to spend on lovely darshans, bhajans, prayers and so on for the remaining days of my stay in Parthi. My mistake was that I had disregarded the message given in the latter part of the dream in which He had commanded me to turn my attention to Aban. The next morning when I made an STD call to Mumbai, dad informed me of Aban's hospitalization for the second time in the past one week and undergoing an operation each time. Taking the first available flight, Nargish Aunty and I returned to Mumbai. (Nargish Aunty sponsored my airfare.)

Sai Accepts Yasmin Aunty's Invitation and Pays a Visit to her House in Parthi

There were two more dreams I had had during my stay in Parthi. On 29.11.97 I dreamt that Baba was visiting the house that Yasmin Aunty had purchased in Parthi. The next morning as I related the dream to her, Yasmin Aunty disclosed to me that the timing of this dream had exactly coincided with the time when she had sat in the room next to ours (we were staying at the same guesthouse) writing a letter to Him. She was in raptures and added that the content of her letter was an invitation to Him to visit her newly bought home. How quick He had been to respond!

The Lord Approves of My Performance in His Own Inimitable Way

Yet another dream confirming His love for me came on 5.12.97. I saw group photographs of Baba's school students being taken with Him in the centre. In one corner of the room, dressed in a school uniform, I stood silently awaiting my turn. Baba blessed me by standing next to me and instructing the cameraman to take our snap. When the students claimed that Baba had obliged to let His snap be taken with those students who had passed the final exam, I felt flattered. This dream was in response to my prayer the night before, asking Him if the work I had done in the past one month had met with His approval.

My Aunt's Complaint Saddened Him

On 14th December '97 at 5 a.m. when He appeared to me in a dream, I begged Him to allow me to touch His feet and He told me to follow Him. He walked up to a chair and sat down. After touching His lotus feet I felt blessed when He didn't reprimand me for placing my head on His lap. A while later He lovingly lifted my face and said, "You are very good in all ways, but there is one complaint against you that I have received from her. She claims that at times you don't listen to her properly. Thus there is that little bit of bad still left in you." While He said all this, Nargish Aunty was sitting next to us. So I assumed that He had been referring to her as the person who had complained.

Nargish Aunty played the role of a mother in my life right from 1993 till 2010 when she finally shed her mortal frame. In every sense of the word, she had indeed been a mother to me – someone in whose company I lived for 17 long years. Today, when I'm at a re-edit of this book, I miss her terribly. Her passing away has left a void in my heart that no one can fill. (This I state with due respect to my own parents with whom I live now, instead of merely spending my weekends with them as before.)

He Confirms that My Actions Match His Expectations

Since I was going by His advice that I act as per my conscience, I did so and on 25th December '97 before going to bed, prayed to Him to let me know if my actions in life matched His expectations.

The next morning when I woke up at 6.15 a.m. after the beautiful dream of the Lord it was with tears of gratitude. I, who believed in the karma theory, even in the dream found it difficult to sit amongst the group of people who merely passed judgement on the behaviour of others who performed to the best of their capabilities. I was sad to note that each one was found dancing to his own tune and not in rhythm with the rest. Instead of guiding their steps, the members of the group where I was seated were busy passing critical comments on the performance. Not feeling comfortable to join any of the groups, I turned my back to both and began to sing a bhajan as taught to me by the Lord. My eyes focussed on the pillar behind which I knew my Lord was hidden from everyone's view, watching our performance. He peeped from there and later came and stood before me. On my part, I continued with my bhajan, oblivious of the happenings in the two groups on whom I had turned my back. After every single line I paused for His approval and He, my sweet Lord, sang after me, word to word, exactly in the same tune as mine. But His voice was only loud enough for me to hear. It did not reach either of the two groups who carried on with what they believed to be their roles in life. All the time that I sang, He continued to nod in approval and a beautiful smile lit His face, His expression implying that He was happy with my performance.

Both, Baba and My Dear Friend Puja Marwaha Helped Me Give up My Fears of Speaking in Public

On 29th December '97 at 4.30 a.m. He appeared in a dream in order to bring to my notice a wrong decision I had taken, of not attending my office meeting to be held at Aksa in which I was expected to speak on HR systems. I had never talked to a group larger than my family and was afraid I would be too nervous to utter a word. Hence, I believed that it would be the right thing to make an excuse and remain absent on that day. In the dream my Lord walked up to the stage and beckoned me to come in the front. Till then I had taken a back-seat. As I reached the stage He announced that now one of His students would be giving a speech and while saying so He turned His gaze upon me. The dream ended. Had Baba not given the timely encouragement, I would have never felt one bit guilty of having taken the decision of not attending the Admin/HR workshop at Aksa.

I feared public speaking. But stage fright was only half the challenge. First, I had to figure out what I was going to say. Here I froze, held back by the idea that it was an impossible task for someone like me who had remained a secretary and not had the opportunity to handle any other challenging roles. Puja, All India Head, HRD (at CRY) was more of a friend than a boss. Time and again, she had demonstrated her faith in my capabilities and encouraged me to be more courageous.

(Dear Puja, if you happen to read these Volumes of mine, I wish you to know that you have played a very important role in building my self-confidence. In the year 2009 as I am at a re-edit of the Volumes, I'm at a stage in life where I manage Sunbeam with a staff strength of 40 and our outreach having expanded from 10 to over 1,000 child beneficiaries. Taking your example, as patiently as you did, I try to empower them in their respective roles and build their self-confidence to bring out the best in them. Therefore, dear Puja, you are and always will remain an integral part of Sunbeam in myself handling the organisation the way I learnt from you.)

An introspection led me to understand my own behaviour of trying to take a coward's way out. When I was a child I had developed a concept about self-worth. I had also formulated ideas about the worth of others. Perhaps my decisions about self and others were made very early in life and hence quite unrealistic. They could be even somewhat distorted and irrational as well. In my case it took a position, 'I am unworthy of love and recognition. I am inadequate.' I felt 'I am not good as compared to the others' and hence felt powerless when I compared myself to others. This position led me to withdraw. This is why the Lord on and often felt the need to intervene to let me know who I was, how I got that way, and where I was going with my life. Even now, He had not completely succeeded in helping me shift that position to 'I'm a capable person. I can speak in public. I have to just give it a try.' He continues with His endeavours to help me reach that healthy position that will help me solve my problems constructively. Very often, dear Puja, it's been Him in your form who has built on my confidence and self-esteem.

Today, I realise that all along I have had a need to be loved and recognised by other people, and the need to do something during my lifetime. Dear friends, you must have noticed in my writings till date that I needed a great deal of recognition from the Lord in order to feel secure. Till the age of 21, I had been ignored, diminished, humiliated, physically degraded, abused, laughed at, called names and ridiculed and in some way always treated as insignificant. Being discounted in this manner time and again had been very painful. But the Lord has not been one to give up on me. Over the years, He has patiently gone about teaching me that it is of no use blaming others or making them responsible for all my problems. He tries to make me believe in myself, all the time drilling into my head that as an individual I have the capacity and potential to develop, experience and express myself effectively. So the above mentioned dream and His message of His student addressing a group of people was one more of His attempts to encourage me to give up my fears.

Not a Single Issue at Our Children's Project Went Unnoticed by Him

The dream that I had on 2nd January '98 at 5.45 a.m. was on the Neighbourhood Project (later christened as Sunbeam). The dream was as follows: Baba sat with the children's attendance register in hand and scanned through its entries. Upon finding me standing next to Him, He queried, "When did Tuljama's family come?" After giving it a thought, I replied, "On the 8th, Baba." He noted down a few details in the register and asked, "What about the other family that is not to be seen since the past few days?" Not knowing which family He was referring to, I decided to give a frank reply. "Baba, I am not too sure." "OK, you may go and carry on with your work with the project" was His lovely response that only confirmed His approval of the work I did with the project.

The scene in the above dream as He sat with a register enquiring about the children (who had not been attending school since the past few days) was symbolic. The same evening for the first time I visited the construction site at Agripada to where Parvati's family had moved. Parvati's younger sister, Kavita, had severe diarrhoea. Hence, Parvati who had stayed back to take care of her baby sister could not attend Sunbeam classes. In a way I had failed to play the role of an effective project holder by not visiting the site earlier. And who was Tuljamma about whom Baba had enquired? Till then I hadn't even met her. She turned out to be the eldest daughter in the family whose siblings Vijaylaxmi and Tukaram joined our non formal education project a week after the dream, i.e. on the 8th – to be precise.

This dream confirmed that the way I ran the project mattered to Him and I went all out to prove that I would never again let Him down but make special efforts to keep in touch with each child that the project had reached out to in some way or the other.

His Advice to Visualise Him in His New form – Sunbeam

On 14th January '98 at 5.30 a.m. the dream I had was as follows: An old lady handed over a letter to me, the contents of which were in a scrawl which I couldn't decipher, especially since it was in Gujarati. A second look at the same letter had me dazed. It had changed itself into a very lengthy sheet of paper with hundreds of pictures of Mother Parvati at different jobs. In some She was seen doing household chores, in others with children surrounding Her, and so on. My eyes now rested on the last photograph of Hers in which She sat at the feet of Lord Shankara, placing flowers at His lotus feet. And then something unexpected took place. The Lord's celestial voice rang out loud and clear. It said, "O Mother Parvati. In this life of yours, you have played the innumerable roles I wished you to play. Now it's time for you to come to Lord Shankara and place flowers at His feet." The next moment the scene changed and I found myself enter the gates of the Sai Temple at Shirdi. A cow rushed straight at me but I was miraculously saved and was left unhurt except for a little wound above the shoulder, on the neck, to be precise. Upon reaching the dhuni (the place where the fire that Shirdi Sai had lit during His lifetime and still has been kept burning) I spotted Him (in Sathya Sai form) lying on the floor. Life appeared to be ebbing away from His body and I was shocked into immobility. Holding on to His feet, I wept. Seconds passed. Minutes. And then the body stirred and He opened His eyes. In a feeble voice

He addressed me thus: "Khurshid, don't cry. Go my child. Get me some flowers and place them at my feet. You have given me all that I asked for. Give me this last offering too." I asked Him if there was anything I could do for Him and begged Him to open His eyes and not leave the world yet. I placed at His feet my offering of flowers as desired by Him. My tears flowed non-stop, because I felt that His moments on earth were coming to an end. Pointing out to a new-born babe in a pram lying to my left, a friend told me, "Khurshid, He has not died. Look He is alive." Her words did not provide the solace they were meant to because I was unwilling to accept my Lord in any other form than His present one. Now as the Lord opened His eyes for the final time, between sobs I asked Him if there was anything else He wished me to do for Him. Gently placing His hand on my head, He said with compassion, "Khurshid, don't cry for me." With that the dream came to an end.

In another dream on 26th January '98 I found myself reaching Whitefield with great difficulty. Some people who were building a wall brick by brick and cementing it properly, stopped me at the gates of the ground itself. In the gap in the wall they placed an iron door with grills. How close and yet how far I felt from my Lord who moved about inside the compound where only permanent residents were privileged to stay. The minute His eyes fell on my tearstained face His own face took on the expression of compassion and love of a mother. And I prayed to Him to show me a way in which I could get the chance to get closer to Him. The next moment the scene that met my eyes stunned me into silence. The devotees sitting next to Him vanished and where Baba stood, all around Him was water. As the level of water rose, He began to drown. As His body submerged into the sea that had suddenly appeared from nowhere, I watched on helplessly from the other side of the gate. Then to my relief, He once again emerged from the waters, walked straight in my direction.

He opened the gate and it appeared as if He was about to walk past me so I made an attempt at touching His lotus feet. Instead of allowing me to do so, He sat on the floor and said, "I am on my way to change my clothes." I replied, "But Baba before you leave, permit me to clarify a few of my doubts. The books I have been writing are complete up to Volume II. After doing the corrections in the computer should I take fresh printouts of the same? And you wish me to carry on writing my books till the end of my life. Isn't it so?" "Khurshid, you had asked me this question before and I had answered you then. My answer still remains the same. You should not ask any further questions. Instead, you may refer to your books in which I have answered your queries as regards the books." So saying, He walked away in hurried steps. A permanent ashramite on her way to reserve a seat in the darshan grounds, brushed past Him, little realising who He was. Soon Baba was out of sight. Later, His car appeared on the scene but He was not in it. Everyone kept wondering as to where He could have vanished and I on my part did not disclose it to anybody that it would be only a while before which He would be back on the scene after changing His dress. The dream ended.

As for His message on 14th January '98 about the cow attacking me, it came true within days. This incident that took place in Delhi, an accident that could have left me crippled for life if not resulting in death. During my short trip to the CRY Delhi office, one evening on our way to the hotel from the office, I didn't notice a cow running in our direction. Puja and Shilpa managed to move out of its way in time but I was knocked down in the first blow when it hit my neck with its horn. Thereafter, everything was a blur. I found myself rolling from one end of the footpath and reaching the opposite one as a herd of cows and buffaloes knocked me about. Within a minute it was all over, leaving me in a shocked state. I can call it nothing short of a miracle. All over my dress there were hoof-marks and at places the material had torn each time when a hoof got entangled in my dress. Except for the excruciating pain in the neck and the large swelling that restricted the movement of the neck, I felt completely normal. I was rushed to the hospital where the doctors confirmed that there were no injuries to the spine and once the swelling on the neck would subside, I'd be able to move my neck.

The other message of Baba wanting to change His dress in the dream on 26th January '98 haunted me for months, but not so later. Because I became aware that He now lived with me in another form – Sunbeam and its child beneficiaries. Now His death and rebirth mystery was clear to me. My attachment to His form had been overcome to a large extent. Selfless love for Him in the form of children of Sunbeam had instead taken its place.

Despite His Busy Schedule, He Never Lost Sight of Me

In the dream that I had on 19th January '98, I found myself strolling out of the college and being met by a pleasant surprise. The unexpected sight of the Lord in a horse-driven chariot thrilled me. The chariot moved from one direction to the other but all throughout my Lord's sight was fixed on me. Sometimes in order not to lose sight of me, He even had to strain His neck. And then, not once but twice, my dear parent blew me a kiss. Tears welled up in my eyes at the thought of the Lord who was busy with millions of jobs in the world, forever keeping a loving eye on me.

'Do not Waste Time in Frivolous Pursuits', is what Baba Appears to Tell Me

On 20th January '98, Aban had a dream of Baba in His Sathya Sai form, except for His hair which looked exactly like mine, the way I had it cut the day before. He stood before the mirror examining His hairstyle and began giving His hair an in-turn. It was a dream that made no sense to Aban but was one which put me to much embarrassment. This is exactly the act on which I had wasted my time the night before – standing in front of the mirror, not too pleased with the way my hair looked and trying to give it an in-turn. Baba, in His mercy, was trying to show that being human, I was bound to have my moments of weakness – my attention being drawn to worldly things, and was willing to forgive me. Thus in His usual sweet manner, He had drawn my attention to the fact that I could spend my time doing better things than standing in front of the mirror worrying about whether my hair was styled in a particular manner or not.

Christ's Appearance to Me

On 2nd February '98, Lord Christ appeared in a dream. And He blessed me with the vision of His last moments on earth, His crucifixion. It was sheer agony to witness His pain, the sight of Him bleeding. But I stood at the bottom of what seemed like a hill, watching it all in silence till the very end, till His head drooped and I knew He was no more.

Serving His Children at the Cost of My Health was not a Wise Decision

In the Neighbourhood Project my endeavour was to fill the lives of the children with warmth and understanding that they deserved from their parents. It was such a pleasure to spend time with them. Now I feel raising kids is the most rewarding occupation. Yet, over a period of time I have realised that there is no full-proof system because all kids are so different. But a little effort and love on my part has paid such big dividends. It is with sadness I note that some of the parents of our project kids believe that their responsibility towards their children ends in providing them with 2 meals a day. One such case was that of 9 year old Padma. With her mother at the village for her 10th delivery, the burden of the family of her younger sister and brother (her other siblings had died of malnutrition) as well as all household chores fell into her lot. This family and one more had joined the project recently and I knew that initially I'd have to spare a lot of time with these kids just as I had done with the earlier lot.

The children used the entrance of the recently constructed building not only for their tuition classes but for their midday meals as well. I didn't want them to bring upon themselves the wrath of the owner of the premises in case they dirtied the place. To ensure cleanliness I decided to have lunch with them at least for a month by which time I would have been able to teach them to eat properly without making a mess all around.

On 8th February '98, in the dream Baba called the project children to have lunch with Him. He distributed almost all the contents of His lunch box to them and in turn took a morsel of rice from each. This scene repeated itself more than once.

The dream was indeed an eye-opener. It spoke of the caring but foolish action on my part which I had been repeatedly performing on a daily basis for almost a fortnight now. As I sat with the children for lunch I couldn't bring myself to eat from my own lunch box that contained proper nourishing meals and not share it with the kids who had only plain rice and some spices. So I used to take vegetables enough for 6 children. But when the 3 year olds, Srini or Balappa demanded the part of the share that was left for me, I felt too guilty to refuse them that either, little realising that since I skipped dinner, it was essential that I have a proper lunch to keep my stamina. Hence, by way of the above dream, Baba had brought to my notice the thoughtless act on my part of not setting limits with the children that in turn had caused damage to my health. Here was my lesson; that it's a good thing to love and serve others, but one also has a responsibility towards oneself.

My Guru's Parting Gift to Me – His Footprints in the Form of These Books

The message that I received at 3.30 a.m. on 12th February '98 is still etched in my memory, a message that expresses the Lord's immeasurable love for me and that my life has not been in vain. And I also believe that the blessing that my Lord has given me in the form of experiences that have shaped themselves into the books titled 'A Glimpse of Joy' is a gift beyond measure. The dream was as follows:

My dear Lord Sathya Sai was moving amongst devotees and I got a clear view of Him every now and then as He passed by me. Then to my disappointment, He decided to leave the stage and go underground. "Baba, Baba," I called out in a desperate attempt to deter Him. He retraced His steps and I asked, "May I touch your feet, Baba?" "But of course, come, come," came the gentle reply. People from the back rushed towards Him and in one corner I stood patiently awaiting my turn. The Lord reprimanded them by saying, "No, no, only the last person," and walked up to me. He stood regarding me with a penetrating expression. As I bent to touch His feet, I said, "Baba, give me something to remember you by, just about anything will do, something you feel is fit to be offered to me." He retraced His steps, and presented me with the most unexpected gift, leaving me speechless. "Here, take this. This is the gift I leave behind for you." So saying He pressed His feet into the ground and as a result permanent footprints were created in the ground which He offered to me as His gift that He wished me to take along with me. For a long time after He had left the scene, I found myself observing the writings inside those footprints. A date, month and year was typed at the beginning of each paragraph mentioning an event. Someone next to me remarked, "Baba has left Parthi, left the scene forever." A Sai devotee walked up to me as I made an unsuccessful attempt to bring to public the Lord's footprints and the writings engraved therein from within the earth where they presently seemed to lay buried and hidden from their view. She said, "Come, let me take a xerox of His writings in black and white. They are meant to see the light of day. They are meant to reach all His children." Suddenly what seemed like a printing machine appeared from nowhere and she provided me with thousands of prints of my Lord's gift to me – His footprints.

The dream continued. My final duty before leaving the scene I knew was to leave behind those footprints for His children – seekers of God's love; children from all over the world, from all walks of life. The copies of the footprints as they kept coming out of the printing machine had turned to Sai's photographs. While on my way to the backstage, I witnessed a beautiful scene. Young and old, people from India and abroad, walked up to the prints stacked on the table and picked up one each.

After the above dream, at this moment, I see things perhaps as the Lord does – in perspective, with all the pieces fitting. I see clearly how blessed I am. To be an instrument to bring about His message to the ardent seekers makes me feel my life has not been in vain. I offer my heartfelt thanks to the Lord for all the experiences and learnings in life and His patience in helping me in my effort to bridge the gap between Him and me. Indeed it has been a gift beyond measure.

Pervin Varma, One of His Blessings in My Life

At 5 a.m. on 4th March '98 the dream was as follows: Baba sitting in a cabin and all alone. This was the opportunity I had been waiting for. Running up to Him, I took my place at His feet. "Baba, may I press your hands into my eyes?" He responded positively. My action of pressing His hands into my eyes didn't seem to make any sense to Him though. "Well, that is not going to help you in any way," He snapped at me impatiently. Taken aback by the rebuke and distraught with fear, I blurted, "But Baba do you mean to say that all my efforts at trying to improve myself have been in vain? Or have they gone unnoticed by you?" In a softer tone, He hurriedly replied in order to calm me down, "No, no, I am not saying that." Making His tone even gentler, He added, "All I have to tell you is that all the time you seem to be worried about something or the other and nothing seems to make you stop from worrying. Don't think too much. Don't worry about what did not happen, things that are happening or might happen in the future. You simply need to let the events in life take their natural course. Let the events come about as they are destined to be. Let people play their roles. Their existence on earth, the way they are and the roles they are playing is all necessary in this world for you and everyone else to learn from." After this there was a long pause. Then He added, "Ah, and one more thing." Before He could go any further, I saw Pervin (Mumbai Branch Manager – CRY), enter the cabin for a while and then disappear. My voice was almost a whisper when I confided in Him the fear that was uppermost in my mind, "Baba, now she is going to be my new boss." He nodded in understanding. (Friends, I had got so accustomed to working under Puja Marwaha that I was apprehensive to report to someone else.)

All that He had said to me in the above dream applied to me. It was true that I worried all the time. Why? Perhaps, it's because I lacked in faith. Today I asked myself that if I was not satisfied with what the Lord had chosen for me, then the fault lay with me.

Friends, before I go any further, I feel the need to introduce Pervin to you. She has been one of the few individuals who has had an immeasurable impact on my life and helped me in my evolution into a better human being. I held her in high regard as a Branch Manager (and later as the CEO of CRY) because she had made it to the top with the kind of values, principles, dedication and determination that few possess. "Pervin, if you ever read this book, I hope that during my lifetime I have been able to convey to you the love and respect I have had for you. Thank you for your friendship."

Pervin has been a friend to me in many ways. I remember the innumerable times when she has helped me by just listening, without judgement or advice. She stressed that I need not ever silence the voice within me that was crying to be heard, or, as I'd myself sense, there would always be a part of me that would remain unfulfilled. Pervin was open to feedback regarding her own strengths and weaknesses. Besides, she was possessed with sufficient humility to see others' strengths and work upon them.

Today, in the year 2009, I perceive Pervin as one of my few dear friends. Yet, just then, in 1998, if anyone had told me that she would not only become my friend, but also would have a huge impact on my life and work at Sunbeam (the Neighbourhood Project), I would have shaken my head in disbelief. But that's precisely the role she played in my life in the years to follow.

Pervin always took delight in the fact that I was growing with my dreams of Sunbeam. She did not try to protect me from pain but by being there when I needed her. She took delight in my successes and comforted me in my failure. And she always made allowances for my imperfections. While she claimed that I didn't really value myself as much as I should have, she also shared with me her own feelings of inadequacy in her role as CEO of CRY. That's simply because she undervalued her own talents and was unaware of her own worth as somebody who was loved dearly and held in high esteem by the Divine.

Not to Disregard the Call of Duty

On Monday – 16th March '98 in a dream I asked the Lord, "Baba, may I come to Whitefield or Parthi wherever you are in the month of April and spend a few days in your company?" He answered crossly, "Do you want to come to me so soon?" "Well then can I come to you in the month of May?" He nodded in the affirmative but the expression on His face wasn't one of great enthusiasm in inviting me to His abode.

This dream was an indicator of the future of which He was aware of, that at the last minute my new boss would request me to take leave a week later than the one I would ask for.

On 23rd March '98 He once again blessed me with granting me darshan in a dream. This time He was in a white robe with golden borders on the sleeves.

Nargish Aunty and I reached Bangalore on 5th May '98 and spent a day at Khurshid and Indravadan Thakur's place in Shanti Nagar, Bangalore. On the 6th morning, after darshan I fervently prayed to Him to allow me to stay at Whitefield one week longer than intended. He in turn granted me permission to extend my stay by 3 days. And the message behind His command to leave on the 14th was clear. Hadn't I authorised my assistant's leave w.e.f. 15th May '98? Then wasn't it my duty to be in the office before she could go on leave?

In order to keep on the straight road leading to perfection, I had to make sure that all promptings I received were from Him, that it was the voice of my conscience and not that of my ego. Also I had to realise that I was not divinely inspired if I withdrew from duties (duties at the office or at home). For these duties were the clearest indication of His will and I did not have to allow anything to supersede them.

This Time the Lord came to Dad's Rescue

At 5.30 a.m. on 14th April '98, in the dream my Lord kept calling out to me, "Come, come, come." Each time He called out, I took a few steps in His direction till I had reached His chair. To my shock, my Lord fell down with a thud and hurt His leg. His cry of pain pierced my heart. But within moments He was back on His feet and my joy knew no bounds.

Shortly after this dream, once again dad had a very bad fall but was saved from any more injuries. It was clear that the Lord had taken upon Himself all of the pain that dad would have otherwise suffered from.

A Heart Warming Message from Christ for Pervin

4th May '98 – 6.30 a.m. The dream was as follows: Hundreds of CRY employees were seen walking, all in the same direction. The majority of them stopped in their tracks after covering a short distance and entered the CRY theatre where they claimed they'd be playing their individual roles in the CRY show. Another group of about 20 employees entered the gates of the next theatre after walking double the distance as compared to the first group. Instead of joining any of the groups, I continued to walk further with Pervin leading the way. Just the 2 of us reached the third theatre. Turning to me, she inquired as to what it was that made me continue my journey. To that my honest reply was, "Pervin, my journey back home is going to be a difficult one, and in the hope that during my period of trial you may prove to be of some help since you have a journey full of enriching experiences, I am walking with you now."

All of a sudden, to my despair I found myself amongst strangers and Pervin was nowhere to be seen. Slowly I retraced my steps and moved out of the CRY theatre to a lonely spot and sat on one of the benches. Within seconds I had company. A tall, handsome, divine looking person in His 30's with long shoulder-length hair and a beard, walked in my direction, who I instantly recognised as my guru in the form of Christ. "Do you know who I am?" He asked in a soft tone. "Of course I do. Don't we meet often? You are Pervin's father."

The answer seemed to please Him but I couldn't stop myself from asking something that had me bothered, "Why have you grown a beard and long hair?" "Well, my child, this is the only form in which she recognises me as her Father." Then He glanced around as though searching for someone. There was a long silence. At length He said, "Where is Pervin? Doesn't she know that her Father is waiting for her?" "Please come and sit next to me," I replied in an attempt to console a Father who felt deserted by one of His daughters. The loving parent that He is, He not only sat next to me but we had a long chat on various issues. Once again He was quiet. And then came up with a request, "My child, go and look for Pervin. Find out where she is and report to me what she is doing."

I went by His request and succeeded in my search. To my amazement, I found her seated on a bench in a very cramped position, allowing someone or the other to sit next to her on both sides. Her eyes were red and swollen so I enquired if she was feeling OK. And I also reminded her that her Father was waiting for her, was looking out for her. She responded with, "I am suffering from a severe headache and have absolutely no time to look beyond it." That was an unexpected and an unusual answer. Walking back to Him, I related to Him all that I had seen and also her response. What she had said appeared to have hurt Him and in a sad voice, He exclaimed, "Ah, she calls my gift a headache! And she has no time for me? Never mind. If she doesn't walk up to me, I'll walk up to her. Come, my child."

The pride I felt in walking with the Lord cannot be expressed in words. Soon He was standing close to the bench upon which she was seated. He had walked and covered almost the entire distance between Him and her. In a very sad tone, in a broken voice, He addressed Pervin, "Child, even if I wish to come and sit next to you, it's next to impossible. You have kept no space for me anywhere; neither to your left nor to your right. If I can cover such a long distance for you, am I asking for too much by expecting you to take a few steps in my direction?" Pervin climbed down and stood facing Him. He immediately held His child in a fond embrace.

The above dream of mine was a revelation to me about the Management Committee's decision to make Pervin the Director of CRY. (This was officially announced to us a week after the dream.) And also a message for her and a lesson to me and others who get so caught up in our duties that we often forget to keep some time aside for the Lord. Another message that I received from this dream was that sometimes one tends to get worried about the magnanimity of the responsibility he/she has to shoulder and forgets that it's His gift to put us in that position so that we can be of some use to society. Pervin was a Christian and so it was natural that my dear Lord had appeared in the form of Christ, the only form in which she could recognise Him as the Heavenly Father.

When I shared the dream with Pervin, she was very touched and stated that now that she knew it to be His will, it would be easier for her to take up the role of the CEO of CRY.

My Efforts at Distributing His Prasad to His Devotees and His Children

On 11th June '98 in a dream I was present amongst thousands of devotees awaiting His darshan. What took me by surprise was that someone behind me sprinkled grains of rice, sugar and kumkum. On turning in that direction I found it was my Lord Sathya Sai distributing prasad in this unusual fashion. A major portion of the prasad had been falling into my outstretched palms and now overflowed into my lap. Considering it only right to distribute it to the other devotees, I did so.

The dream signified my gratefulness to the Lord for showering me with His blessings and my sense of duty towards the society by completing His books (editing) on the computer, and, in my spare time after office hours to carry on with the Neighbourhood Project work, thus justifying my Lord's faith in me.

The Mother's Heart in My Guru Could See Only the Good in Me

In less than a week i.e. on 16th June '98 at 2 a.m. the Lord blessed me with His darshan in a dream. I was travelling by car and I peeped out from the window to find the Lord's car following me and He, my Divine parent was smiling at me. The scene changed and I found myself seated next to Him in His car, asking His permission to touch His feet. In response to that He slightly tugged at His gown to reveal His lotus feet and I pressed my eyes on them. Holy ash flowed from His hands and after applying some of it on my forehead, I swallowed the rest. "Aren't you the ash producer and not merely an ash applier?" To this unexpected question of His I had no reply. Finally, I asked in a choked voice, "Baba, do you think so?" He nodded in the affirmative and smiled very lovingly.

My Lord in His mercy saw only good in me, a mere human and I resolved to work harder to come up to His expectations of me.

She Could See Goodness Only in Those Who Would Dance to Her Tune

No amount of effort on my part could convince Rupali, a relative of mine (name changed), that I was not as selfish as she at times believed me to be. So I prayed to the Lord to show me a way to bring back her lost faith in me, that she may see and understand that the same spark of God that she visualised in a few others was present in me as well.

In response to the above prayer of mine, I had a dream on Saturday the 18th of July 1998 in which I saw her and myself both in the front row, in the Parthi crowds. To my puzzlement, she looked in my direction right beyond me as though at someone standing behind me who apparently had caught her attention and with a nod of approval she remarked, "This is the only God I believe in." Soft music could be heard all over the Parthi grounds. The music suddenly took a very different note with fast beats and then once again changed its tune to softer notes. I turned to look at the lucky person in whom she claimed she could visualise God. The scene that met my eyes left me speechless. It was my Lord Sathya Sai dancing away exactly to the tune of the music! It was the most unusual spectacle that I had ever witnessed!

The above message in the dream indicated that dancing to Rupali's tune would be the only way to please her. But that's something that I could not bring myself to do which is why she could not visualise the spark of the Divine in me or many others who expressed their own views and opinions.

It was Baba's Wish that I Identify Myself with a Lotus

The dream that I had seen on the 18th of July 1998 was in two parts. The latter part of the dream was as follows: Baba handed over an examination paper to each devotee. Not just that, He also handed over an object to everyone, claiming that He wished each individual child of His to learn to identify himself / herself with that object. Then approaching me, He handed over a lotus to me along with the examination paper, saying that it was the lotus He wished me to identify myself with. With that the dream came to an end.

Even after growing in murky water, the lotus is untouched by its impurity and symbolises purity of heart and mind. Therefore, what He expected of me, was to live like a lotus – living in the world and yet above the worldly desires and attachments.

Baba Blessed My Parents with a Long Life

On Thursday, 23rd July '98 in a dream my dear guru walked up to me and embraced me. "Ask me whatever you wish to know," He told me. To that I responded with, "Baba, bless my dad with a ever happy, healthy and long life." Nodding in the affirmative, He placed His hand on my head, thus granting me my desire. "Baba, bless my mum too with a ever happy, healthy and long life." Once again nodding in the affirmative, He blessed me by placing His hand on my head. "And what about me? Baba, what do you have to say about me?" "For an answer to that I shall come to you at 2 o' clock tomorrow." Then, as if to add to my confusion He said, "Well, tomorrow means tomorrow according to me and that can come any time." So saying, He laughed merrily and was soon out of sight.

My guru was aware about my pain-filled future, full of major health problems which I was in the dark about. Perhaps that's why He postponed His answer to an indefinite time.

His Vigilant Eye Ever Focused on Me

Once again within a short span of a week He appeared in my dream on 30th July '98 at 5.30 a.m. At top speed I ran in the direction of His car in order to get a close view of my dear Lord. I found Him smiling. To my shock a few seconds later though I could see His back, in place of His crown of hair it was His face that was visible at the back. His eyes were fixed on me and a smile of love and approval lit His face all the time. Perhaps this dream indicated that nothing goes unnoticed by Him.

He was Referring to His Rebirth in the Form of Sunbeam when He Addressed Me as His Mother

On Thursday, 4th August '98 in a dream Baba once again came to reiterate His promise to me that He had made almost 15 years ago. He was lying on a bed looking very ill. Both of us, i.e. Aban and I were in tears at the sight of His critical condition. "I am not going away forever. I shall take rebirth and be back with you." Aban asked Him who His mother in His next incarnation was to be. To that He replied pointing out to me, "Khurshid, you are going to be my mother in my next birth." God alone knows how much these words meant to me.

The scene changed and suddenly out of nowhere a patient appeared next to His bed. It seemed from the appearance of the patient with tubes all over his body that the chances of his survival were very slim. Baba's astral form came out from within His body and watched from above as the Divine body took on all the suffering of the man lying next to Him. Baba's body now had all the life saving machines attached to the tubes to His body and the sick man sat upright, completely cured. Unable to see my Lord in pain, I cried out in anguish, "O Baba, what is happening?" In a calm voice He replied, "This man was about to come to me." As I walked up to my Lord, lying in agony, He said, "Bhakti (devotion) can take different forms." He seemed to be very happy with me. With that the dream came to an end.

In the former part of the dream He had been hinting at His rebirth in the form of Sunbeam. In the months and years to follow, I could never be close to Him in His Sathya Sai form, but He had stated that He would be with me in the form of my child. Indeed, He did live with me in the form of my brainchild, Sunbeam which now (i.e. in November 2011) reaches out to over 1,300 child beneficiaries.

The latter part of the dream signified that He had rushed to the rescue of a devotee by taking his suffering upon Himself and granting that child of His, a fresh lease to life.

"All the Dreams that You've Had of Me and Noted Down in Our Books are Correct," Sai Told Me

Dream on Monday 10th August '98 at 6 a.m.: "Baba, I have been coming to Parthi or Whitefield to have your darshan as often as once in six months. Is it OK?" I asked. "It's not good for the popularity of the book," He replied gravely. Full of remorse I said in a subdued tone, "Then, perhaps I should be coming to you only once in a year." To that He merely smiled. "Baba, how do you find the book I am writing?"

"What is the book all about?" He queried. "It is a book on my life. Baba, I have been writing about each and every message of yours since I was about 16 or so. Do you mean to say that something that I have written is not correct?" I asked in panic. He attempted to reassure me by saying, "Of course all the dreams that you have had of me and noted down in our books are correct." After a pause He added, "Mother." "Baba, may I touch your feet?" "But of course." So saying He allowed me to be at His lotus feet. "Baba, do you think I have improved spiritually?" "No," was His quick answer.

Baba Blessed Me with the Title of Motherhood

On 20th August '98 at 5.30 a.m. He once again took the trouble to come and draw my attention to my faults. In the dream as my Lord spoke to mum, I decided to take down notes of His messages. This annoyed Him and in anger He chided me by saying, "While I am talking if you intend to keep writing in the book then you better stop writing." Scared stiff, I immediately shut the book. His anger was justified since I didn't pay much attention to what He was saying as I was merely bent upon taking down the notes and at times, I even missed out on some of the messages. Now I listened to Him attentively. "May you bear a child." (In Gujarati He had said "Taari Goad Bharaai".) The next moment He sat at my feet with a bowl of water in His hand and requested me to stretch out my feet in order to give Him a chance to wash them. In my enthusiasm to obey Him and surrender to His will, I even went to the length of removing my slippers and extending my feet. But the minute I realised my error, I pulled back my feet in shame. The audience sat dumbfounded, watching the scene as the Lord requested me to allow Him to wash my feet! Fear of the conclusion that people may draw at the Lord's strange behaviour and my embarrassment at being showered with so much respect by Him, made me withdraw my feet further away. The dream ended.

Though the Lord had given me more than one message via the above dream, the latter part of the dream depicting His humility had moved me to tears. I could not think of a single act on my part that merited such an action on the part of the Lord and this overwhelmed me even more. But what I do know is that in my life I feel like a small child, insecure in many ways. If He doesn't appear to me for more than a fortnight or so, I begin to feel abandoned by Him. I long to be accepted and recognised by Him in ways that are important to me i.e. via dreams and visions of His. And within the grip of this fear I often turn to Him for validation. He has never failed me and I know He never will.

Over the past two decades, just when I thought I had stretched myself enough, so to speak, or had lifted my consciousness to a certain level, my dear guru had raised the standard a little higher. Here again, to meet the new standards, He had given me His full support. Yes, Baba had taken upon Himself the almost impossible task of making me reach His height. He understood that I was not able to manifest my true nature every moment of my existence. Very patiently, He had always made me understand that perfection was what I had to strive for. Today, by acknowledging the spark of divinity within me and requesting that I allow Him to wash my feet, He had humbled me by His own utter humility. The only way to respond to His love would be to constantly strive to live up to His standards.